ENGLISH TO GO

INSIDE JAPAN'S TEACHING SWEATSHOPS

Craig Currie-Robson

Craig Currie-Robson

Copyright © 2015 Craig Currie-Robson

All rights reserved.

ISBN-13:978-1505350937
ISBN-10:150535093X

No part of this book may be copied, written reproduced or distributed without the author's permission. English to Go is the intellectual property of Craig Currie-Robson. This book is a non-fiction work.

Cover design by Jean-Paul Dennis and Craig Currie-Robson; Proof by Gareth Shute

Published at Amazon CreateSpace; available on Kindle and print-on-demand.

For further information visit the author's blog:

craigkneedeep.blogspot.com

For all those still fighting

Craig Currie-Robson

CONTENTS

Acknowledgments   i

1	A New Breed	7
2	Champagne Supernova	33
3	Berlitz Battery Hens	65
4	Aeon's Cult of Impersonality	101
5	Life on Mars	127
6	Gaba Moves the Goalpost	147
7	Love, Marriage and Charisma Men	177
8	Stalkers, Gropers and Serial Masturbators	205
9	ECC – Appetite for Compromise	231
10	Interac's Phantom Jobs	253
11	How Does Eikaiwa Get Away with it?	291

Glossary	311
Appendices	313
Notes and References	317

Acknowledgments

Nobody writes a non-fiction book all by themselves. First I would like to thank Ian Raines and Chris Flynn at the General Union, as well as Adrian Ringin at Gaba, for their insight and clarification. Thanks to Ben Stubbings at the Japan Times and Ken Hartmann of the Hokkaido Insider for their support and assistance. I would also like to thank Gareth for last-minute editing and proofreading, and Paul for his help with the cover art. Thank you to my friends and loved ones who have stood by me in this project and offered advice and support.

And finally to all the current and former teachers who contributed, on and off record, with their candid stories and observations. You are the ones who have built this industry, fought for it, and this is your story.

Craig Currie-Robson

Foreword to the Second Edition

It has been almost three years since beginning this project and a year since the first edition was released. Despite the bumpy start, the book has been generally well received. In the year since it hit the shelves (or your Kindles) there have been a few large developments in the industry and a couple of small victories for teachers that I see as very much a continuation of a worsening pattern of behavior.

Firstly, the good news. In several cases in 2015 the unions successfully asserted the rights of individual teachers or small faculties. Though these may seem a drop in the ocean, great things come from small beginnings:

Waseda University was forced to retract a five year employment limit. This was put in place to circumvent a labor law in Japan that stipulates after five years, part-time or contract workers must be offered full-time roles. One employee at a smaller school, IES, was not enrolled in the mandatory national social insurance scheme, despite being a full-time employee for over a decade. With union help in the courts, the teacher was finally enrolled and awarded in arrears. Managers and supervisors at both Nova and Interac have been forced to apologize for ill treatment of staff.

Both ECC and Berlitz have seen strikes as the union pushes for small improvements. In the case of Berlitz, the union has finally won a small pay rise, less than five percent, after many years of struggling. A lot of companies hand out such increments every year as a matter of course but in Eikaiwa, a foreign teacher is not seen as a valuable asset. It remains to be seen whether these small improvements will snowball into something greater, but the General Union continues to labor tirelessly for the betterment of the teachers, and despite them, their employers too.

Secondly, a change in Japanese Labor laws means that access to social insurance may be on the cards from October 2016 for English teachers. All companies with more than 501 employees will be obliged to enrol anyone working more than twenty hours per week. Several chapters in the book outline the struggle for teachers in the industry to get enrolled: benefits include subsidized healthcare, a pension scheme and unemployment coverage. This should be good news, however English schools have for many years tried to avoid this responsibility and look set to keep trying:

One the largest employers of foreign teachers, Interac, has announced it will split up into at least six smaller firms ahead of this change. The General Union suspects that because the new regime will apply only to large companies at first, Interac is trying to dodge this bullet by spreading more than 2,500 teachers around the 'subsidiaries'. Other large employers of foreign teachers may take note. Nova is now having teachers sign contracts that list them as 'independent subcontractors' in order to avoid accepting them as 'employees' at all. We don't know yet whether the government will uphold these regulations and monitor compliance. I suspect it won't and the fight will be left up to the unions and teachers themselves.

There is as always some pushback from 'Big Eikaiwa' – and smaller schools. Those who challenge illegal company 'policies' without union backing (even with it) still risk summary dismissal. Though Gaba and Nova have both instituted procedures to handle sexual harassment complaints by staff, Gaba still seems determined to protect clients accused of harassing its teachers and has attracted union attention for trying to intimidate its teachers into remaining silent. Part-time teachers in large firms continue to fight for recognition of the five minute 'breaks' between lessons as paid working time, and Nova has recently amended its contracts to also claim that the six-minute breaks between its lessons - during which teachers can be seen frantically logging notes and preparing for the next lesson - are also unpaid 'down time'.

These events demonstrate that with union help and the courts on their side, teachers can get their due, but they also highlight the industry's dogged determination to reduce pay and working conditions. Major English schools in Japan continue to flout labor laws, treat their teachers dishonestly and to look for loopholes wherever a blatant breach of employment regulations would be too obvious.

Japan is a wonderful place full of generous, compassionate and welcoming people. Unfortunately one major gateway for foreigners who wish for an extended career in Japan – the English teaching business – is not. This book is still for those teachers that continue to tough it out year after year in what must seem at times an uphill battle. For those who are planning on going to Japan and working for any of the major national chains a word of warning: look at the websites, get informed, know your rights before you commit.

For further information and ongoing news make sure you visit the General Union website, now amalgamated into one excellent clearing house for all developments in the Eikaiwa employment situation: http://generalunion.org/Joomla/. Forewarned is forearmed.

Auckland, Oct 2016

1 A New Breed

First came the rumors, then the late pay checks. The teachers huddled in staff rooms and around water coolers talking about finding new jobs. There were even rumors of *yakuza* involvement. The Japanese staff members were always flustered, fielding angry calls and facing students demanding answers at the front desk. It was with these fears that Duncan headed into work one morning, just before lunchtime.

He got off the train and battled his way through the underground, past hurrying salarymen and old ladies jostling their way into basement food markets at high-end department stores, and bound his way up the stairs to the lobby of his office building. He needn't have bothered. When the lift opened the doors to the language school were closed. There was a notice in Japanese and English that his workplace, language school Nova was closed for business indefinitely. He couldn't even get inside to pack up his desk.

It was autumn, 2007 and Duncan had been in Japan just under two years. Now, he was suddenly unemployed, with no income and an apartment he'd soon be evicted from. At least he could take comfort in the fact he was not alone: everyone else he knew was also out of a job. Four and a half thousand English language teachers in dozens of cities across Japan had just seen the rug pulled out from under them. It has never been put back.

In the beginning they trickled in. There had always been English teachers in Japan, even before the war. In the early seventeenth century, the first Tokugawa shogun kept shipwrecked Englishman William Adams as a sort of cultural ambassador – a life famously fictionalized in James Clavell's *Shogun*. In the mid 1800's another shipwrecked sailor, this time a Japanese returnee known as John Manjiro, brought English back after more than a decade in the United States. At the turn of the twentieth century, the American Leonie Gilmour, mother of famed artist Isamu Noguchi, blazed a trail where few had gone before; supporting herself as an estranged wife and single mother by teaching her language to the children of the elite. After the war, interest in English steadily grew as Japan sought to rebuild and modernize. But it wasn't until the 1980s, when Japan's economic boom created the wealth and for some, the leisure time, to pursue interests such as foreign languages and travel, that the gilded age of commercial English teaching truly began.

Eikawa. The word translates as 'English conversation', in the abbreviated form that the Japanese are so fond of giving to all things new and chic. A curious mish-mash of genuine classroom teaching, earnest cultural exchange, seedy fantasy and business bottom dollar, the teaching of English in Japan has lured westerners for several generations. It ascended the dizzying heights of the bubble years and plunged the depths of the early twenty-first century economic slump, and carried along with it on its tumultuous, white-water journey, a mish-mash of adventurers, educators, martial artists, pick-up artists, *manga* geeks, backpackers, snowboarders, Zen Buddhists and lost souls that would sit at ease in any science fiction bar scene. Why did they come? Adrenaline, career, women, enlightenment, mere curiosity. They joined the ranks of acronym-hungry corporate giants such as NOVA, ECC, GABA and a raft of smaller schools, local education boards, private colleges and government-sponsored exchange schemes. They hit the ground running, ran out of steam, found love, failed, succeeded, got laid off or just got laid. These people - mostly young men and women from the English speaking world - had the courage to go out and try something new. Some were lured by money, some by love or lust; others by the promise of something just different. Some left their mark; many just left. Some are still here.

When Troy arrived in Tokyo in 1993, the bubble years were just winding down. Buoyed by its rapid industrialization and stunning economic success in the seventies and eighties, Japan was still riding a wave of wealth and consumerism. Japan's bubble never really *burst* - save a few high profile financial collapses - but rather slowly deflated over the coming decade in what cannot properly be called Japan's recession. But when Troy first landed, he remembers that, 'Times were still pretty high and you could still make good money teaching. Japan was more global then and people still felt they needed the language.'

Troy was not long out of college in Oregon and had arrived on the JET[*] program, which brings graduates to Japan to teach in public schools. In those days, employment at JET was limited to several years but Troy felt there were better opportunities downtown and left after only a year: his JET posting had been at the edge of Saitama, a prefecture that stretches out from the western suburbs of Tokyo, giving way to villages and farmland, and Troy wanted to be where the action was. 'Back then a lot of schools were still not paying much less than JET, around 300,000 yen a month and always looking for staff, so you wouldn't go broke if you left. Plus you could pick up private lessons for 5,000 an hour, or teach doctors and lawyers, who paid up to 8,000 yen for ninety minutes.

---

[*] The Japan Exchange and Teaching program.

Schools were still charging upwards of a hundred bucks an hour for one-to-one lessons so private lessons were a good deal for students with the cash'. Even in Tokyo, these alternatives opened the door to a lifestyle and potential savings that English teachers could only dream of in later years.

Working at large chain ELS, Troy taught four or five lessons a day and after a while was earning over ¥280,000 a month. He supplemented his income with lessons at a local college that paid a good ¥10,000 an hour (about $80) for about four lessons a week. He also found private students on his weekends. Rent wasn't cheap. Troy paid about ¥80,000 a month for a tiny one bedroom flat near trendy Harajuku. 'The place was run down but girls didn't seem to mind. I didn't think I was working too hard, but looking back it was a lot. I would have preferred not to work weekends but the money was too good to pass up. A few months, I was getting over ¥400,000 and a big chunk of that was cash in the hand from private students.'

In Japan's so-called bubble years, foreigners flocked to Japan lured by the easy money fueled by a rampant property boom that saw Tokyo's real estate prices skyrocket to the highest in the world. This resulted in a lot of people having a lot of money to spend and English lessons became another status symbol like golf or tennis lessons, or a personal trainer. Entrepreneurs sought to cash in on Japan's new outward-looking affluence and saw a language school as a low-cost, low skill investment with potentially quick returns. Anyone could start a language school – there were only commercial matters such as business registration and no academic oversight or accreditation. Smaller schools rose and fell all the time.

Almost anyone could be a teacher too. Language schools weren't always as interested in teaching English as selling the fantasy of the foreigner. One researcher noted advertising tactics based on the *appearance* of being foreign to the point that anyone with blond hair and blue eyes could land a job. It was not unheard of for potential employers to approach foreigners on the street and offer them work as long as they looked like the smiling westerners in the commercials and on the posters: 'Such superficialities and images of the English-learning business are confused with genuine learning activities.'[1] This was never meant to be rocket science.

It helped that Troy really did look like the models in the advertisements. He was young, fair-haired, handsome and in good shape. At twenty-four he was very much the poster child English schools were looking for, and increasingly what the students wanted. A face like his was easy to market to consumers in a Japan that was still obsessed with stereotypes of Western beauty. He quickly learned the game. 'You learn some methodology, how to teach from a textbook, how to run a classroom. But mostly you learn to perform, how to keep the energy levels up, to entertain.' Troy hadn't even been that good at English in school. 'I basically learned on the job how to explain grammar from the same textbooks the students were getting it from in class. It was learn as you go.'

He learned more about the value of a pretty foreign face as well. 'Young women would request my classes. I was very popular in the beginning. After a while students at a school would get tired of a new face and move on to the next one, but for a while I was the *it* guy.' But even fleeting initial popularity wasn't enough to deter a string of on-the-job relationships, the kind that eikaiwa would later become famous for. 'I dated one student for a while, a dental assistant. At another place I used to go out with the receptionist,' he confesses matter-of-factly.

In one assignment he was sent to the home of a businesswoman to teach her teenage daughter. 'She was a high school senior and really attractive. I don't know in what world this was normal but her mother would leave us alone for the lessons and go out to her yoga class or something. I was sort of nervous about being accused of anything inappropriate being left alone with a schoolgirl, but the mother watched the first lesson and decided she trusted me. The girl was precocious, cheeky and flirting all the time. In lessons she'd talk about her boyfriends and even ask how many women I'd slept with. She'd ask me if I liked Japanese girls, that sort of question. One lesson a few weeks in, she just started coming onto me. We ended up having sex right there in the living room and she was definitely more experienced than I was. That became the template for every lesson after that, we'd spend about half the time doing the materials and getting worked up and the other half in her bed.' Sex for English lessons – these were high times indeed.

Grant is a gregarious Liverpudlian in his fifties who also arrived on the last wave of the bubble years. The holder of two degrees, one in performing arts, he first came to Japan in his early thirties after working in various theater productions in London. He had come to Japan because a friend had asked him to come over and join the party. 'This guy had it all. He was good-looking, well-liked and enjoying the lifestyle in Japan. We all thought he'd found his little slice of heaven. He had girlfriends, steady income. He eventually married an American woman – Chinese American. Good family: lawyers and other high achievers. After moving to the US with her he kind of lost his place. They had kids and the family had high expectations, but he'd left his niche and he wasn't happy.' The friend fell into drink and depression and died of a hemorrhage at forty-nine. But that was all in the future for Grant in his first days in Japan.

We took one weekday afternoon to sit on the veranda outside a Starbucks coffee shop in downtown Sapporo. During the short summer in a city famed for its long snowy winter, the veranda seats are the best in the house. Yet because these were outdoors they were given over for a time to smokers and Starbucks even provided ashtrays for customers on request.* We soaked up the passersby and the smokers behind us, and talked about Grant's experiences and his take on the direction of the industry.

Grant recalls a job interview back in the day, for a small school in Tokyo. 'It was this little hole in the wall place. While the receptionist had me filling out a form in the lounge, I could clearly see and hear the teacher in a cubicle a few feet away having an animated lesson with an older Japanese gentleman. He was an Aussie kid, straight off the boat. Couldn't have been more than twenty four. He just kept on talking and talking about his family and his sister and all sorts of things while the student was trying to get a word in edgewise. Whenever the poor man started, the teacher would actually tell the student to hold on a minute while he finished.'

Such a lack of professionalism is not uncommon among new teachers. Many have been misled by the friends who came before them. 'They've been told teaching is easy money and you just have to go in and chat to

---

* Starbucks Japan finally went smoke free at all branches the following summer

the students,' says Grant. Even those who harbor no such preconceptions before arriving, quickly find that the small schools have no training budget and expect them to learn on the job. Some learn, others don't. One complaint I've heard at every school is that a teacher talks too much and too fast and the student gets no chance to practice and no real instruction.

Finally the student had had enough. 'He put up is his hand and told the kid to stop. He said - and he had very good English - "I'm a doctor, I didn't come here just to hear you talk. I want another teacher." The kid looked utterly dumbfounded and asked for confirmation. The student asked again for another teacher. So he steps out to reception and within earshot, tells the girl, "This wanker says he wants another teacher." It's still the most shocking thing I have heard a teacher say. I gave up on applying at that place.'

While Grant's anecdote reflects a lack of training, it also demonstrates a very colonial sense of entitlement. People come from western countries and expect the locals to accept everything they do. Cultural differences aside, personal prejudice often contributes to misunderstandings, as much as the expectation that any foreigner can simply turn up, start talking and get paid. Among some, there is the fantasy that the Japanese will be satisfied with just listening to the awesome wisdom imparted by a mighty westerner. Grant didn't want any part of that.

He found himself in Sapporo's *Kokusai Plaza*, an information center for cross-cultural relations that maintains a job-board for foreigners looking for work.[2] He asked on the off-chance if there was any theater-related work and to his surprise, was introduced to an actor/director on the spot. The director had been involved with the center and was in that day. This was the start of a two-decade friendship and collaboration that saw Grant involved in theater projects in Japan as a coach, an actor, director and producer doing productions and workshops in the UK, India and Singapore.

Yet theater didn't pay all the bills. Grant still had to work at the main game in town for foreigners: teaching English. In this case a reasonably-sized chain named American Club. 'From the start it wasn't the most organized of places, but they offered a great variety of books to students, even if the curriculum wasn't strictly set. We were encouraged to choose from the available materials and develop our own lessons. You couldn't just waste time: there was an evaluation system of sorts, wherein students were encouraged to give feedback to the center. If a teacher was deemed to be slacking off or otherwise failed to meet expectations, he was told.' It was an interesting contrast between feeding the fantasy and actually being committed to language learning – a business model all but vanished today, in the large corporate language schools. American Club ably attracted high caliber students such as doctors and lawyers, yet still kept a relaxed atmosphere.

In early 1994, Grant was invited south to the Sendai branch, where replacement teachers were needed. 'I was comfortable in Sapporo,' He tells me, 'We all had it made. I didn't really want to go south because of my involvement with the theater. Things were okay just where I was.' Yet for the time being at least, a substitute was needed. So the company flew Grant to Sendai, a comfortable city of over a million people that is the main center for the Tohoku region, where he was to spend a week or so filling in. 'The day I got there, the head instructor showed me around. I remember the girl at the front desk looked incredible. He asked me if I thought she was cute and I said yeah. He told me he could hook us up that night after dinner.' Though Grant never took him up on the offer, he was becoming aware of eikaiwa's reputation - at least in the nineties - as a potential meat market for promiscuous foreigners and the women who sought them out.

Though it was not a unique example at the time, the Tochigi based American Club, a mid-sized operation spanning three prefectures in the northeast, could be viewed an as early bellwether for industry troubles. Starting in 1986, it expanded to six cities including the northern economic magnets Sendai, and Sapporo where Grant was posted. But by the mid nineties it was unable to pay teacher's salaries. This wasn't necessarily because the school itself was doing poorly. Like other large chains, American Club was a subsidiary of a company that suffered from financial troubles in its other business ventures.[3]

On the first occasion in 1994, the employees' union filed a lawsuit and eventually won back three months' unpaid wages. The second time, in 1995, also resulted in a lawsuit, but the company directors never turned up at court and ignored orders to pay. The president simply resigned and nominated a figurehead in his place to avoid taking any heat for the collapse. This apparently was the end of American Club's responsibility to the foreign teachers employed there. Compensation was paid by the Ministry of Health, Labor and Welfare - in Japan, laid-off employees can receive up to 80% of unpaid salaries if a company collapses - but American Club itself never paid a cent and the courts never chased up truant defendants.[4]

Such leniency can be baffling to the western mind, but Japan Inc. has been known for siding with big business. Don MacLaren, who led the teacher's union in its first lawsuit, wrote to *Business Week* drawing on his experience to comment on an article covering corruption in Japan:

> I think you should devote more space to the institutionalized corruption here and the reasons it has been allowed to go unchecked--which I see as follows:
> 1. The Japanese tend to protect any authority figure, no matter how corrupt.
> 2. Japanese companies and their employees tend to cover up anything that might make them look "dirty"; bad loans, fraud, etc.
> 3. Because no one person or institution takes responsibility for crises in Japan, they are allowed to fester.
> ...I was amazed that neither our lawyers nor the Japanese newspapers covering the story made efforts to address the issue of the land the company held as assets, which should have been seized and sold off in order to pay us. Apparently, they were more concerned with protecting our employers than with exposing them.[5]

MacLaren was not just venting. American Club was still in existence as late as 2011, at least on paper: Its business registration indicated the company was still a legally operating entity, with 30 million yen in equity. The Shimotsuke Shimbun, a newspaper that had ironically run stories on the lawsuits, still advertised American Club's services in its pages.[6] With the company sitting on all that equity and other assets without being forced to pay their obligations, MacLaren could be forgiven for thinking the courts preferred to protect the directors when they should have been punishing them. Across the industry teachers have faced a similar fate. The company simply dumps them and without the financial resources, language skills, local legal knowledge and crucially *time*, teachers are forced to throw up their hands in disgust and just get on with their lives: they find another job or give up and return to their home countries, but they seldom get their last paycheck from their employer.

'I didn't really see a drop in students or in the English market till about '97 or '98,' says Troy. 'The recession took a long time to catch up with English schools. The college reduced classes around that time and one or two private students quit. Numbers were about the same at my branch.' The big chains were even expanding. Aeon and Geos were still opening new branches all over the country even as the signs of a drop in demand must surely have been on the horizon. Buoyed by student fees paid in bulk rather than per lesson, English schools were buying up or leasing prime locations in all major cities and employing foreign instructors in ever-increasing numbers.

Back at American Club, Grant and his coworkers had not yet been touched by the company's financial troubles. The job and the company seemed to be hanging on to the hedonistic spirit of the bubble years. 'There was one woman who signed up, a bored housewife in her early thirties. She was good looking alright. In those days the students would buy their lessons in bulk and she paid about half a million yen (around $4,000 at the time) for a year's worth of classes. On her first day she spotted me in the lobby and asked to take my lesson next time she came. On the day, she was all dressed up and suggested we go for drinks after class, since it was the last lesson of the evening, as if she'd had it all planned out. She took me to a bar, introduced me to all her girlfriends there, like they'd been waiting for me all along. She got roaring drunk and we went back to her place – God knows where her husband was. She literally staggered through the door, was naked in a flash and pretty much demanded we do it on the spot. The next day, she canceled her whole contract, a year of lessons and we never heard from her again. The manager asked if it had anything to do with my lesson.'

Grant didn't find out how much of a refund the student was entitled to, but the days of such freewheeling waste were coming to a close. That students would sign up for English lessons just to facilitate hookups with foreign teachers was mind boggling enough, but they were also paying vast sums to do so. A typical yearlong contract at a language school could easily run up four or five thousand dollars in tuition plus several hundred in a membership fee. Wily schools charged more still for texts, especially materials developed in-house. With such money at stake it is no wonder language schools eventually started to write non-fraternization clauses into their teacher contracts, to protect their pool of customers from the apparently 'predatory' clutches of teachers.

Meat markets or otherwise, there was no shortage of language schools. Despite the soon-to-be sagging economy, branches opened in response to rising demand. Students needed to study overseas, travel on business, get a leg up at school or just get a leg over with a foreigner. Instructors were willing to take a leave from their careers at home, spend a couple of years experiencing Asia after college or just take some time out from life to teach in Japan. Now the schools were in place, the rogue's gallery of teachers was in town and the business model was established. But how to turn such a personal service into a marketable nationwide brand?

In the late eighties and early nineties Japan saw astounding success, as both a financial powerhouse and a manufacturer and exporter. Brands such as Sony and Mitsubishi were sold around the world and hardly a house in the developed West went without a microwave from Toshiba or a vacuum cleaner by Hitachi. In the world of finance, companies such as Daiwa securities and Mizuho bank featured regularly in the *Wall Street Journal* or the *Financial Times*. Western economists and businesses were scratching their heads, wondering what was so different about Japan Inc - what made it so successful, that they could emulate and transplant to their own operations.

But they overlooked the fact that Japan was also learning from them. A new form of business model was sweeping the world, one that took advantage of standardization both in product and service. A successful company would look the same whichever branch you walked into. You'd be greeted by the same smiling staff in the same corporate wardrobe, giving the same service and delivering the same quality, anywhere in the world. It was this fundamental shift in the way business was conducted worldwide that prompted sociologist George Ritzer to write his seminal 1993 book, *The McDonaldization of Society*.

The Japanese of course, are known to value conformity. In a country where practically every school had the same uniform, where 'office ladies' all wore matching attire to work, and where the typical salaryman who rebuilt postwar Japan was so used to his suit and tie, it was reputed he could scarcely decide what to wear on his day off, the principles of McDonaldization would have looked at once attractively new and comfortably familiar. The new model easily fit and complemented the Japanese way of doing things. It was on the cusp of this global change that freewheeling foreign teachers rode a tide of standardization into the language teaching business in Japan.

Language schools were quick to see the opportunity for change.

Today the global industry known as English as a Second Language or ESL, provides an important stepping stone toward integration into the societies and economies of the USA, Canada, Australasia and the United Kingdom. It is also an ongoing hobby for language enthusiasts around the world and a necessary tool for businesspeople and travelers. Language centers are found in practically every country in the world, and are a growing market in the up-and-coming economies of Asia, Africa and South America.

The idea of ESL in Japan however, has been almost entirely eclipsed by the concept of eikaiwa. Thousands of language centers across the archipelago cater to the students' rather more limited English needs with a mix of entertainment and genuine tuition, with varying degrees of success. The eikaiwa business is now dominated by a number of large chains such as ECC, Nova, Aeon, and Berlitz, collectively known to some observers as 'Big Eikaiwa', or the 'Big Four'. But if these institutions sound like centers for learning and development, that would be a coincidence. Their primary aim was to make money and in the strict pursuit of profits, eikaiwa chains tightened and refined their operations to become veritable production-lines.

They did not need the most effective way to *teach* English. They had identified – or perhaps decreed – that learning goals were secondary to their students' other reasons for signing up. Rather, what was needed was the most efficient way to *market and sell* the idea of English to the masses, and to draw in as many customers as possible. In the new world of English teaching, presentation would reign over progress; convenience would trump competence. There would be a branch beside every train station or in every shopping center, and they'd be open all hours. Busy Japanese workers and students could duck in for a lesson as easily as they could stop for a coffee or a burger, and expect the same type of lesson from the same type of teacher wherever they went. The age of eikaiwa had arrived.

The 'McPrinciples' could have been lifted directly from Ritzer's book. First, efficiency: every aspect of the organization is geared towards satisfying the customer in a timely manner and moving on to the next customer and the next one after that. Language schools have refined their lessons into bite-sized nuggets of English lasting forty or fifty minutes. Students can roll up and get their English fix for the day, with or without sauce, and make way for the next customer to be satisfied. This process seemed detrimental to teachers. Bruce who worked at a Nova affiliate found, 'you really can't do much in forty minutes. If the class has more than a few people someone always complains they didn't get enough talk time in. It's just a way to squeeze more lessons out of us in a day for the same pay.'

The second principle of McDonaldization is calculability. Even relatively objective results, such as personal development and English improvement take a back seat to something far more easily measured - profits. Though customer satisfaction does come into it, such satisfaction is judged from the *experience* of being a customer rather than actually improving one's English skills. Success is not based on matriculating students who will go on to better things, but keeping the customers coming back for the same product or slightly modified updates, year after year, guaranteeing revenue. At some chains, table ratios are set as targets and the more students to a teacher, the more money the company pockets. James, who worked at Berlitz, notes teachers were judged, 'not on how well the students learned English, but how "happy" they were and how many signed up for more lessons'. Money matters more than educational results.

The third McPrinciple is predictability. Customers must expect the same product or service wherever they go. They expect to see the same, fair-haired, suit-clad foreigners smiling in front of them. Formulaic lesson plans, rote-trained teachers following a script; standardized texts and leveling with a one-size-fits-all philosophy have made expanding and marketing easy. According to Bruce it was tricky matching up groups of students with lessons tailored not to their needs, but toward the bottom line. 'You had about ten minutes between lessons to choose the lesson materials for the next class. You had to be careful to find a lesson plan that none of the students had done before, because they'd complain if they repeated the same lesson twice in six months or a year.'

Finally there is control. Large chains use their own in-house texts and market their own self-study supplements. Lessons are done by the book and teachers who deviate from the script are disciplined or reprimanded. Other facets of behavior, such as dress codes are enforced as strictly, all so as to remind the customer they are getting a quality product, while reinforcing the teacher's role as not an educator, but a representative of the company, a salesperson delivering front-line over-the-counter service that is superficial at best, and often impersonal. Andre, who worked at Aeon, summed it up: 'You're not a teacher. You're there to project the company image. There's a corporate culture in every sense.'

To Ritzer's observations one could also add *convenience* - a cornerstone of eikaiwa. Large chains strategically place their branches in major business and shopping districts or beside public transportation hubs such as bus terminals and train stations. In a nod to the fast food industry that inspired so much of its business model, some branches of eikaiwa share floor space with Starbucks coffee; in one ingenious stroke of product tie-in, a children's eikaiwa chain even held lessons inside McDonald's restaurants, with lessons based around the menu.[7] English with a side of fries.

Or English to go, if you will. Dispatch agencies such as Interac send thousands of foreigners to public schools as ALTs (Assistant Language Teachers). The teachers sometimes have greater classroom freedom, or are at least subject to the needs of the local school boards they're sent to work for, rather than the company's lesson plans, but the hiring, training methods, discipline and pay scale are all similar to eikaiwa. Teachers are brought in from outside Japan in recruiting junkets; their housing is arranged, they are trained in basic company methodology regardless of former qualifications, and are sent out as the face of the company. Dispatchers that have modeled themselves on eikaiwa contribute to the uniform nature of the English teaching industry.

Dispatchers service not only public education, but increasingly private institutions such as universities, junior colleges and technical schools, even some national universities. As funding for English education is slashed, foreign staff in the tertiary sector are often first to feel the pinch. Gone are the days of tenure and permanent contracts: even teachers with an M.A .or Ph.D. can find themselves reduced to part time work, with no holiday pay and yearly contracts that can only be renewed twice. Institutes that don't want to spend even that much are turning to dispatch agencies, local language schools and large chains to send them teachers on a part time or temporary basis, at a cut-price eikaiwa rate. Naturally the quality of teachers varies and not all are vetted. In one case, an unqualified former mailman landed a job at a university and when briefed to teach a 'writing class' was caught giving lessons not in composition, but penmanship.[8]

English teachers in Japan are largely a mix of Anglo-Saxons or native speakers from an Anglophone country. The USA, Canada, Australia, New Zealand, the UK, Ireland and even South Africa are represented. Many from Europe, South America, Asia, Polynesia, the Middle East and Africa can also get work if their English is up to scratch. Schools vary in their qualification requirements. Immigration laws require a bachelor's degree in any discipline for a teacher to have a work visa sponsored by a school. This means the employer does the paperwork and ensures that the foreign teacher is gainfully employed. Though large chains prefer university graduates for bragging rights, it is possible for almost anyone to teach, if they have a working-holiday visa or a spouse's visa and do not require company sponsorship.

A few schools also prefer pre-trained teachers and those holding a recognized ESL certificate such as the Cambridge CELTA (Certificate in English Language Teaching to Adults). However the casual nature of eikaiwa and the Japanese perception that any foreigner can teach English make such a certification an added bonus at best – after all, any teenager can serve a burger and fries. It is rare to be paid more for extra qualifications and it is not unheard of in smaller schools to see a new graduate working alongside a teacher with an MA and ten years experience, or a reformed high school dropout with a spouse visa, all for the same pay. Just as in fast food, where all customer service positions are entry level, all foreigners in eikaiwa have the same value.

Since there can be no such thing as an 'expert burger flipper' who requires a higher grade of pay, in most large eikaiwa chains, turnover is high by design. Fresh graduates are usually preferred and many of them are hired overseas at recruiting drives in their home countries. ESL certification and experience are not necessary – in fact are sometimes shunned - as the chains prefer to train the teachers to deliver lessons according to their own methodology. Though most teachers are pretty smart, holding degrees in unrelated disciplines such as chemistry, engineering, even MBAs, those who hold an internationally-recognized qualification such as CELTA or even a master's degree in linguistics are not necessarily valued any more for it.

Motivation for coming to teach English varies. Most foreigners are looking for a bit of adventure. Many come to Japan to follow up on Asian studies programs at university; some because they have a fetish for Japanese culture. For a few it is a stop on a worldwide jaunt before taking up serious work in their home countries, and others have followed a Japanese spouse or lover they met overseas. There are some who have an interest in *manga, anime* and other forms of Japanese pop culture and want to be in the middle of it. There are others who just ended up in the role by accident and found it comfortable enough to stay.

Student motivation is almost as varied as that of the teachers. College graduates may take lessons for a few months to brush up before going overseas on a home-stay or working holiday. Housewives and retirees might do the same before a short trip, though being out of the workforce they are likely to sign up for longer. Large companies and government departments send their employees to class or contract schools to dispatch teachers to their own premises. Big names like Fujitsu and Toyota obviously need English, but so do individuals in the police, fire departments, the armed forces, medical and legal professions, and local or prefectural governments. Parents send their children to keep up or get ahead in school, or to prepare for Japanese-standard English tests such as ACET and *Eiken*. Adult lessons can be in medium-sized groups, small circles or one-to-one lessons. Children's lessons are usually held in small classes of four to eight students.

Some individual students take lessons as a hobby, to keep their minds active, to socialize with other people who have the same interest, or to meet foreigners for friendship or romance. Some attend lessons out of boredom and habit alone. Students may study at a school from a few weeks to more than twenty years. Hopping between schools as work/life circumstances change or because the service was unsatisfactory or a favorite teacher has moved is not uncommon. Many students seek private teachers outside of schools and take lessons in cafes or even at home. Students can be any age from toddlers to pensioners. As a rule, people in the prime of their working lives have less time for classes; they may take lessons very early or late or on weekends. Those with free time on their hands – housewives or retirees - make up a larger portion of students in the middle of the day.

Eikaiwa is marketed to all ages, with newspaper and TV spots, billboards and posters at subway stations or on trains. The schools use targeted marketing, with brands such as ECC and presenting the faces of smiling children to advertise kid's lessons, and a relaxed comfortable classroom with attractive young people and a well-groomed foreigner to appeal to young professionals. Industry giant Aeon has spent heavily on celebrity endorsements over the years, using Japanese TV and pop stars; even big Hollywood names like Cameron Diaz and Ewan McGregor have graced billboards and subway posters. Advertising often contains mildly suggestive images - the young Japanese woman getting an intimate lesson form a handsome blond American - feeding Japanese perceptions that language studies can be a gateway to foreign adventure and romance. Young women who work but live at home are a prime group of consumers with money to burn on hobbies and travel, but have few financial responsibilities, making them as natural a target for the eikaiwa business as they are for Louis Vuitton.

The advertising is naturally a response to the needs and desires of Japanese people with an interest in English. Many have a genuine need for English and some advertising is geared towards that. For many others, marketers seek to push their buttons in other ways. In a survey collected by one researcher, some respondents reported concrete needs for learning English – to run a surfing shop in Australia, to open a dental practice catering to foreign clients, or to get a job in California. Others had woollier goals. Several young women cited an interest in marrying foreigners; others simply spoke of raising their children overseas, as though learning the language were the main barrier. Yet others wanted to watch DVDs without subtitles or visit Broadway musicals. One hoped to somehow see her salary increase 'a hundred times'.[9] Whatever the goal, career or lifestyle, eikaiwa would position itself as being the best way to achieve it.

Texts and teaching materials are as varied as the needs of the clients. Large eikaiwa chains almost exclusively use in-house materials. This reinforces the brand and highlights the differences between 'our' school and 'the competition'. It also provides a marketing opportunity to on-sell further educational products and put more money in the chain's pocket, such as at Peppy Kid's Club, owned by a company that publishes educational materials. Smaller schools make use of hundreds of off-the-shelf ESL titles available from notable educational publishers such as Longman, McGraw Hill and Oxford University Press. Some schools choose from these a series of texts to be used as the center's standard curriculum that students can follow as they 'level up'. Others let students choose their own texts or let teachers prepare lessons from various books from the school's shelves.

Teaching standards vary from highly professional teachers using their ESL training in conjunction with internationally recognized texts, to snowboarders who roll up to class with a hangover and some good stories to chat about after the weekend. Large eikaiwa chains train teachers to deliver standardized, formulaic lessons in accordance with their corporate image. Their quality control involves student feedback and supervisor observations with ongoing training. Any creases are quickly ironed out and deviation from the script is usually discouraged. Ensuring quality at smaller schools varies from similar broad efforts at feedback and pointers, to simply letting untrained teachers loose in the classroom and leaving it to whatever gods oversee language lessons. Gary, a teacher who has worked at several eikaiwas and a teacher dispatch service says, 'Be on time, smile, make them laugh...you know, English.'

Perception of the industry over the years has been shaped by the large chains, not least by their scandals and meltdowns. Though the massive marketing campaigns by the likes of Aeon, ECC and Gaba continue to draw thousands of students a year, many also leave for smaller schools to get a more personalized experience. In their race to embrace the fast-food like standardization of business practices and service delivery, the large chains have undermined their own efforts to differentiate their services from one another. This has tested the patience of students who move from school to school and brand to brand, but get the same old sales pitch wherever they go, see the same cookie-cutter lessons, and find the same suit-clad foreign teachers pretending not to be bored to tears.

Financial scandals and public collapses have further shaken consumer confidence. The hiring of so many inexperienced teachers and the lack of quality control (especially in smaller schools) has also hurt the profession in general and foreign instructors are no longer seen as dedicated professionals. English lessons were once a sign of prestige, but are becoming just another hobby, like park golf* or mahjong. Part of the problem may be a lack of need for English. It has never been a priority in public education and most Japanese will never work abroad or interact professionally with foreigners. English remains the preserve of travelers and language enthusiasts.

Japan has suffered over two decades of mild economic slowdown since the property boom of the late eighties fizzled. It has also slipped from the second largest economy to the third, behind the US and China, and if you count the Euro zone as a country, Japan finds itself in fourth place. As in most stable, developed nations that do not embrace immigration, the population has been shrinking and aging. Already a quarter of Japan's citizens are over 60 and the birthrate is one of the lowest in the world. According to the Ministry of Health, Labor and Welfare, the population is expected to drop from 127 million to around 90 million by the middle of the century. It could be more than halved by 2100.[10] While a less crowded country would probably be more desirable in the long term, in the short term, the shortage of workers and surplus of retirees will put a massive strain on the economy and pension services. This has affected all sectors of the economy but in addition to its other woes, eikaiwa has experienced a steady drop in its client base and the declining population does not point to an increase in the future. Going

---

* A watered down version similar to mini golf popular with the elderly.

forward, there will be less money to spend on English lessons and fewer consumers to spend it.

In the early days of the post-bubble 'recession' of the 1990s, Japan reacted as it often has over the centuries when times got tough: the nation turned inward along with the national sentiment, and an intense, two-decade bout of obsessive navel-gazing ensued. This is not new. When the Tokugawa shoguns took over in the early 1600s, Japan closed its borders and limited foreign contact for over two centuries, a period of political and social seclusion known as *sakoku*. The modern return to an insular approach was bound to spell trouble for language schools - a service that thrived on a commitment to globalization, and there were inevitably casualties.

In 2002, a peak of sorts, eikaiwa amounted to a 670 billion yen industry (over $50 billion at the time), with almost two million students enrolled nationwide and tens of thousands of foreign teachers employed. The market share of the major players – the so-called Big Four - stood at 25%. The market itself has contracted considerably since the large collapses a few years later but the share of major chains has more or less held and they continue to define the industry. ECC and Aeon have stepped in where Nova and Geos have floundered; these two chains have individually increased their slices, yet many students have returned to smaller schools with a more personalized touch.

To understand what eikaiwa has become in today's terms, it is necessary to go back to the end of the gravy years. How does a large chain grow and expand? How does it keep its customer service standards? How does it prepare its teachers and how do they fare under its watchful gaze? Crucially, what happens when it all goes wrong? The direction of the industry has been defined by a chain that was the first and last word in the business but went spiraling into bankruptcy, almost dragging its competitors down with it. Once the biggest of the Big Four, its brand has endured in the public consciousness and is still synonymous with English teaching and learning in Japan.

2 Champagne Supernova

Patrick from Seattle arrived in Tokyo in the mid-nineties. 'A friend who was already working there invited me over. The way he told it, it was easy money, mad partying and hot women, 24/7. I had just finished college so I thought I'd give it a try.'

He had worked a few years after high school then put himself through a degree in International relations. He was a passionate rower and wrestler in college and carried on with bodybuilding afterward. He started rooming at his friend's downtown flat and they spent a year together, 'drinking, laughing and chasing girls'.

Then as now, one of the easiest ways to get a start in Japan was with the 'Big Four': Berlitz, Aeon, Geos and the undisputed champion, Nova, where Patrick's friend already worked. 'Most teachers were hired from overseas, but didn't get to choose where they'd be posted. Since I had a place to stay I applied from inside the country at the Nova branches where I'd like to work. It wasn't hard to get the job, and though my friend and I ended up at different branches, we were both only a few subway stops from the apartment.' In the interview, Patrick had the impression the head teacher was desperate for recruits. 'He basically launched into a pitch about how the language was a "product" and the students were "customers". He talked about the schedule. There were no public holidays, they or official weekends. In his words, "We don't recognize them." There would be two split days off a week and seemed to assume I was already working there. The place was expanding and really needed teachers. He said there was very little planning, just follow the steps. It sounded like a sales job - all service and no substance.'

One of the first people to apply popular modern business practices to the English-teaching industry was a plucky young entrepreneur by the name of Nozomu Sahashi. After returning from university in Paris, which apparently took five years and failed to net him a degree, Sahashi found himself unemployed. He was no doubt feeling left out of the Japanese corporate culture, which prescribes school then a local or national university, followed by lifetime employment in a big name economic engine like Mitsubishi Electric or Daiwa Securities. The bubble years might have passed him by had he not hit upon the idea of starting his own language school. With two expat acquaintances, a Canadian and a Swede, Sahashi opened the first Nova branch in Shinsaibashi, Osaka in 1981.

Sahashi patented what he called the 'System Concept', a direct teaching method that he thought would make language learning easier. Based on what he had seen, and his own linguistic experience, Sahashi believed that the Japanese and English languages elicited different brain wave patterns and this made it difficult for Japanese to distinguish English sounds from background noise. Such nonsense, along with the popular myths that Japanese have longer intestines than other races or that they alone are capable of subtle, nonverbal communication fills a whole category of pseudoscience known locally as *nihonjinron*, which has largely escaped rigorous questioning in Japanese science circles. Sahashi may have been following the dubious teachings of Tadanobu Tsunoda, who argued that language was processed in a different hemisphere of the Japanese brain to that of westerners. A simpler explanation would be that they aren't used to hearing a native speaker. Junk science aside, Sahashi correctly identified that putting the learners in a classroom with a native speaker and having them hear and repeat stock phrases and sample conversations, teachers could bypass many of the ingrained learning difficulties and bad habits developed by people who'd learned English the Japanese way in high school.[1]

Such teaching methods were not unheard of, but the real genius was in the marketing strategy. Sahashi aimed to get big, fast. Lessons were sold in packages of up to 300 sessions, paid in advance, and sometimes financing the cost with loans from credit agencies allied to the school. This created a pool of funds with which to hire more teachers and open more branches. Money was spent on advertising - billboards and TV spots - that emphasized the uniqueness of the method and the convenience and speed with which students could learn English. Branches sprouted up all over Osaka and later nationwide, conveniently located near rail and subway stations so customers could pop in for quick lessons after work or even during lunch breaks. The school was run like a shop, or a hair salon. Lessons could be booked at short notice and classes consisting of several students of (at least in theory) similar levels, cobbled together depending who had signed up for that afternoon. Lesson content and format were simplified and standardized; foreign hires didn't have to be professional teachers as they could be trained to deliver the 'lessons' the way an encyclopedia salesperson is trained to pitch to customers, or a cashier at McDonalds packs Happy Meals. Teachers hardly needed preparation time as the materials were ready to go out of the box; a *salaryman* on a business trip to another city could theoretically stop by a local branch and get the same quality of product he would in his home town.

Staff and teachers worked hard to keep the operation running smoothly. The school relied on multiple classrooms hosting 50-minute lessons from morning to night; teachers became service providers valued for the number of lessons they could crunch through in a day. The hours racked up and the profits rolled in. Teachers came and went, ads were pumped out and the company expanded on into the nineties. At its peak in the early 2000s, according to the company's website, Nova could boast over six hundred branches, five thousand foreign teachers, half the market share of the entire industry by revenue, and 66% of the country's English students.[2] There was even a branch in Honolulu for customers on vacation who needed to pop in for a quick bite of English. It was the kind of efficient money-generating machine that was proud to announce it had reopened Kobe branches 48 hours after the 1995 Great Hanshin Earthquake that killed thousands in the city. But as Nero fiddled away, new fires were smoldering at the foundations of the Nova business model.

Duncan from Edinburgh and Jarrod from the DC area were coworkers at Nova in 2007. Both had transferred from Honshu branches to Sapporo, shortly before its collapse. Duncan was a physics graduate who at first took the job to fund his travels in Asia. 'I had planned on going to Europe after university, but a friend suggested Asia, so that's where we went. She had quite a challenging interview with Geos and got the job. Everyone said Nova was easier to get into.' Jarrod grew up near the US capital, in a small town where he had lived all his life. He studied education in college and went back to teach at the high school he had attended. 'My world was just too small. I was a colleague of my former teachers. My kid brother went to the prom with one of my students. I had to get out so I did a rush application for JET (Japan Exchange and Teaching).' Jarrod didn't manage to secure a position on the JET program, but he did get into Nova.

For many teachers, it was just a job to support living overseas and other youthful adventures. Jarrod recalls one talkative young woman at his Washington DC recruiting session. 'She was just out of university and wouldn't stop yapping, about anything and everything. She commented on the recruiter's "cute" Scottish accent. I assumed she didn't get the job…but you never know.'

Duncan's own sexy Scottish accent was not a stumbling block to being hired, but he quickly had to adapt it to the classroom. 'My accent has changed a lot since I arrived. At first I was writing everything I said on the board because the students didn't understand me at all. After a couple of months I thought, *fuck this*, and started to dilute my pronunciation for them.' In Japan a North American accent is preferred, though any will do as long as it can be understood by non-native speakers. Sometimes the schools themselves request certain accents, or students ask to learn 'British English' or 'Australian English' ahead of a trip. One former JET teacher from New Zealand recounted that her trainers even asked her to sound 'more 'American'. But while in eikaiwa looks are still more important than a specific accent, Duncan recognized the need to adjust his so that students could follow him.

Training for the new recruits was reasonable compared to many schools. 'We got over a week,' says Jarrod. 'It was very detailed and the whole operation looked really corporate. The system translated well from paper to classroom. At first, I was proud to wear a suit to work every day

– I was part of something big. After teaching the same student seven times in a month without a hint of improvement it started to wear on me a bit. Some lessons were altogether soul-crushing.'

'But at least we got the training,' Duncan adds. 'It gave us something to fall back on and it was easy for new teachers to follow the steps. If you had no background in teaching, at least they made sure you were ready for their lessons. It gave me a grounding for my teaching ever since.' Duncan was also enamored with the corporate image to begin with. 'I thought this was the real deal, a big company and a chance to go places, so I followed the rules as best I could.'

While Jarrod was already a teaching professional and Duncan had the sense to water down his accent and learn the trade, not every teacher was as dedicated. Some teachers frequently called sick so they could go skiing or visit a hot spring or because of a hangover and others just didn't show up for days on end. Students complained of quality gaps between branches and even individual lessons at the same branch. The teachers weren't always happy, but no job is perfect. Instructors would pump out lesson after lesson with only a few minutes between. Discipline was uniformly tight. Staff had to dress in dark business attire, stick to the lesson plans and follow other corporate rules and regulations, such as smiling and greeting any passing student in the lobby.

Bruce from New York recalls his training session at a Nova affiliate in Hokkaido. 'The Japanese woman in charge of training kept pushing me to smile more. We had to smile all through the real lessons, and so we had to practice. They'd leave each new teacher in a room with a cardboard cutout for half an hour or more just to practice our greetings. At every step in the training process, she'd say, "That's good, but could you smile more?" My face was aching at the end of the day.' From a customer-service point of view, many rules made sense and it is true none of these were hardships. But for the exhausted teacher just finishing his sixth lesson of the day, third in a row, and about to go back in for the last, it was frustrating to be reprimanded for failing to smile at a passing student in the hall, or for looking tired in class.

Teaching was not always a chore, but it is easy to recall the difficult students. 'Most students were normal, well-adjusted people interested in learning English,' Jarrod says. 'Like all jobs, some were a headache. There was one pairing of students – The Dream Team - not a couple but they had a lot of lessons together because they basically couldn't integrate into regular group classes. The man had definite mental issues – he had a seven-inch surgery scar across the side of his head; the woman was the kind who took forever to make a sentence. When they came separately they were nearly impossible to teach. But when they were there together they somehow seemed to complement one another, in a weird parallel universe kind of way. Without that dream team, you couldn't make it through the lesson without wanting to bash your head against the table.'

One complaint from a lot of eikaiwa teachers is why so many 'crazy' people seem to be interested in English lessons. Everyone has met the student who sits quietly and doesn't participate; the one who pauses a minute or two or three before giving a single-syllable answer; the students who come week after week, year after year and never improve and don't seem to be enjoying themselves - every language school seems to attract its share. Duncan may have found the answer. 'A student I had was a psychologist or counselor. She told me that doctors advise mental health patients to get a hobby: go out and take flower arranging classes, learn to paint or learn a language. A lot of these people end up in

English classes.' This makes perfect sense of course - if you're miserable then there's no better advice than to just get out of the house. But it does beg the question of what need a person has for another language when they rarely communicate with others in their own.

Jarrod remembers a woman who was, 'Very frank - she basically used me for her personal counselor…talking about everything from her periods to infidelity…nothing seemed to be off the table.' Duncan adds, 'I think for a lot of them they're more comfortable talking about problems in another language. The Japanese can be very shy and may not have anyone to open up to. Even if they do it seems unnatural in their own language because it's just not done.' Speaking about personal issues in English may just give the Japanese chance of release while putting some distance between the speaker and the problems.

Patrick didn't rock the boat. 'There were times I wished I could request not to teach this student or that, but it was a business and you had to keep the customers happy. Some of them could be a real chore, though. But there were some supervisors who absolutely *breathed* Nova. They ate, slept and shat it. We had one supervisor at our branch and he'd say stuff like, "That tie, why don't you leave it at home next time?" I thought we were all in this together, so why was another foreigner riding us?'

The company had a long list of things it could ride teachers for. Some ran afoul of Nova's notorious 'dating policy' which forbade socializing with students. The rule is common among eikaiwa schools and is enforced to varying degrees from polite discouragement to contract-stipulated bans. It makes some business sense to stop students making private study arrangements with their teachers or quitting because they now have an English-speaking lover and can practice for free (though that would be rather venal justification for disciplinary action). It should also curb would-be Lotharios among the mostly male faculty from sleeping around and damaging the company's reputation. Patrick recalls, 'One guy was seeing two girls from the branch and they caught wind of each other. They got together and trashed his apartment while he was out one day. Another guy broke up with a student and she came to the front desk in tears claiming she was pregnant trying to get him to come back.'

Teachers carrying on like this can make a language school understandably cautious. Nevertheless, boys will be boys and girls will be girls and in a business where most teachers are single men in their twenties or thirties and most students and support staff are single women in the same age group, enforcing such abstinence is quixotic at best, if not a violation of human rights. In Nova's case teachers were not to share details with any students or meet them outside of school hours and Jarrod found this policy at odds with the company's stated goals. 'Eikaiwa schools talk of multiculturalism but then put all these restrictions on intermingling. You ended up living in a bubble. It doesn't foster multiculturalism.' Jarrod was first posted in rural Ibaraki prefecture, with limited options for socializing as it was. When he transferred to Sapporo, he found himself in a big city surrounded by attractive women.

Duncan, who started his Nova career in a Kansai branch, found socializing difficult too. 'It took me seven years to just find a social football team. The only Japanese we knew were our students and the staff, and we weren't allowed to hang out with students. That kind of forced teachers into dating the Japanese staff. In another way, it at least allowed a social life to develop. Coming over, knowing nobody, you're instantly thrust into this preexisting clique revolving around Nova staff.'

Neither Duncan nor Jarrod recalls anyone being disciplined for dating students at their branches but both conceded there was enough of it going on. Yet at Nova, teachers have been punished or even dismissed in the past for having relationships with students and have taken legal action as a result.

The National Union of General Workers is well-placed to assist foreign workers. Many do not understand Japan's complicated labor laws and run into trouble with employers due to unpaid wages, unfair treatment or general misunderstandings. Though Japanese law upholds the right to form or join unions, most foreign teachers feel their position is too tenuous. They lack the financial resources, language ability, local contacts and visa security to challenge their schools. Employers discourage teachers from joining unions with misinformation. Some have even gone as far to stipulate in their contracts that staff will under no circumstances be permitted unionize. The General Union involves itself in collective bargaining, industrial action and disputes at the courts or labor boards for individual cases of unfair dismissal, wage discrepancies or non-enrollment into the national health and pension plans.

The union was quick to address the consequences of anti-fraternization rules at Nova. In 2004, the Osaka Bar association ruled in a case brought by the General Union, that Nova had violated Japanese law over the policy. Six teachers had been dismissed in a crackdown on hanky-panky: cases included a teacher who was engaged to a student in a different Nova branch and a teacher who was forced to quit for dating a woman he had first met in a bakery, who just happened to be a Nova student. The association ruled that not only should Nova reinstate the two union members who had filed the suit, but that the anti-dating clause be removed from the contract.[3] When one teacher was transferred for his relationship with a woman who was a student at his branch, the court awarded 400,000 yen - about five thousand Australian dollars at the time - and a letter of commendation from the company as he had already left.[4] However, big business in Japan has rarely felt obliged to follow court rulings where workers' rights are concerned and according to current employees of affiliated schools, the non-fraternization policy remains intact. Boys and girls being what they are of course, the teachers and students continue to quietly undermine them.

Buddha 360 was a chic drinking spot just around the corner from Sapporo's nightlife and red light district of Susukino. In the short hot summers of Japan's frigid north, there are tables on the sidewalk where office workers unwind in the evening air. Over drinks, Bruce, an American, who worked at a Nova affiliate in Sapporo for four years, told me his center had also seen its share of bed-hopping. In just the time he'd been there, his first head-teacher was married to a former student, and the next, had been seen on a date with another student after hours. One young teacher had a fling with a female student, leaving her for another student, and a teacher who was married had at least two affairs with women taking lessons there. The anti-fraternization rule extended to female staff as well and was equally disregarded: at least four teachers had all had relationships with women working in the three downtown branches; another had dated two of the office girls successively, and another of the girls had dated two different teachers in as many years. Yet another female staffer at a suburban branch had a reputation for sleeping with a number of the male teachers - usually when they were still new - before getting bored and moving on. Some of this was surely just gossip, but Bruce's workplace was not even a very large school, with four branches and perhaps two dozen teachers at any given time.

No action was taken because, 'nobody in the office really cared about the policy.' Bruce was currently dating the sister of one of his students, whom he'd met at a company party, and they'd been together over a year. When asked if the center guards students' relatives as jealously as it does current ones (on paper at least), after all they're potential customers too, Bruce shrugged. 'They probably would if they could get away with it. But the truth is everybody does it. I think they recognize you can't just throw away experienced teachers over little things, you can't really control people or stop them hooking up, and let's be honest, that's what a lot of girls come for anyway'.

Because the union has challenged Big Eikaiwa directly, union membership itself can be a black mark and has been blamed in some cases for dismissal. Union supporters protested outside Nova's Shinjuku Branch in Tokyo in 2004 after five union members had been dismissed. In the case of teacher Kara Harris, who had asked to be made a permanent employee upon her sixth consecutive yearly contract and lost her job instead, the courts found Nova in violation again.[5] Despite having a good record, Harris was not renewed and was not given a solid reason, but held that it was because she had asked for her due. Her case illustrates how the yearly contract is used as heavy leverage by eikaiwa schools. If they don't like you, they have the option not to renew, which cuts into a legal gray area between dismissal and redundancy. Foreign teachers are in a weak position and most simply accept their fate and leave. Union membership would be helpful in such cases, but there is a high turnover of English teachers in Japan, with many staying a year or less, and it can be hard to maintain a union presence at many schools: It may take months to net new members, who would likely be gone a few months later. In many cases teachers don't join the union until they've already run into trouble.

Sometimes foreign instructors dig their own graves. In 1994 after two Nova teachers were arrested on drug charges, the company demanded all 3,100 foreign teachers sign a drug test agreement. While 90% signed and none were ever tested under the regime, the measure was seen as intrusive, especially as it only applied to foreign staff. It was also illegal - a fact that didn't prevent the majority of staff from feeling pressured into signing.[6] According to Bruce, the Japanese are ever suspicious of foreigners. 'They see it as perfectly natural that only the foreign teachers get drug tested, because well, that's what we get up to right? I don't think the Japanese have a different understanding of human rights, as much as a different understanding of *human*. It doesn't occur to most people that labor laws might apply to foreigners in Japan as well as citizens.'

In 2007, seven Nova teachers were charged with possession of marijuana after their dealers had been arrested. While the youth and adventurism of the typical eikaiwa teacher might explain them smoking a little weed or even popping the odd ecstasy tablet, such shenanigans do little to assuage the insular Japanese public's natural mistrust of foreigners. The Japanese are famously uptight about even the mildest narcotics (tobacco and alcohol excepted) and the law is strict: jail time and deportation await the unwary foreigner. Like sleeping around with students, drug use becomes a black mark that's hard for the industry to live down. It certainly didn't help Nova's image that it already had a growing body of students who were disgruntled over the way it was doing business in general.

One of the more successful Nova features was its scheduling. Different from the traditional format of each teacher 'owning' a regular class, students could book a day or two in advance, sometimes even a few hours. A group other students of about the same ability would be cobbled together and a teacher assigned to it from the roster. The teachers were on salary and knew when they'd be teaching, but the exact make up of the class could be left until almost the last minute if need be. This convenience suited the target market of busy young professionals and college students, in the same way as locating schools near major subway and train stations to catch people on their way home from work and school. The system required students to sign up for a package of lessons, paid in advance; lesson 'tickets' were sold in lots of up to six hundred and needed to be used up before the contract expired, usually a year from the start date. Buying a larger lot of tickets meant a lower per-lesson price, from around 2,300 yen ($23) per lesson on a 100-lesson plan, to 1,200 yen per lesson on a 300-lesson plan.

By selling bulk lessons in advance to thousands of customers, Nova collected millions to finance its rapid expansion, literally flooding anew the market that Nova itself had already saturated. According to the *Mainichi Daily News*, the school sought to grow from an already bloated 300 branches to a staggering 1,000 centers around the country. In one lawsuit, the parents of a young male employee who committed suicide in 2004 attributed his death to the stress of working up to eighty hours overtime each month to help achieve this goal.[7] The hefty number of lessons bought was a big commitment for both parties. Students tended to underestimate how busy they'd be when signing up at the start of a year, and found it hard getting to class once work had really kicked in; Nova saw a slight reduction in teachers around 2004 and this affected lesson availability. Often people would call to schedule and there would be no teacher to fill that slot. The months would go by and the yearlong deadline crept closer as unused lessons mounted. Many customers would decide to cancel their contracts early, but to get a refund they'd have to learn the Nova two-step.

Naturally customers expected to be refunded for unused tickets. But students who had signed for 600 lessons found that when they canceled after only a hundred or so, the company would calculate the value of the lessons already used differently from the contract stipulation. Regardless of a student's package, the lessons used would be calculated at the smaller lot rate of 2,300 yen per lesson. This would take a bigger slice out of the expected refund, the remainder of which was calculated to the company's advantage at 1,200 yen per lesson for a large lot. Simply put, Nova overcharged the customers for the lessons they'd already had, and then underpaid their refund. In such cases the disparity could be as much as a thousand dollars.[8]

Between 1996 and 2005, the National Consumer Affairs Center received 7,600 complaints about the refund policy. Lawsuits were filed and after two appeals and a Supreme Court ruling, Nova was found to be in violation of commercial transaction laws. In June 2007, the ministry of Economy, Trade and Industry imposed restrictions on Nova soliciting new students: the school could no longer sell packages of more than 70 hours of lessons or lasting longer than six months. Since 1999 over 70,000 students had received government subsidies for adult education that could be redeemed at Nova schools. The labor ministry announced the same month that it would no longer subsidize English courses at Nova, a sanction that further eroded the client base.

On top of refunds and scheduling woes, there were grave misgivings about the quality of the teaching. Students would complain of teachers who seemed apathetic, bored or disinterested in class. They were charged with being unprepared, hung over or still drunk from the night before; scruffy, unprofessional or just plain incompetent. That few of the teachers were trained professionals became apparent to many students as time went by. Though the main requirement for teaching eikaiwa had always been that you look the part, Nova was in some cases taking the 'any gaijin will do' philosophy to a new level.

'We had them all,' Bruce recalls. 'One guy called sick almost once a week to go snowboarding and once didn't turn up for three days straight without calling in. He wasn't fired.' Others used the lessons to chat up female students. People would do no preparation and simply bluff their way through lessons. Lateness became endemic as conditions worsened and salaries fell. According to Patrick, 'with private students or guys that run their own schools there's accountability, but when you're working for one of the big chains it's just a job. There is a sense that it's not real, that you'll be gone in six months, a year, two years and what happens in Japan won't affect you back in the real world. So why not milk it, live it up and save your energy for your real goals.'

Customer complaints are justified, but shouldn't be wholly blamed on the teachers. A company's failure to motivate its own workforce is an institutional failure. Teachers were numbed by working for an organization that robbed them of incentive. Bruce lists some of the complaints he saw when the office made a halfhearted effort at quality control: 'They posted a list in the teacher's room of all the customer complaints from a satisfaction survey. Some were real complaints, like the teacher spoke too fast or the student had repeated the same lesson on too many occasions. But others were just insulting: a teacher had his tie on loose with the top button undone, someone sat cross-legged or we "looked tired." I was even told a student complained because I'd put handouts on the carpet for a moment and not the table. That was bad because apparently the floor is dirty.'

Patrick offered similar sentiments: 'If I've done something wrong, fine, tell me. But I don't want the front desk to come to me with chickenshit like I yawned or my shirt was wrinkled. There has to be some oversight, but they also have to remember we're human beings.'

It is a sign of the industry's commitment to the idea that English teaching is purely customer service that makes small change like wardrobe transgressions so important. When an English lesson is reduced to practically an over-the-counter transaction, the teacher becomes the person *behind* the counter or worse, the product itself. Window dressing becomes the most vital part of the corporate image. Other schools such as Aeon and Geos have been very strict about dress codes and presentation, requiring teachers to wear a full suit or even stand at all times in class. The underlying assumption is that teachers are not professionals, sharing their knowledge and experience, but merely company representatives, molded into a product or service. Or perhaps given that in Bruce's words so many teachers, 'roll up to work looking like they just jumped off a skateboard', a dress code and a little discipline are all that stands in the way of complete chaos. Yet the nexus of staff apathy and financial complaints was brewing into a tempest.

Perhaps the first inkling foreign staff had that Nova might be in financial trouble was a step taken in 2005 to reduce labor costs. It is often a complaint that the first place an eikaiwa school looks to save money is in teacher salaries and benefits - ironic when one considers that the teachers are the star attraction, the reason the customers come in the first place. The Ministry of Health, Labor and Welfare requires that all employees in Japan who work at least two thirds of a full time schedule be enrolled in the national pension and social insurance scheme, *shakai hokken* for short. According to labor ministry guidelines this equals roughly thirty hours a week. Under the compulsory scheme, the company withholds a portion of the teacher's salary equal to half the individual's *shakai hokken* commitment and pays that into the national pot, matching it yen for yen.

By reducing the lesson times to forty minutes and insisting (on paper at least) that preparation time would be only a few minutes either side of a lesson, Nova was able to redefine all its teachers as part time-employees. Officially they now only taught 29.5 hours a week and their total office duty time was also just under the minimum, as prep time had been cut and previously paid working time between lessons was now designated as unpaid intervals. The company thus excused itself from paying pensions and union sources estimate this saved the company billions of yen. In real time spent at the office, in and out of class, the teachers were not working any less than before. Even the government, which rarely takes issue with the 'smooth' operation of big businesses, exercised an interest in how a company can arbitrarily declare its staff are suddenly 'part time' without any change whatsoever to workloads or schedules.[9] In theory the teachers could still pay into the national public health insurance scheme, but would have to register individually, and crucially, pay the entire amount themselves. In practice, few foreigners on limited contracts feel they can afford the burden.

Many part time workers or self-employed people in Japan are also forced to pay their own health and pension costs and it seems a glaring inequality to make those without a steady income pay more for public insurance than full time workers. The price for the health insurance stands at ten percent of the previous year's average salary – in ten installments, not twelve - and comes without some benefits the full cover offers. On top of regular income tax, workers can end up paying over twenty percent in total for pension and health. Living in Japan is not cheap and saving to leave can be prohibitive if foreign teachers commit to paying all their obligations as residents. Many delay, some default and not a few simply 'do a runner'.

Teachers could also register for a private insurance offered by the company but that meant paying medical costs themselves and chasing up the money later. Workers on *shakai hokken* simply flash their insurance cards at the doctor's office and get billed for only thirty percent of the cost, with the government paying the rest. Getting private insurance may mean getting reimbursed less, later, or not at all. In less scrupulous schools, teachers who thought they were covered have had their pay regularly docked, but have gone to the hospital only to find they have never even been registered for any kind of insurance. One teacher at another franchise in Sapporo found this out the hard way when he fell ill and learned that he'd never been covered at all despite having over eight hundred dollars in premiums deducted over the course of a year.

In September 2007, many Nova teachers around the country were notified their salary would be delayed. People started booking flights or looking for a new job. Those who had already resigned and were awaiting a final paycheck never got it. Those who were still employed at the school were paid late or by installments – up to 3,000 teachers by some estimates. 'If the insurance was the canary in the mineshaft, this was like the man next to you keeling over,' Patrick says. The news caused a minor stock panic and Nova share prices declined. CEO Sahashi mortgaged nine million shares of company stock, including more than a million of his own personal shares to raise capital, but salary payments were late again in October. Both the Tokyo union NAMBU and the General Union filed complaints on behalf of some 4000 workers. Half of those were still waiting for September's salaries as well.

The foreign teachers' 'Nova bubble' was compounded by a lack of communication. The Japanese newspapers were all carrying stories of receivership and lawsuits, but most foreigners couldn't read them. Those that did have access to media or a Japanese person to translate for them got the information second hand and perhaps couldn't comprehend the gravity of it. As late as 2013 teachers I spoke to said they'd heard rumors of involvement by the *yakuza*, Japan's organized crime networks. Such concerns reflect a general mistrust among foreigners of the Japanese business and power nexus more than any genuine allegations of underworld involvement. Yet in the absence of solid information, imaginations were free to run rampant.

There was no explanation from the company, only cryptic emails circulated by the directors exhorting teachers to pull together and ride out the storm. The foreign instructors were effectively the last people in Japan to know the place was going under. 'I was naïve,' Duncan explains, 'even on the last day I still thought things would pick up. The students started giving me their email addresses because they knew better than we did which way the wind was blowing. The next day the place was closed. I couldn't even go inside and pick up my stuff.'

A good number of those teachers were living in Nova-sponsored apartments. Nova deducted rent from paychecks and paid the landlords directly, and now it was going unpaid. Eviction notices came swift and fast, but many teachers were left without money to pay the rent, fly home or support themselves till they found another job. The cash flow stopped suddenly - even before Nova declared bankruptcy. According to Patrick, 'If we had been warned before the money stopped coming, we could have looked for another job or gone home, but they sideswiped us. Suddenly, all these foreigners were out on the street and there was nobody to turn to.' One local language school reported some four hundred applicants to a single position, as desperate Nova teachers cast about for a lifeline.

Jarrod explains, 'They even kept hiring till the end. One guy had just signed up. He was into snowboarding and was keen to shred some powder and in a week he was out of a job. He'd paid for his own ticket and everything.' By then over four thousand foreign teachers were in the same boat. It was not long after that some airlines such as Qantas began to offer discounted flights home to stranded expat teachers.[10] Duncan was evicted along with his roommates. 'On the day of the "check out" we were told we were responsible for ten years worth of wear and tear to the apartment that we'd lived in for 6 months. In the end we just paid a few thousand yen for the last month's water bill and walked away.'

With teachers dropping out, students leaving and debts mounting, chairman Nozomu Sahashi began casting about for a lifeboat. In the summer of 2007, several months before the first overdue salaries went unpaid, Sahashi approached travel agency HIS to suggest a business tie-in but talks went nowhere. He also pursued a partnership with Benesse Corporation, the owners of rival Berlitz, but was rejected. He even considered selling off some property the company owned and issuing more shares to generate income to make up for the shortfall in sales, and called a meeting of stock holders. Though one shareholder called on Sahashi to resign, the majority rallied around Nova and 170,000 new shares were sold.

Absent any other market impetus to move the new Nova shares one way or the other, the scramble to buy pieces of a damaged brand even as the scandal broke looked decidedly suspicious. Daily trading of Nova shares on the JASDAQ exchange usually ranged between 100,000 and 1.7 million. But on August 29 the volume rose to 10 million and peaked at 60 million on Sept 7. Sahashi sold a large volume of his personal shares as well, but failed to report this transaction to the authorities, even though he was legally required to notify them of any major changes in shareholding. [11]

Nova had also spent big on TV advertising, continuing to ramp up the campaigns even as the school's income dropped and the refunds skyrocketed. According to the Yano research institute however, the industry had already been in decline some years. It had peaked at 375 billion yen in 2003 but had already shrunk by around ten percent by 2006. After Nova's 2007 collapse, the shockwave shrunk the industry by a staggering 61%.[12] Did Nova know it was going against the trend, by continuing to spend on expansion in a saturated market? Patrick believes that there was certainly, 'far more money going out than they could hope to recover with new sales.'

Wasteful spending was also personal in nature. Sahashi was reputed to have a 330 square meter office with a double bed, sauna and traditional tea room in his presidential suite at Osaka headquarters. The HQ itself seemed over the top for a language school, sited on the twentieth floor of a downtown tower block and costing 2.7 million yen a month in rent. By the fall of 2007, it was like trying to outrun one of Japan's famous bullet trains. Tens of thousands of students across the country were demanding five billion yen (around USD $40 million at the time) in refunds. Payments to business partners, banks and advertising agencies were delayed; Sahashi tried to recall eight million shares from an asset management division of French bank BNP Paribas, but the shares had already been legally sold on. Nova's most recent quarterly report, from the first quarter of 2007 showed the company's recurring profits had dropped 19%, and it was over four billion yen in debt. It may have only been a fraction of the actual damage.[13]

Shareholders as well were finally lusting for blood. The Nova board held an emergency meeting and removed Sahashi from leadership of the company he had founded. On October 26 shares were delisted and Nova effectively ceased to operate. On November 5, Japan's largest paper *Yomiuri Shimbun* reported that Osaka police had filed embezzlement charges against Sahashi over a 320 million yen staff welfare fund – paid into by employees - that he allegedly used to pay student refunds. It didn't help that according to the paper, Sahashi made 159 million yen in 2006, while his company lost almost 3 billion.

It must have been an ignoble end to Sahashi's dream, but the careers of thousands of English teachers and staff had already ended; the hopes of hundreds of thousands of students that they could improve their English were quashed. Nova had personified the industry, but if the teachers were all womanizers and drug users and the bosses all thieves and fraudsters, public confidence in the very idea of studying English was undermined. The collapse sent Big Eikaiwa into a spiral that sucked in several other major chains as well as dozens of smaller schools and continues to affect the industry and image.

Patrick survived with some cash to spare. His hobbies weren't expensive and he had lucrative private students. 'I was still getting ¥10,000 an hour from a group of doctors I taught twice a week. I started looking for work when the late paychecks came in and lined up some alternatives by the time everything hit the fan.' It started as part time work: the money wasn't great but it was flexible, and it was better than unemployment. He got in before the glut of teachers started beating at doors.

There was chaos for Jarrod and Duncan in those first few weeks. Duncan started looking for a new job. 'I didn't want to go to another big school. I had been offered jobs at Interac and Heart [as a dispatch teacher to public schools]. I thought it would be a nice change but look how they turned out.' Dispatch agencies bid for the contracts to supply native teachers to local school boards each year. That school year, Interac lost the contract for the Sapporo board of Education to Heart in a bidding war. The following year, Heart lost the contract because its low bid meant low pay and many teachers had quit mid-semester: Interac was back in. Had Duncan taken a job with Interac he'd have lost it to Heart by the time the semester started. If he'd gone with Heart he would have lasted only a year.

So Duncan went into business with his roommate and a private student of his who'd been interested in starting a school. 'Because it was a start up, we worked without pay for a few months to get it up and running. We went hard out recruiting former Nova students and anyone else we could get our hands on. Then the student's husband got involved and decided it was *his* business.' Being foreigners, it had been difficult to get official business registration, so the help was welcome. 'There were a lot of legalities we weren't aware of, and requirements we couldn't fill even if we'd had the language ability. When the registration papers were drawn up the husband's lawyer changed the names of the business owners and made us just employees. But we had no employment contract with the now "legal" owner of the business, because we didn't believe at the time we were his "staff". The other guy just dropped it and walked out. I gave four weeks' notice and taught till the end. They didn't pay me so I went to the labor department.' But because Duncan had no employment contract and with it no fixed salary or hourly rate, the arbitrators could not determine how much he was owed. He got a settlement based on the minimum wage in lieu of anything else to go by – about ¥750 per hour. "It was a good experience, a learning experience. The school apparently survived but I heard they sold it in the end. It must have done okay.' Due to the settlement he is unable to say any more.

After that Duncan worked various jobs and taught private students. Like most part timers, it involved a lot of chopping and changing, and dropping gigs that weren't profitable for those that offered more stability or better cash. 'One kids' school I worked at part time, said they'd fine me for leaving early. I pointed out it was illegal and they backed down. They really just think we know nothing so they can try anything on us, but I'd learned the game by then.'

Jarrod quickly secured a transfer to EC, an affiliated chain of schools owned by G.communication, the company that stepped in to buy up Nova branches immediately after the collapse. 'A lot of branches were closed but some were kept open. Others were amalgamated with the chain of schools they already owned in Hokkaido. Some of us got placements immediately in the local operation.' The affiliate wasn't run too differently from Nova. Lessons were fifty minutes instead of forty, but the basic eikaiwa structure was in place: in-house curriculum, pretty girls at the front, and a lot of smiling and ego-stroking. 'The first few weeks I was in a kind of limbo. They gave me keep-busy tasks like checking lesson plans and filing student records. They didn't want Nova teachers doing the new lessons yet because the fifty minute lessons didn't match our contracts which stipulated we were to teach forty minutes.' It was unusually thorough accounting – other schools would have just had him teach the extra time and pocketed the difference. At the time many teachers would have been happy just to have work at all.

Jarrod even found himself teaching some classes under the old Nova system. G.communication needed to woo the surplus of eikaiwa students suddenly loose on the market. 'Part of the plan was to take them in, along with their teachers, and keep teaching them Nova lessons till their remaining Nova lessons had all been used up. Then I guess they'd be offered new contracts at EC. It was messy having a teacher in one cubicle teaching the EC lessons and another next to him doing Nova. I'd step out of my lesson ten minutes before the next guy had finished. It confused everyone.'

G.communication kept over a hundred Nova branches open and also acquired branches of rival chain Geos when it collapsed in 2010, incorporated them into the 'NovaXGeos brand. Both were later bought by Jibun Mirai Associe Ltd, and integrated with other brands that had been acquired. Despite its tainted name, Nova would come out on top. EC, which had enjoyed decades of market leadership in its own region, was assimilated, effectively becoming a Nova franchise. Jibun Mirai rebranded itself Nova Holdings in 2013.

After being passed around so much Nova teachers were long overdue for some pain. The package seemed to get progressively worse. Salaries were reduced and cuts to benefits were dressed up as performance bonuses: teachers were told if a class has a certain number of students then there would be a 'bonus' of a hundred or two hundred yen per lesson. These 'table ratios '– the number of students per teacher per lesson – were of course designed more to gauge fiscal efficiency than educational benefit: the schedulers and the seasons had more control over table ratios than teacher popularity and in any case, a month of full tables would be unlikely to make back the pay cuts for long term teachers.

New hires were easy victims for the so-called incentives and bonuses, teachers who didn't call sick all month got a bonus of up to 25,000 yen (about $250 in late 2013). Bruce taught for several years under G.communication and Jibun Mirai, and soon realized the incentive 'was also money they'd already taken away in pay cuts'. The regularity bonus was simply a portion of what had previously been the teacher's regular salary set aside, and renamed in order to discourage absenteeism for any reason. Without a doctor's note - sometimes even with one, since such a condition was never specified - a teacher could stand to lose a day's worth of wages (up to $100), plus $250 of the lost 'bonus'. It amounted to a fine for calling sick, an illegal labor practice under Japanese law. Bruce could see the real reason behind the changes: 'The whole idea was to hold us hostage to the company's scheduling needs.'

Year after year of such nickel and diming irked the staff and smacked of discrimination. After another round of post-revival trimming, Bruce complained of the company giving the receptionists and counselors a bonus whenever they re-signed a student for a year, but the teachers - the people who worked hard all year to keep that student and who spent all the time with them - got a pay cut. 'It shows just how far down the hierarchy we are when these twenty-two year old girls are given all the credit for our efforts,' Bruce says. 'It's like, "Nah, a foreigner couldn't have done that. It must be something the Japanese staff achieved".'

Being 'offered' several contracts in a year was the final straw for Bruce. 'They were trying to strong-arm us. It was either take the new contract or get fired. You couldn't argue with them, and each new contract cut more than the last.' Since it was no longer financially viable to work in Japan under such conditions he resolved to finish his contract on his current salary and leave. Yet he had to quit even earlier, when Nova tried to force him to sign yet another contract six months before the old one was due to expire. 'We all knew it was illegal and they probably knew we knew. What can you do? The house always wins.'

The new Nova continues to hire and expand, though under the new pay conditions turnover is predictably high. On August 26, 2009 Sahashi was found guilty of embezzlement and sentenced to three and a half years in prison, later reduced to two. He has since appealed and lost. Sahashi may be discredited, but the structure of the company he built remains intact. Bruce muses, 'with all the schools out there, name recognition is still a big thing and people will go for the big name, the one that spends on advertising, even though it went through all those scandals. The company should have disappeared by now, but people just instinctively trust a big name.' Echoes of Don MacLaren's charges against American Club a decade earlier.

Nova's collapse was a boon for the competition: ECC, Geos and Aeon all took a chunk of Nova's market share. Nevertheless, up to half of the students and a third of the teachers found continuity under the G.communication rescue package and some are still there years later under the newest owners. The object of buying a language school, even a tainted brand, is to make a profit and the new management has sought to squeeze every yen out of the teachers, much along the lines of other market leaders. Bruce feels teachers have lost out, even since Nova's revival. 'There are two eras in the business – before the collapse and after. They used the decline in enrollments and consumer confidence to pull all manner of benefits out from under us.' But with a small recent revival in fortunes – Nova is expanding again – teachers have yet to reap any rewards.

Patrick has moved on to a public school job. Bruce has resumed a career in physical-therapy in the US. Duncan has a secure position at a national franchise that opened fairly recently in Sapporo. He is head teacher after three years, is married to his Japanese sweetheart and a new father. He is not on a salary and doesn't have full employee benefits, but the flexibility suits him. 'I don't want to be a salaryman. I want the freedom to work other jobs, teach privates and so on. I have a good position and the school is still growing so who knows?' The couple has already bought their first home.

Jarrod now works at a small, but well-established language center in the north. 'The place has a real family atmosphere and I'm comfortable where I am. I teach 25-30 hours a week and have all the freedom I need in between. I can go boarding before work, study Japanese or work on my own book.' He is not sure about the future of the industry, but for his own part, he is considering a permanent resident's visa, which he should be eligible for after seven years in Japan. 'I like the city and I love teaching. It's just a shame there's so much mismanagement in the industry.'

This hasn't of course stopped the new Nova's expansion. According to Bruce, the natural upshot of growing at the expense of the staff's career development is declining morale and a student body that picks up on it. 'We stopped having regular team meetings, training was reduced. Student numbers went down. This is what happens when you're not included in the process. Their whole system is designed to keep you off guard. No meetings, no job security, zero control of your career path.' Still, Bruce credits his time in eikaiwa for learning to teach better English. In addition to his day job in occupational and sports therapy, he teaches ESL a few nights a week as an adjunct professor at a college in the US. 'Most of the students are Hispanic and they're all there because they need English to survive. The training I got in Japan didn't do anything but despite that, more than four years on the job taught me vital classroom skills. When I got to the classroom, I was prepared.'

Ironically, Bruce received an email from Nova over a year after leaving, exhorting him to apply for hire again. The offer for rehires was truly astounding: 300,000 yen a month and a completion bonus of 400,000. (around $4,000) This was far better than most eikaiwa schools offer, but still less than Bruce was already making back in the US. Reading between the lines it was not hard to see the cracks: eight lessons a day – '44 minutes' each. While the figure of 44 minutes suggests preparation time is paid, it also suggests a part time wage based on lessons booked. The conditions state that absences will not be paid but do not say whether that means teacher or student absence. The completion bonus is generous but travel and start up costs are all to be borne by the teacher and conventional wisdom says it costs at least that much to get started in Japan. Moreover, taking a page from Gaba's book, the bonus is contingent on steady lesson evaluation averages. If the industry is any indication, any school worth its salt will make any excuse to avoid paying such a generous bonus.* Bruce is skeptical, 'it might look like a good offer to a teacher already in Japan, but there are too many ifs and buts.'

He has good reason to be skeptical. In recent years Nova teachers have been busted down from full-time to part-time status, seen their sick days and holiday pay eroded and finally evaporate as they are renewed as 'subcontractors'. Any hopes that a per-lesson rate could be more profitable in the short term were quickly quashed by Nova's announcement that it would charge subcontracting teachers a dollar a lesson (out of the fourteen dollars or so they now earn) for use of the classroom facilities, amounting to a further loss of around $150 a month.[14] There's no way I'd go all the way back just for that,' Bruce laughs, 'who would?'

---

* See Chapter Six

Craig Currie-Robson

3 The Battery Hens of Berlitz

The supervisor shifted uncomfortably in his seat. He was fairly new to the position although an old hand at the company. James, though an eikaiwa veteran, was fairly new to Berlitz. 'We've had a complaint from a customer,' his supervisor said. A day earlier, James had been kept over after a long shift to cover for another teacher. His first mistake had been stating that he was covering for someone. 'I thought they'd wonder why it wasn't the scheduled teacher but apparently that was taken to mean I didn't want to be there.' The next was mentioning a student had a different hairstyle to her picture in the class file. 'Fair enough, she might be sensitive about her appearance, and it didn't need saying anyway.' The third complaint was that he looked tired and demotivated, 'And that's where I nearly lost it. It was the end of the night and I was tired and blindsided. I told them I'd mull my response. I went home stunned wondering why the hell I'd come back to this industry. I'd fought like hell to be here and now this? I thought, just what – not who, *what* - do they think I am?'

A year later at a different school, he was reprimanded for just the opposite: being too energetic and apparently not serious about the lesson. That's when he finally did snap. 'I told them they can fire me if they like but I would not accept a dressing down for trying to keep the mood light.

They needed me so they backed down. Now I run a whole team of teachers at that place and every time the front or the scheduler comes to me with complaints about someone's energy levels, I tell them that's not a valid concern. I'm not going to my teachers and telling them they look tired when they all know they're tired and why. I'm not helping a Japanese company disrespect them on my watch, and I have no time for any foreign head teacher, in any school, who does.'

Kieran from the US has worked In Japan for over a decade. 'I had always wanted to teach overseas. I thought Europe might be nice, but I didn't have an EU passport so it would have been a lot harder to get a job there. I found a program with a school district in Chiba, so I decided to try Japan.' This is a fairly common route for teachers of ESL: a can-do attitude and the guts to get on a plane and try something new. Chiba is a prefecture adjoining Tokyo where many of its towns serve as bedroom communities for the metropolis and for the bustling Narita airport. As you head toward the south and east, the region becomes increasingly rural, with picturesque farms and villages, and forested hills in the distance. Kieran's first stint lasted a year at one of these country schools, and he enjoyed the work and the students.

But after having problems with a tenant of the property he owned back home, Kieran returned to the states to sort out the trouble. He was back in Chiba the following year but he was not placed so well. The next school they sent him to didn't use him as much and he was 'bored and feeling wasted' – a problem familiar to many ALTs in public schools. 'There was a lot of down time between lessons, students and teachers weren't motivated. The quality of the schools can vary widely.' He left after a year and moved to the big smoke, taking a job with Berlitz in Tokyo.

Education in his home state was unionized so Kieran was naturally attracted to *Begunto* – the Berlitz branch of the Tokyo General Union. At first he was in his words, 'gung-ho', putting up posters and handing out pamphlets. Union membership was never as high as he'd have liked it to be. 'A lot of people think the union can't change anything so they don't join. Many aren't in it for the long term and see no need to get involved or rock the boat.' But the difference in benefits for union and non-union members is a marked one and those who don't join the fight don't get to share the spoils.

Maximilian Berlitz could never have imagined his school would be an international brand where western teachers challenged Japanese bosses. The German émigré opened his first language school in Providence, Rhode Island in 1878. At first he catered to Americans learning foreign languages, and with his French teacher, Nicholas Joly, developed the direct approach. Joly taught French *in French* and avoided lengthy grammar explanations in favor of drilling and practicing useful phrases and dialogues. Even beginners were thrown in at the deep end. It was perhaps the first time modern language study was recognized not as another school subject, but a gateway to international communication. Today most language centers around the world employ the Berlitz method, or 'communicative approach' to some degree.

The school expanded to other American cities and included English teaching to immigrants in its curriculum. After Berlitz's death the company was headed by the founder's son-in-law and grandson in turn. In 1966 it became a subsidiary of Educational publishers MacMillan, Inc.

In 1993 Fukutake Publishing of Japan, now known as Benesse Corporation, began purchasing Berlitz stock. Benesse became sole owner of Berlitz in 2001. One of the 'Big Four' language schools of the nineties and noughties, Berlitz still maintains a large market share in Japan, with 1800 employees and 62 branches nationwide as of 2013.[1]

When Benesse took the reins, Berlitz was a reputable school with a solid corps of dedicated, full time teachers. There were steady base-up pay increases and benefits such as a seniority bonus. Teachers were happy and productive, students were satisfied, and it was a coveted place to work. Something had to be done.

In a traditional Japanese corporation everyone gets a share. The workers knuckle down and put in long hours. In return employers pay them well, with steady increases each year and twice-yearly bonuses equal to several months' pay each. The company is obliged to enroll full time employees in the national health and pension plans and match their contributions. In the highly productive seventies and eighties, the so-called 'bubble' years, this relationship was a key component of Japan's astounding economic growth. Everyone benefited, so everyone chipped in. With harder times in the decades since, this arrangement has slowly eroded; in eikaiwa, the practice was scrapped as soon as possible – especially when schools realized foreign teachers would work for less.

Under Benesse, Berlitz followed the industry standard throughout the nineties. Not only was the apparently prohibitively expensive practice of paying bonuses and giving longevity raises scrapped, the company aped other eikaiwa schools in their 'under thirty hours' policies, avoiding the responsibility of paying into the national health and pension schemes on behalf of teachers. Yet while the contract stipulated that teachers worked 29.5 hours, up to 35 lessons, the union later argued that teachers were frequently on duty up to forty hours when unpaid preparation time and gaps between lessons were counted. This went on for *sixteen years* until the union fought back.

At the time Kieran joined Berlitz, pay was set at around ¥250,000 for starting teachers. They taught thirty five 'units' a week and were paid for five units of preparation time. After 2005, the five 'preps' (preparation units) per week were paid only at the discretion of the branch manager and depending on lesson demand. This was intended to improve the quality of lessons by allowing new hires time to actually prepare, especially for children's lessons. Those who had been at Berlitz since the bubble years of the early nineties had it better. 'There were teachers who had been there forever and were just raking it in,' Kieran remembers. 'They had salaries way above ours and all the standard employee benefits. They'd sit around bitching about the job but couldn't leave because the money was too good and they knew they couldn't get the same deal elsewhere anymore.' According to the General Union web page, Berlitz teachers in those days earned ¥318,000 per month, with a ¥15,000 per month housing allowance and a further ¥165,000 per year in transport allowances – a salary package unimaginable today.[2]

It can be hard to bump a permanent employee down in salary. By law in Japan, this cannot be done without the consent of the worker. Schools have figured out since the good years how to avoid this. New teachers are hired on a contract basis rather than as full time or 'permanent' employees. This allows the company not only to avoid pension and health benefits but also to renegotiate the contract each year. If a pay cut is the only way to keep the job, a teacher has little choice but to sign. If not, they'll find another teacher. For full timers there is a nominal annual contract completion bonus but it only adds up to a few hundred dollars. Such old-timers are an increasing rarity in eikaiwa: few remain who arrived in the good old days and have kept their old contracts.

Other benefits are fleeting and hard to attain. These day Berlitz offers three to five paid sick days per year, but it only kicks in after three years of service. The average length of stay for a Berlitz teacher is two or three years so many never get a single paid sick day. Kieran suspects this is deliberate. 'It's as if the company has tied the requirement right to when, statistically, people are most likely to leave anyway.' Such benefits are granted to Japanese employees from day one. Across the industry disparity remains between 'full time' Japanese staff in a large corporation and 'part time' foreign teachers.

Even standard 'base-up' raises or increases to the per hour rate depend heavily on student evaluations. This also irks Kieran, 'I think they do everything to keep you at the current level. Evaluations are subjective and increases go to "excellent teachers". What is an "excellent teacher"? Can't those who do better teach the rest of us to be as good? Favoritism seems to be as big a factor as actual performance.'

The catalyst for union action, other than a boiling resentment at having no pay increase in a decade and a half, was a windfall profit for the company. In 2007, Benesse's net sales topped ¥380 billion ($3.8 billion) and owner Soichiro Fukutake was on the Forbes list with a personal worth of $1.4 Billion. At 11% profit over the previous year, it was the fifth consecutive year of increasing returns. While the Berlitz branch of the General Union, *Begunto*, was negotiating for a base pay rise in light of these profits, a lavish party was held for the Berlitz management at the luxurious Roppongi Hills Grand Hyatt in appreciation for their role as a leading division in the corporation's success.[3] Foreign instructors were incensed that the managers were being fêted while the front line teachers had not been given a share of the profits. In an English school, where students pay to be taught face to face by foreigners, and the teachers work hard all year to make it happen, it was those very foreign teachers who were left out when it came time to divvy up the spoils. Berlitz and Benesse were patting themselves on the back without considering the contribution of those who had made it possible. It was time to ratchet up the pressure.

Union teachers began by picketing outside the hotel where the party was being held. The union formulated a list of nine demands. Chief among these were a 4.6% pay increase, a one-off bonus equivalent to one month's pay and to be enrolled in the national pension and healthcare schemes. Over the following months union teachers conducted 'spot strikes' at Berlitz branches that snowballed until scores of teachers were participating. To make striking painful however, it had to be guerrilla warfare: the union had to hit hard when and where the company least expected it.

Under the Berlitz system, students were able book a lesson as late as 6pm the day before, and teachers' schedules for the next day were posted on the notice board the night before. This flexibility worked well for students and many teachers but made it difficult to notify the company of a strike. If the time, date and location branch of a strike were known, the school could simply reschedule the lesson, assign it to non-striking teachers or move the student to a nearby branch where possible. For an organization built around such flexibility, it would be the same as the teacher simply taking time off for a doctor's appointment. Worse, strikers could be preemptively singled out by having their schedules reduced or receiving other forms of punishment.

In order to meet the definition of stopping work effectively, teachers would therefore give only five minutes' notice before walking out on a lesson. This kept the company on its toes: instructors would walk out on one class and be back for the next two, away for the following one and so on. It made it difficult for the company to bring in substitute teachers and break the strike, because they didn't know who would strike, when or for how long. Students were notified of the practice and the reasons for it in a leaflet handed out by union members in front of the buildings where the language centers were located.

Industrial action is not unheard of in Japan, but it must have been novel for downtown lawyers and bankers to see foreign teachers striking outside their office towers. Kieran recalls the mood over the strikes at the time was, 'excitement. Finally we thought we were getting somewhere. I handed out leaflets outside the building and some students expressed solidarity. But It was a big office building and unless you saw a face you knew, you couldn't be sure everyone who took a leaflet was a student. We couldn't know how many people we got through to.'

Berlitz came out swinging. The company was quick to deploy part timers and non union teachers as strike busters. Sometimes even managers and staff from other branches were drafted in. These teachers would wait in nearby cafes and coffee-shops – somewhat fittingly, Starbucks was a favorite – and would be called in to cover a class at a moment's notice. There was some resentment toward these 'caffeine cowboys' as the union strikers dubbed them, but many other teachers who weren't union members showed solidarity and some even downed chalk and walked out as well.

After eight months of strikes and bargaining, only two demands were still standing, the pay increase and the bonus. This was not because the strikes had been particularly effective: the union had dropped most of its demands but the company was still stubbornly unresponsive. To a company that had made 8-11% increases for several years running, a small pay rise for the teachers - about a hundred dollars a month - should have been not only affordable, but a token of appreciation gladly given. Berlitz made a counter-offer: a pay rise of less than one percent, effectively no offer at all.[3] The gut punch came in November 2008, after nearly a year of walkouts that had involved more than a hundred teachers and cost the company thousands of lesson hours. Berlitz sued the union, individually naming several union executives, foreign and Japanese, and demanding ¥110 million in damages from each. The company also circulated a letter informing teachers that the strike was 'illegal' and threatening dismissal. It may sound ironic that a company seeking so hard to keep its teacher's wages down would ask for a million dollars or so out of an English teacher's meager salary, but of course that wasn't the point.

The union immediately responded to this intimidation with a claim filed at the Tokyo Labor Commission charging the company with unfair labor practices and that the cease and desist letters were an illegal interference. The Berlitz suit against the union was widely recognized as intimidation. A slew of legal experts noted in op-eds that it is highly unusual for companies to sue because a strike is 'illegal'. The right of private sector workers to strike is protected under a raft of Japanese labor laws dating back to 1946. The right to form unions and take industrial action is enshrined in Article 28 of the constitution; Article One of the Labor Union Act (revised 2005) ensures workers have the right to collective action; Article Seven states that union members may not be discharged simply because they are union members or have formed a union.[4]

Nevertheless the union felt compelled to stop the walkouts, fearing that individual strikers would be terminated. Even with union protection, the eikaiwa teacher is in a tenuous position. Few can afford to go without work while a court case drags on, and many would have had to throw up their hands and go home had they been summarily dismissed. After a year of Tokyo District Court hearings, beset by delaying tactics, late paperwork, 'miscommunication' and other shenanigans from the company, Berlitz and the union finally entered formal talks in December 2009. In October the following year, talks broke down and litigation resumed. In February 2012, the court released its findings in a 43-page ruling that unequivocally confirmed the union's right to strike. All strikes that had been conducted were recognized as legal by the court and all of the company's compensation demands were dismissed. Within a week, Berlitz lodged an appeal at the high court.

In the meantime two of the union executives on the case had already been fired by Berlitz. One had to take an unpaid leave of absence because he was a US Army reservist and had been called up to serve, although that had never been a problem when it had happened before the union action. Another was dismissed because she had to take time off to undergo cancer surgery and chemotherapy, which ought to have been a good enough excuse to put before any employer. In both cases the company claimed it had dismissed them for being away too long, but the union viewed it as an attempt at union busting.[5] The courts also oversaw 'reconciliation talks' between Berlitz and the union and collective bargaining began again in earnest. By late 2012, after four exhausting years of industrial action, court battles and collective bargaining, Berlitz capitulated. It was a mixed victory wherein the company agreed to a base pay rise of 3% and the one-off bonus proposed earlier; the union agreed to give three weeks' notice before any industrial action and 45 minutes before an actual spot strike.

The union also scored a small victory in ensuring all negotiations would henceforth be carried out in English. The 'language barrier' is something eikaiwa schools have traditionally sought refuge behind when they don't feel like playing straight with foreign employees. Berlitz frequently brought in local lawyers during bargaining and interpretation across the boardroom table got tricky. The union felt the company was stonewalling by bringing in outside professionals who didn't understand the language. Since Berlitz has plenty of Japanese employees with fluent English and few of the teachers speak fluent Japanese (not to mention the fact that Berlitz is an English language school to begin with), it has been forced to recognize that English is the logical choice for communication with its foreign staff.

The union cannot rest on its laurels. As with any corporation, complacency means letting the management dictate the terms, and in eikaiwa, management has gained a reputation for taking advantage of foreign instructors when their backs are turned. There are relatively mundane demands such as training seminars, English fire drills, and courtesy calls when a student cancels late and a part time teacher needn't turn up. There are also more serious cases that continue to run through the courts, such as discrimination, wrongful dismissals and teachers who have been removed from the national insurance plan against their wishes. In smaller schools, or those without unions, teachers with such complaints usually find themselves disgruntled and on the next plane home. There is strength in numbers.

Kieran feels that, 'if the union publicized better, more people would know the benefits. Berlitz settled after the strike action, but only union members benefited. People have a point of sale mentality when it comes to joining: they think "What can I get now?" They don't realize that it's a long and involved process.'

James from Australia has been in the industry over a decade. He's had his share of ups and downs, part time jobs and small schools, as well as a few brushes with Big Eikaiwa before rising to the position of head instructor at a mid-size city language school. 'I had worked in Japan once before taking jobs in Southeast Asia and the Gulf, but I really loved Sapporo so I came back. It was in many ways a big mistake. I knew the market would be smaller and harder but I underestimated just how hard. All I wanted was a steady salary and an easy life teaching in the place I loved, maybe take a job in a country school or something.'

But he came back in 2008 to find a cutthroat market of part time hours and dispatch agencies. 'There were no high school jobs left anymore. They were all taken up by the dispatch agencies like Heart and Interac. Jobs that used to pay ¥270,000 or ¥300,000 a month were now farmed out to temps for ¥220,000 or ¥230,000'. Big chains had long waiting lists and all he could find was one small school to sponsor his visa and they couldn't even provide enough work to get by. He needed other jobs. 'I had come with pretty modest goals I thought. All I wanted was a standard job: an average salary and paid holidays. Even that was a mountain to climb.'

James' sponsor did a common piece of footwork to ensure the availability of teachers: the immigration department required teachers to have at least enough hours a month to earn ¥180,000 or so. The school couldn't provide that much work but agreed to help with the visa, on the understanding that James would give first choice to them for hours, but still find other work. 'It was run by a helpful old lady who was committed to international exchange. She couldn't provide much work, and couldn't really run a school, God bless her, but she wanted to help foreigners get a foot in the door.' After several months of looking for work, staying at an expensive guest house and watching his funds dwindle, a chance finally materialized at Berlitz. In Sapporo, Berlitz was a franchise owned by the now defunct ELS Japan, rather than Benesse, the owner of most Berlitz branches. Nevertheless the school employed the Berlitz curriculum, schedule and pay scale for its Berlitz lessons and teachers. 'Berlitz was definitely on my short list because I wanted to work for a big name company. I had no idea about their curriculum but I assumed they'd pay more. Even when I was only offered part time work there I snatched it up. They offered more hours and I was encouraged to keep my schedule open. I'm not proud to say it, but I dropped the other job like a stone.'

Berlitz, like the other major schools, reinforces brand identity with its own in-house texts and materials. As with the competition, teachers are graduates from western universities, but do not need to be linguistics or even literature majors to teach: the school trains them to its own standard and to deliver its product. They didn't even need to be native speakers, James recalls. 'They taught Italian and French, German and Russian. The non-native teachers were so good they could teach English too. One Czech guy taught English German and Russian, there were teachers from all over Europe who had gone through the doors. I was really impressed with how global the place seemed.'

But Berlitz/ELS in Japan had a decidedly different idea about teaching, even with the communicative methods that the company pioneered and that James was used to. One of his first hurdles was the text: 'I didn't want to "sell" the lesson to the students, which is what my trainer told me I had to do. What I'd learned in my TESOL training and what I'd experienced in teaching in several countries is that students are supposed know why they're taking English classes and don't need to be told the value of the lesson.

Berlitz lessons were designed around 40-minute units, with four units to a chapter and a dozen or so chapters per level. Each contained practical survival skills such as renting an apartment or going to the bank: neat, bite-sized nuggets designed to be delivered within the forty-minute time frame following a set script in the teaching manual. According to James, 'These lessons would have been mildly useful to someone going to the US for work or study, less so your casual conversationalist. The lesson revolved around a short role play scenario or two and – as best I could make out – a couple of pictures. You had to be constantly engaged, constantly drawing the student into the lesson and trying to get them to speak, especially if the target skill didn't look immediately useful, which it often didn't. The trainer was right; I really had to *sell* the lessons.'

In eikaiwa, the idea is to have the student speak more than the teacher, to give them a sense of having used the lesson time well. But teachers will tell you many students are reticent, shy or otherwise not particularly talkative. Many simply don't answer a question when it is put to them. 'I was exasperated at times when had to repeat a question several times – one I knew the student understood – and received simply a wall of silence.' James recalls. 'This leaves it to the teacher to fill the gaps with his own voice or risk a long silent lesson where the language goals are not met.' A lesson where nobody talked at all would generate a front-desk complaint at any self respecting language school.

But by filling that silence, teachers could run afoul of the required teacher/student talk ratio. 'This was a big no-no. The head instructor listened outside a lesson once and pulled a teacher up for speaking too much in class. The student was a beginner who could barely put a sentence together. But with a text that relies so heavily on speaking – and so few examples of how to do so, the teacher is constantly battling against the lesson content to get something done. If an experienced teacher can't get his head around the text, perhaps there's something wrong with the lesson materials. The teacher's manual recommended all manner of repetitive drills and activities that would work better in a group lesson than the usual one-to-one, and that was still squeezing blood from a stone. There was just not enough content in most units to fill 40-minutes.' After a couple of months of battling the textbooks, James says, 'I wanted to break into the ELS side of the company: it paid a bit better and we got to use Oxford texts. ELS was considered real teaching'

Another problem with the text, James alleges, was the price. 'Students had to pay I think ¥15,000 or ¥20,000 ($150-200) for these texts, which were developed in-house of course, and couldn't even be used for self-study because they were designed entirely around the teacher's classroom delivery. For a fifth of the price they could get much better text in the bookstore, but ours was "special" because it was the Berlitz method.'

Grant, who worked a stint at Berlitz in the nineties recalls the texts were, 'great for beginners, with constant drilling and repetition, a good way to establish a foundation in English. But anything above that, forget it. The brand name attracted high-level professionals like doctors and lawyers, but they were too advanced for the texts we had. Berlitz traded on its name the way French restaurants do – attracting people who will pay extra just to say they went there, or because they only trust big names. It's snob value.'

Texts weren't the only thing expensive. Most lessons at Berlitz were one to one or in small groups of two or three students. At James' branch students paid over ¥8,000 per private lesson, for which the part time teacher would get only ¥1,750 as a starting rate, before tax – less than a quarter of the lesson fee. The gulf between what students pay and what teachers get is a constant sore point, especially in light of the quality of the text and the effort needed to teach a Berlitz lesson. Speaking from years of experience, James explains, 'People in the business will tell you it's the *teacher,* not the text. That begs the question of why the teacher got so little and the text cost so much. In any case a poor text makes the lesson harder for everyone.'

With such engagement, each lesson was an intense 40-minute presentation. According to James, 'it was quite stressful because just looking at each unit, there was really only 15-20 minutes of material on the page at most. You'd come into class thinking, *I have to do this and only this for the next 40 minutes. I can't bring in supplements, or deviate from the script. I'm not allowed to use half the classroom tools I've developed over the years; I'm not even allowed to push ahead once we get through it, so I have to stretch it out.* You'd open the textbook before class and see what lesson you had to teach and start dreading the classroom, because you knew it was going to be a grind.'

James was sent out to corporate clients: an air-traffic control center, a software developer, district courts, and had to teach the same lessons as the in-house students got. 'I got more money for commuting, but they didn't need lessons in how to rent a flat or cash a check. They needed practical English for their jobs interacting with foreigners in Japan. The course wasn't flexible enough to allow that, and I felt like we were cheating them out of a good lesson.'

Stretching out the textbook wasn't the only way to keep people coming to class. 'Berlitz always underestimated student levels at assessment to encourage them to stay longer,' James recalls, 'so they ended up studying a text that was too easy. If you burned through that at a sensible pace you'd have half the lesson time left to fill. Some students would be happy just to spend the time chatting, but with others you had to be really creative to find new ways to make conversation out of an eight-line dialogue and a couple of photographs. They were extending the student's stay by starting them on stuff below their level, then capping the amount of the text that could be covered in each lesson.'

While James felt the text was often going too slowly for the student, Kieran observed as many cases of the opposite: 'It doesn't matter whether the student is ready or not, you have to follow the steps. If at the end of the year they're still struggling with their level, and it's time to move up to the next, you move them up because that's what they've paid for. A lot of students just want to chat, but the company's insistence on following the script and sticking to the text doesn't allow time for that. You were almost forced to break the rules.'

Grant, who put some time in at Berlitz, also remembers the lessons were very good for beginners, because it forced them to talk. But the curriculum didn't always suit the students' real language needs. Kieran notes the texts have improved since James' time at Berlitz. 'The new series of books is much better, and each chapter is laid out just as it needs to be taught in class, making it more intuitive for teachers. It progresses fluidly from chapter to chapter rather than presenting a jumble of unrelated scenarios. But the dialogs are more realistic now and more challenging for the students. The eikaiwa model is to keep pushing students through the curriculum, whether they master the material or not. Students often blame the teacher for the curriculum's shortfalls.'

It was the classic fast-food service model. You can't ask for a custom-made burger: everyone gets the same dishes on the menu. Kieran found the front-desk staff didn't help students find the right level course either. 'The girls at front don't listen to students. They just push them through the curriculum. Students have to have hundreds of lessons, spend thousands of dollars and stay for years to get that much freedom. You can't move them up too fast even if they're ready, because if they get to the top there's nowhere to go but out. You have to keep them on the books. It's all about revenue stream. Our branch was downtown. The students were business people and highly motivated. These people knew what they wanted and why they were coming to class. The materials didn't always live up to their expectations so I had to fill in the gaps.'

Weak teaching aides were compounded by heavy schedules. A teacher would have up to ten 40-minute units in a day, and lessons were back to back with only five-minute breaks in between. In an eight hour shift, James would teach a block of six lessons, practically non-stop, then have a 50-minute break (one unit plus the five minutes between units) then go back on for another four in a row. Or they'd teach four then six in reverse order. James and his colleagues had a name for this, 'we used to call it a six pack. My throat was raw and I was exhausted most nights when I got off. Worst of all, for all the effort I hadn't achieved anything. I can work hard. I don't like working hard for nothing.'

James took issue with the short lessons. 'The whole idea of 40-minute lessons itself is a joke. An hour, fifty minutes even is a reasonable time slot to get through a language function and grammar point, and allow the students plenty of practice, provided you have good materials. They make it forty to squeeze the maximum number of customers in. It also depersonalizes the experience: sorry, there goes the chime, times up. It's actually counterproductive even from a customer service point of view. They had these small rooms with white boards where the lessons were conducted and you'd do one grueling forty-minute session, a chime would sound, you'd pop out to the staff room, another chime and you'd go back in. You could almost hear the register going *ka-ching*. It was like being a battery hen. You're cooped up in a little booth all day, all night laying little golden eggs for Berlitz.'

Such a schedule quickly led to student complaints that are common in the industry and often baffle teachers. 'You come to Japan, looking to work hard, impart knowledge and improve international communications, then get called into a supervisor or manager's office and told with a stern face that a student said you looked tired or weren't energetic enough. The first reaction is *I didn't even know they could complain about that sort of thing*. I'd never have thought that was a valid reason.'

Amid all the chimes and fear of trivial complaints, one would imagine a quiet spell would be welcome relief but for part time Berlitz teachers, no work meant no pay. 'We had to keep a block of time open and the company filled it with lessons. Students could book up to the evening before, so we couldn't plan any other work or arrange a private lesson. We'd find out the night before if we had a full day or only a handful of lessons or none.' This led to wild discrepancies in income from month to month and strange working shifts. Some teachers would teach mornings then nights, some would have only a few hours in the evening. James, who left his schedule open from 2-10pm got most of his work on weekdays between 5pm and 10pm, and on weekends had to work 10-6pm. 'Because I was practically the newest, everyone kept their sweet shifts. Weekends didn't rotate, and most other teachers were always off. I ended up being one of the weekend guys and since I had to work Saturday and Sunday, basically found it hard to eke out a social life or enjoy any cultural events. Come and enjoy Japan: work six days a week including weekends.'

James says his income ranged between ¥130,000 in a very slow month and ¥270,000 at the busy end and he adds, 'I was always behind or running out of cash at the end of the month. The good months only covered the bad ones. I think the most I made, for a killer month, was ¥280,000 yen but there were only several months when I earned over ¥200,000, and that's about the minimum you need to get by in Japan. I wasn't even getting that. I often had to borrow fifty or a hundred bucks from a friend until pay day and that's very demoralizing when you feel you're working so hard.'

Day-to-day teaching was conducted under the sometimes watchful eye of Berlitz's Instructional Supervisors – subalterns in charge of the other foreigners at each branch. These careerists could be team players or company men. For Kieran at his central Tokyo branch, 'My first I.S. was great. He could walk the line between the corporation and the foreign staff. He had come up through the ranks and knew what we and the students needed and he really focused on my strengths, gave me the best classes for my ability and tried to develop me that way. This is not education; it's PR, it's sales. But he realized I could actually teach, could bring something to the table, so he let me use that despite the standard way of doing things.'

Kieran ran into trouble after a new supervisor took charge at his branch. At many schools, the role of head instructor comes with the risk of being labeled an 'Uncle Tom' – someone who has sold out to the Japanese management. At Kieran's center, the new I.S. was more than happy to throw the teachers to the wolves. 'Our contract guideline was to get five paid lesson slots per week for preparation. But the new supervisor cut those slots to shore up the bottom line. Managers' bonuses are calculated on how well a school does. It was widely held among the teaching staff that the plan was to increase margins by making it look like costs had been cut.'

Another hurdle was Kieran's Asian-American heritage. In Japan it is often expected that English teachers look 'Western'. Customers are paying not just for the language, but the image and they want to see the smiling blond Adonis from the poster or TV commercial in the classroom as well. Yet according to Kieran, Berlitz hires a lot of people of east Asian descent, any ethnicity in fact. Corporate may have decided the Benetton look is good for the image, but in the classroom, this often translates to disappointment when the student meets the teacher for the first time, and sees someone that looks too much like themselves. 'There's still this idea in Japan, where there is no line between culture, language and ethnicity, that only a white person can be a "native" speaker. They somehow feel that because my ancestors came from Asia then I'm not a real American.'

A long-term Fukuoka resident once related a story. He spoke fluent Japanese but his colleague, an American of Chinese descent couldn't speak a word of it. Yet at a restaurant, while ordering, the waiter kept looking across to the Asian face for confirmation despite the fact that the customer with the "western" face was communicating perfectly well. He just couldn't comprehend that the person who looked more like him was less able to communicate in the same language, so he kept trying to connect with the Asian.

James once offered to help a fellow foreigner at his local supermarket. 'It was a black guy, had these Jamaican dreadlocks and all, and there was a staff member at the supermarket dealing with him with a stunned expression of utter incomprehension. I went to offer help with my own Japanese ability and got there to find the customer was speaking fluently and I wasn't needed. I wondered what was wrong with me assuming that my Japanese was better than his, then realized that wasn't it. It was the look on the attendant's face: that same deer-in-headlights shock they have even when you speak Japanese to them. Their eyes and ears can't reconcile a foreigner pulling it off. A lot of the time their brain just shuts down completely and they don't even hear you speaking their language because, well, that's impossible, we can't do *that*. I've had bus drivers and security guards just ignore my Japanese and revert to hand signals. It can be very frustrating.'

On the other hand it is this presumption that 'foreigners' (as opposed to 'Asians') cannot speak Japanese that lies behind the insistence that only those with western features are fit to teach English in class. For

Kieran, he felt that this inherit cultural bias was at the root of some of his complaints from students. 'A lot of these were non-specific like the student just "didn't like" the instructor. If someone doesn't like me that's not a *complaint*, just get them another teacher. Sometimes if a student just doesn't understand I give them the Japanese equivalent, but this is not without risk, however well intended. You can be reprimanded for speaking Japanese if the lesson is being monitored.'

Any trained instructor will tell you that it is preferable to avoid using the student's native language in class. However in eikaiwa it has become both a mantra and a selling point that not a word of Japanese be spoken in an English lesson. This is effective until the student simply cannot understand a point, despite the teacher's best efforts. The 'no Japanese' rule is also all too often just another stick used to beat eikaiwa teachers with, and in some schools is even used to financially penalize them (see chapter 6). In another run-in, Kieran found himself teaching a graduate student. 'In a discussion about healthcare, I commented I didn't like the American system. He complained that I had been too opinionated, and I was reprimanded.' It was small stuff, but enough to get into trouble in eikaiwa, and enough to rub a teacher the wrong way.

Kieran can't help but wonder whether a lot of these petty complaints might have been overlooked if he'd been Caucasian. It might also be a difference in Instructional Supervisors. An earlier I.S. didn't mind if he brought in non-Berlitz supplementary materials when needed, but a later one did. Even changes in the hiring policy couldn't really buck the trend. 'Berlitz has hired more Asians, so the company is clearly trying to diversify. But a lot of students don't come for diversity. Some still say they don't like my "style." I don't want to say it's because I'm Asian, but a lot students seem to prefer white people. I've listened to some other teachers and they get away with a lot that I'm sure I'd have been pulled up for if I had tried it.'

James confirms the bias exists across the industry. He now heads a team of teachers at a smaller school where, 'we had a guy of Filipino origins. He was American, third generation, but to the passerby, he looked Japanese. Though he was great with kids' lessons, being a father himself, some of the adult students told the receptionists they didn't want any more lessons from him. They didn't say why – or it was never communicated in words – but they just preferred another teacher. The look on their faces said *it's that again*. It was an open secret that it was because he just didn't look the part.'

James also feels the inherit bias against all foreigners is reflected in the corporate vocabulary. 'The word they use is *customers*. Once our position is reduced to that of mere *server,* then anything a customer complains about becomes valid. Perceived wants are more important than language needs. We're not professional teachers, because that word in Japanese carries connotations of respect. We're instructors, contractors, or in some cases just foreign staff. They're not *students* who need to be guided, but *customers*, whose every whim must be satisfied. We're just the help.' James echoes the complaints of many working for the large chains. 'I was delivering a product, a service. It wasn't even a language service. It was some sort of ego stroking service designed to lull people into giving the company money. I was a salesman. The idea was to squeeze as many 'deals' out of me in the form of 40-minute lessons as they could before one of us cracked. The learning goals of the students were secondary to the money. The chimes never let me forget that.'

Between the chimes, James had his share of oddball customers. There was one woman in her late forties but looking ten years older. She'd come in carrying this Styrofoam soda cup with a lid on it. The other teachers swore she had beer in there, even though she usually came at about eleven on weekday mornings. She claimed to be suffering from narcolepsy or some sleep disorder, and certainly looked sleepy. But the general consensus was that she was a lush.'

Another was a 'sulky, bipolar chick. She was in her early thirties, unmarried, and had to take care of her dad because her mother had passed away. Basically she was his housewife because Japanese men that age often don't know how to cook and clean and they need someone at home when they come back from work. It stifled her own goals in life so she was miserable. Everyone hated teaching her because she was dark, moody, disengaged and always looked dissatisfied with the lesson. You could feel the tension in the class. And if there's one reason to teach English for a living is because it's not supposed to be a stressful job.'

There were good students too. 'We had a lot of doctors and researchers. I think they were a group contract or something, because they all came from the same university hospital, although different departments. One guy, a little overweight, thirtyish, shaved head, dressed like a gangster. He had baggy T-shirts and loose jeans and wore these thick gold chains. He even drove a Subaru sports car like the boy racers and young toughs. He looked like a real bruiser and you'd walk around him if you passed on the street. But he was actually a transplant surgeon who had vowed to take up medicine when his grandfather died of kidney failure. It was almost a shame to be teaching a guy this smart from the same text as everyone else.'

Apathy and disillusion deepened when, for two months running in late 2009, the paychecks were late or partial at the Sapporo franchise. James laughs, 'I turned up one Wednesday to find a teacher missing in action because he had done, in his own words, "a heroic amount of drugs" the night before and was so hung over he couldn't get out of bed. The supervisor was running about like a headless chicken because he'd had a lot on his plate, as we were about to learn. He cast about for substitutes to cover the guy's evening classes. There wasn't much need. The IS got off the phone, called us into a classroom and announced, on the edge of tears, that the place was shutting down on Friday – two days away.' James had been there exactly a year.

His few lessons that night were surreal. 'We went back to work, with basically nothing else to do and not knowing if we'd even be paid for it. One guy who came in just for the meeting was wearing khakis and a polo shirt. He ended up subbing for the teacher who was still at home and incommunicado after his big night out. The supervisor insisted he wear a tie, over a pink striped polo, and even lent him one. I don't think he was being finicky for the company's sake; he just had a strong work ethic. I snapped, "Look fuck the damn tie, we're all out of a job now. If he has to wear one, I'm taking mine off." That's how we taught the rest of the evening. The next day the hangover case finally turned up. The supervisor told him if we hadn't all been laid off he'd have fired him anyway. Good times.'

The collapse of ELS Japan and its Berlitz franchises was Nova in miniature: late pay, poor service, apathetic staff and dwindling numbers of students. The management had been unwilling to accept defeat and dragged it out till the last possible second, ensuring staff had no safety net and students would have to lobby for refunds. Overspending was also a factor: the company once splashed out on a trip to Las Vegas; for the Japanese staff only of course. Though several Berlitz branches went down with ELS, the main stakeholder Benesse and even the international ELS offered no help as they were already tired of the franchise's fiscal irresponsibility.

Berlitz/ELS teachers eventually got some money. The Japanese Ministry of Health, Labor and Welfare offers something of a safety net in cases of companies going into receivership. Laid off employees can get 80% or so of their last paycheck if the company no longer exists or has no means to pay. James and his colleagues got that, and received a letter in spring 2009, with a statement showing how much more they were owed on paper. In his case he was entitled to a good month's salary in compensation – about ¥240,000. But because the company no longer existed and what money there was had been swallowed up by creditors, he only got a quarter of that.

James' year at Berlitz was a stepping stone as far as experience goes. 'The joke is even though I think I've taught better English before and since, having a big brand name on the résumé opened doors.' He was also quick to stress that difficulties with teaching students better English were not entirely the fault of the organization. 'You can lead a horse to water. The students have to not just be taught English, not just study it, but really try to *learn* it. They seem to think they can just turn up to class and become an English speaker by osmosis. The communicative approach *does* work, but it requires the cooperation of the students. The Japanese learn to sit and listen in school, and they expect an English class to be the same. The methodology most eikaiwa schools use just assumes the enthusiasm of the students, but they've been trained by their education system not to speak or ask questions. The Japanese learning approach is different from the western one. They've brought bad habits in from their school days, but the training doesn't really prepare teachers for that. It assumes they're all eager beavers.'

Eikaiwa teachers find themselves between a rock and hard place when an uncooperative student comes to class, especially in a one-on-one lesson. They know they can't waste the lesson talking, but feel pressure to fill the silence if a student won't talk, otherwise they'd be stuck with an hour of silence and inevitable complaints. Even in group lessons, it can be tempting to ignore the shy member, but this can lead to the common student gripe of not getting enough 'talk time'. At some schools, where hourly pay is constantly adjusted up and down according to customer comments, this can be a costly dilemma.

James fell on hard times after the ELS collapse. 'For a couple of days I was in a funk and didn't know what to do. But my visa had just been renewed for three years and I was free of that restrictive environment, so I suddenly started to look up. It was time to go freelance, and carve my own niche.' He soon realized he'd been too optimistic. Working for yourself can be hard and being freelance sometimes just means having several bosses. The competing demands can cause schedule clashes, conflicts and a lot of hard work, all for basic hourly pay. James found himself working several jobs, running all over town. 'You teach anywhere just to survive. Big places, or scummy little rented classrooms and so-called schools run out of converted flats. I would sometimes work three different jobs at up to four locations between nine and nine in a single day. I worked six days a week and was still often behind on bills. The few busy months had better paychecks but for about three grand did I really need to be wearing myself out? That's what you get in ESL back home just for working nine to four. In the quiet months like school holidays I enjoyed the free time, but my income tanked. It was impossible to save.'

After a couple of years James finally progressed into full time work at one of the small language schools he was rotating between. 'You have to compromise. I taught kids and at kindergartens, song and dance stuff. I hate kids but you have to take what you can get. I let one place pressure me into giving up valued breaks to run across town and teach a corporate gig: they got more money than their usual rate for such classes, but I only earned the regular pay. Another freelancer who the client had gone to directly was making more for the same work because there was no school taking a cut. Disparities like that lead to resentment.' James dropped work that wasn't panning out or that clashed with the 'better' work. He cut one job altogether because, 'I liked it least and I needed the sleep. A dozen years of living overseas I never got homesick, but around then I started wondering why I was wasting my life in a country and economy that doesn't seem to want me to succeed, but for a time I was also stubbornly determined to make it work.'

James is now head instructor at a local language center, but has already set a date for leaving. He makes an average salary, though at least it is steady pay. 'It's a tradeoff, because middle management comes with its own stresses.' He is working on his exit plan, but concedes he won't leave with much. 'It took my first year working full time just to pay of the previous year's tax bill. I'll take out my pension contributions and a few thousand in savings, but basically I'll be leaving with as much as I came, six years older and burned out. In hindsight, I shouldn't have come back at all.'

For a time, Berlitz seemed to have accepted the fact of the union and acknowledged staff grievances. This didn't mean the union always got what it wanted and collective bargaining is ongoing. Nevertheless there have been considerable strides in eikaiwa terms. A union leaflet in circulation lists a raft of problems solved: senior full time instructors have been enrolled in the national pension and private health insurance is extended to all teachers working over 30 hours a week. Whereas strictly part time teachers previously had no paid holidays, there are now provisions for paid time off. Overtime is paid at a higher rate. Most importantly the company's union busting teeth have been pulled, or at least blunted, with new procedures for grievances and dismissals. An agreement with the union is now a required step before 'terminating, transferring or changing the working conditions of any union member.' [6]

The union is also gunning for guaranteed breaks after long strings of lessons and more importantly, recognition of the five minutes between lessons as paid working time. This could have huge implications for the company's employment conditions. Not only would it add up to typically one more paid lesson slot per eight hour day, but could in many cases push 'part time' teachers into the full time bracket, obliging the company to spring for more pensions and health insurance enrollments. If the union achieves progress on the five-minute breaks, it may open the door to a new era. Even Berlitz teachers on a monthly salary are not enrolled in the national health and pension schemes. Kieran explains, 'If the company recognizes those breaks as paid working time then we'll be working over the thirty hour a week limit. Berlitz will be forced to admit we are full time workers and that could end up costing them even more money.'

It could also set a precedent that reverberates throughout the industry, should it turn into a court battle of any significance: unpaid administrative time is a favorite method of squeezing more out of teachers: competitors Aeon and Gaba have also found themselves under fire from courts and unions. The so-called break between lessons is when teachers fill out forms, answer student questions and prepare materials for the next class. This is work that can't very well *not* be done, yet instructors do it without getting a cent because they're not in the classroom.

Could a positive outcome ensnare the whole industry? James is skeptical, 'don't bet on it. I can imagine one company, even a big one like Berlitz falling into line if it's ordered to. But the rest won't make any changes until they're dragged up in front of the courts themselves. It's just too lucrative to keep teachers listed as part timers. The courts don't enforce industry-wide rulings.' The idea that teachers who are there all day, and busy all day, five or six days a week are part time is now commonplace. While the union hopes to get payment for the five minute gaps between lessons for all its members, teachers have already challenged the company privately. A few kept records, went to court and received hefty payouts amounting to the statutory two years of unpaid overtime a worker can claim in Japan.[7] But being in the union is a big advantage; an unprotected teacher risks dismissal if he challenges a school alone. Union members can go to the labor department knowing someone has their backs, but the rest remain on shaky ground.

In early 2015, Berlitz tried claiming that each paid unit would now be 45 minutes at the usual rate, thereby 'including' the 5 minutes unpaid paperwork per lesson. This comes despite teacher contracts that clearly stipulate their paid work is 40 minutes per unit and continued union efforts to get teachers paid - and back paid - for the extra time in between lessons. The company was forced to back down on unilateral changes, but the union has continued to challenge Berlitz for avoiding the responsibility to pay teachers for lesson preparation.[8]

How did it come to this? Kieran says, 'The old days of feudal patronage in Japanese companies have passed. Workers are now expendable. Ironically, this is because of globalization: more foreigners have flocked to Japan, but as Japanese companies seek to emulate the American model, employment conditions look more and more like Wal-Mart. It has been happening in eikaiwa for a while because these schools were early examples of the American model. Now it's everywhere.' The number of part time workers in Japan has exploded and many rights and privileges employees used to enjoy have evaporated in the ensuing fireball.[9]

Kieran agrees times have changed. 'Companies evade social security contributions because the law is not enforced, as it is in the United States. Rather than raise the consumption tax to pay for the shortfall in pensions [Japan raised its sales tax from 5% to 8% in 2014 and to 10% in 2015], the government should tie contributions to hourly wages and salaries, regardless of the amount. part time and non-contract workers are falling through the cracks and will not be able to collect when they retire, because they are not paying into the system. But according to the western business model, that's the trend. Put the burden on the worker or future generations, but don't interfere with the holy grail of profits.'

On the future of teacher pay in the industry, Kieran asserts, 'it's not like we're greedy. Just pay us the same as everyone else. Large portions of the workforce still get benefits, but as income producers, we don't.

We're just asking that the law be obeyed. All too often when it comes to foreign workers, this is not the case.' Though it seems to him teachers no longer come just for the money, Kieran holds that there is also change in the type of people doing the job. 'New teachers are savvier and they know what they're getting into. They look on the internet and the chat sites and they are choosier about the company they sign up with. They're also more cynical; to them it's just a job from day one. They come with fewer illusions and no long term plans.'

James thinks the industry is heading for another big shakeup. 'With salaries dropping and teachers leaving, quality going is down among those who stay because they care less about their work, something has to give. I think some big names will go under and the smaller, leaner companies will weather it and profit from the change. Salaries will hit rock bottom and when schools realize they keep getting monkeys, they'll stop paying peanuts and conditions will improve. But it'll get worse before it gets better, and will never get back to what it was twenty years ago. Smaller schools that care about staff and students might be a good place to work after that, but in the next crash a lot of those will get dragged down as well. We'll see who's left after that.'

He has some advice to English teachers: 'start your own business or start planning to leave. Nobody here will give you a good job and you'll be lucky to make a living wage. Teaching in Japan should be a temporary experience and you get it out of your system and get back to the real world without delay. If not, you wake up and you're over forty and a have a wife that won't live anywhere else and kids to feed and barely enough money to keep a roof over their heads. I've seen guys like that. They're all miserable. They all dream of going home, but they're stuck.'

In late 2014 the Berlitz union renewed its demands: pay increases, paid preparation time between lessons and better job security. Berlitz responded by issuing a new decree to all staff, outside the bargaining process. The company offered part time teachers a ¥200 per lesson increase, about US $1.80 at the time, perhaps to compensate for the five minute space between lessons while still refusing to admit that these were not actually breaks. The 200 yen 'raise' came with a raft of claw backs. Among conditions both stipulated in labor laws and hard-won by the union when the company didn't comply: paid national holidays, overtime for working on usual days off and a flat rate commuting allowance – all benefits that were removed under the new plan, or in the case of transport allowances, pared down.

The union argues that not only does the extra money per lesson not even cover the breaks between lessons and other preparation work required, but would not make up for the potential loss over the year of paid holidays, overtime and transport allowances. It also holds that the company simply bypassed its legal obligation to negotiate and unilaterally changed conditions. Moreover all teachers were being asked to sign the new contract in March 2015, regardless of when their current contracts expired – a further breach of labor laws.[10] It is easy to imagine a not-too-distant future, where, citing financial woes, Berlitz cuts back the per lesson rate to recoup its two dollars, leaving the teachers with nothing but a per-minute lesson fee the same as it was before and no benefits whatsoever. The union threatened a strike for February 1st and according to its Facebook page, new enrollments had tripled in the weeks leading up to the date. The company backed down to avoid a strike and the claw backs were removed from the negotiations.

In one handbook for new teachers titled *Overview for New Instructors,* Berlitz reminds teachers, 'We have chosen you to work for us because we think you are special. Thousands of foreigners in Japan are looking for work, but only a small percentage of those have the commitment, the flair, the professionalism and the unique character that we believe our instructors need. We expect that you will look upon your work as more than just a source of income. We expect you will care.'[11] Teachers can only expect as much of their employers too.

Craig Currie-Robson

4 Aeon's Cult of Impersonality

I found on an international job forum a New-Yorker who prefers to be known as Stan. Stan's experience with eikaiwa was brief and intense: he was hired by large chain Aeon, paid his own way for a flight to Japan and was sent home with a company-paid ticket less than a week later. How on Earth did it come to that? 'I've had some teaching experience before, but nothing to prepare me for their way of doing things.'

Some experience is an understatement. As well as working in sales, marketing and economic research, he has taught in Saudi Arabia, China and the Gulf, where he was a director at a language center. As is often the case with big eikaiwa schools, Aeon hires exclusively overseas and prefers recruits who've had little or no experience in Japan. Those who have done any kind of teaching at all may still be at a disadvantage, as learned habits may be put to use in an actual classroom. This is the last thing Big Eikaiwa wants. In Stan's case, 'my experience actually hurt me, because anything I came up with would be anathema to Aeon's methodology.'

The interview and the recruitment phase were challenging but didn't raise too many alarm bells. He had researched the company beforehand and felt that this had given him a leg-up in the interviewing process. However the last part of the interview, 'Almost spelled my end'. Candidates were given a lesson to teach in five minutes, just a quick grammar point or language function. They asked me to rate my own lesson, then a Japanese staffer told me what was wrong with it and where

I could improve. I stumbled badly because I was expected to copy their methods, on the spot, and leave my own experience at the door. But I was given a chance to do the lesson again and did it better the second time.'

There was also a degree of weirdness among the foreign recruiters. Stan noticed in the group interviews that everyone was watched closely. 'Whenever someone was making a presentation, one of the Aeon staffers was observing all the other candidates.' The pattern recurred through orientation, where there was always someone taking notes on everything the trainees did. 'The way the recruiters spoke to one another in a certain code was a little creepy. Their interaction seemed to be rehearsed. There were a lot of leading questions which the candidate was encouraged to answer in a certain way. In my opinion this cements a certain power arrangement that gets more intense over time. It was kind of *cultish*.'

Though he was starting to suspect he wouldn't fit in, Stan pulled up his bootstraps and passed the interview phase. A month later he was on his way to Japan. After arriving at the Aeon training center in Omiya, Saitama prefecture, Stan lasted four days. 'I arrived with the flu,' Stan explains, 'so I wasn't in the best shape for a grueling week-long training session. On one occasion I was a minute or so late back from break, because I'd been blowing my nose in the restroom. On another occasion I was pulled up for standing with my hands in my pockets and for leaving a bottle of water in front of me on the table. I was generally thought of as not being *genki*, or energetic enough, because I was suffering from the flu at the time.* It seems the Japanese equate sickness with a kind of moral weakness.'

---

* Appearing *genki*, - lively, happy or outgoing - is considered essential in eikaiwa. Teachers are often exhorted through training, student feedback and performance reviews to be more 'energetic' and put on something of a performance in the classroom.

Japan's rate of absenteeism is among the lowest in the world, largely attributed to its vigorous work ethic. People with colds tend to drug up on over the counter remedies, put on a surgical mask to limit the spread of germs, and trudge into work regardless of how poorly they feel. Companies traditionally offer few days off per year: the law requires a minimum of just ten days' annual leave, and sick days are only to be used as a last resort. Even workers who have sick days expect to use up leave days first. Some companies offer separate sick days – at my last job in Japan I got a whopping five per year – but the general understanding seems to be that a worker should be bedridden, hospitalized or worse to use them. The Japanese idea of what constitutes bedridden may be different from western norms: there is even a word for the concept of working oneself to death - *Karōshi*. It is considered a common end for many middle-aged executives.[1]

Stan was in no danger of dropping dead during training, but he could hardly be expected to perform at optimum levels with a cold. His biggest concern however stemmed from the expectations in training. Though Stan concedes he failed to meet those expectations, while the other trainees managed, he holds Aeon partly to blame. 'I had to provide a full lesson on the second day of training, but we weren't given the script to follow until the first day. There was a period of months in which Aeon could have supplied us with some materials before we actually got there. If Aeon really prizes its product then why not provide the teachers with the methodology in advance, so they can get a grip on it?'

The Aeon system is similar to that of Berlitz. The lesson is divided into steps that anyone in theory can learn to deliver. First is a presentation stage, when the teacher introduces a language point, phrase or piece of vocabulary. This is followed by a practice phase in which time is spent drilling the point, role playing and so on. The final step is the production, where the student is required to reproduce the language and use it accurately in context. The 'Three Ps' are fairly standard and with many variations, this is how most schools teach, how most textbook chapters are organized and what any half-trained language teacher already knows. The problem lies in rigidity. In Big Eikaiwa the system is considered sacrosanct. Any problems that arise must be the teacher's fault for deviating from the script: the method itself is infallible. There's only one way to deliver a lesson once you get to Aeon, and flexibility is not tolerated. According to Stan, 'The methodology can be helpful in any TEFL environment, though following it line for line would be counter-productive outside the Aeon bubble.'

In the Aeon bubble, Stan's past experience and training was working against him. In this brief encounter, he had come face to face with the corporate bias of Japan. A company likes to train staff to do things its way and its way alone. Often these skills are not considered transferable. Rarely can a manager from one big company get a similar position at a competitor, because past experience is often dismissed as bad habits. Companies prefer fresh graduates who can be molded.

'The older one is, the less likely one will be able to adapt to Aeon's requirements,' according to Stan. 'I believe they'd be better off recruiting only young people as the environment would be less appealing to those already set in their ways.' Stan feels that apart from the flu, or perhaps because of it, his training instructor had deemed him unfit from the start, and his fortunes spiraled downward from there. When asked if he considered it deliberate hazing he didn't go that far. He does however hold that 'They don't want individuals, they want drones - people who don't ask too many questions and just accept what they are told. I had certain habits as a teacher that they wanted removed, and I was uncomfortable with the company's attempt at deprogramming.' Another Aeon teacher corroborates, 'It was like boot camp: they break you down so they can build you up again.'

Though Stan's past experience was anathema to Aeon, he still feels that had he been given more time to prepare, for example if he'd received the materials weeks or months in advance, then he would have coped better with the training. Why doesn't Aeon provide its new recruits with such information, when they're clearly organized enough to send a cultural handbook and dress-code brochure? Stan believes, 'they guard their own methodology very jealously. Secondly, and I might be cynical here, I think they want to keep their new employees on their toes and off-balance. Not too much so, but just enough.'

Finally, as Stan tells it, the trainers and supervisors told him that it wasn't working out, and they'd have to let him go. 'It was much less about becoming a good teacher than being a good *employee*. I simply didn't buy what they were selling and that showed in subtle ways. One of the major paradoxes of Aeon's recruiting and selection process is that they seek people who are both self starters and compliant. These characteristics don't often appear in the same person.' It should come as no surprise that most ESL teachers in Japan, in and out of eikaiwa, are the kind of people who have the courage, confidence and independence to pack up and move to a job overseas. That is practically a prerequisite just for getting there. Yet the large chains also need teachers who are comparatively meek, willing to do as they're told, often without question, and in some cases to act against their better instincts to serve the company's needs. It is a rare combination of guts and spinelessness. Most eikaiwa teachers learn to simply fake the latter in order to get by with the minimum of fuss, or they simply switch off and stop caring about the politics of the workplace.

Aeon was reasonably good about sending Stan back. Though dismissed workers are supposed to be paid a month's salary under law, Aeon did at least cover the plane ticket home instead. He was told he would have to relinquish his work visa. 'An Aeon representative said that if I didn't cancel the visa, I'd be liable for Japanese taxes once I returned.' This is not the case. Stan could, if he wished, have found another job in Japan, but he concedes that it would have been hard to apply at other schools and explain that he'd been fired by Aeon after just a few days. 'I'd told everyone I knew I was off to Japan to teach. To come home again so soon was genuinely humiliating.'

Aeon traces its roots even further back than Nova, although it was born out of the dissolution of a previous enterprise. In 1973 roommates Kiyoshi Aki and Tsuneo Kusunoki hit upon the idea of their own school. The company would be named AMVIC, for *Ambition* and *Victory*, which must have sounded better in Japanese than it does in English. Later the school broke into two divisions – one for teaching various foreign languages and one specializing in English. Kusunoki would head the English division, and he eventually entered into partnership with Warner Pacific College, a Christian college in Portland, Oregon. It soon became clear that Aki and Kusunoki had different visions for the direction of the company and not long after, the company split entirely, and Kusunoki's vision was realized in the founding of Global Education Opportunities and Services, or Geos.²

While Geos' main competitor Nova could only boast one overseas branch in Honolulu, catering for Japanese customers who wanted to pop in for a lesson while on vacation, Geos successfully expanded overseas in the UK, North America, Eastern Europe, Asia and Australasia. Eventually it had over fifty schools and affiliates abroad with varying language courses tailored for ESL students of all nationalities.³

In Japan, however no tailoring was necessary because the market had already chosen the one size fits all model: ready-made lessons, youthful, energetic teachers, and flexible schedules. Like Nova, Geos Japan had entered into the McEnglish business. There were some differences, for example the *tanninsei* system, whereby students could keep the same long term teacher instead of swapping out every other lesson. Geos insisted this built a better bond between teacher and student and promoted continuity. Many smaller schools still use the formula, but larger chains tend to favor flexibility in scheduling.

In the bubble years the school expanded rapidly. Geos had regional headquarters in Tokyo, Osaka, Sapporo, Nagoya and Fukuoka which managed the various branches and centers in outlying cities. Aside from English, Geos also offered lessons in several European languages, Chinese and Korean, and even taught Japanese to foreign students. There was also a cultural center and language institute that took in foreign boarding students. By 2007 there were over 500 branches, 90% of them in Japan.

Opinions vary on just why Geos continued to expand after Nova's spectacular implosion. Perhaps Kusunoki saw opportunity in the collapse of his biggest rival and, seeking to step into Nova's shoes, fell into the same trap of getting too big too fast. But Nova wasn't completely gone, and under G.communication still had more than half its branches open. Moreover, Geos had been expanding the whole time Nova had and there was no sudden burst of enrollments in 2007. Nevertheless Geos must have been hopeful that Nova's diminished reputation would send former students and potential customers its way. Perhaps, like the large construction firms and bloated government departments outlined in Alex Kerr's *Dogs and Demons: the fall of modern Japan,* Kusunoki may have just been unable to stop. According to eikaiwa veteran Troy, 'companies like Geos and Nova know only how to do one thing: expand. They don't consolidate or slow down. For them the market is an unlimited playground and there's no such thing as saturation.'

Like Nova, Geos had other investments and they weren't always sound. There were the requisite financial problems that were reported in local media and in hindsight might have been red flags. As early as 2001, the Japan Times noted that around twenty Geos affiliates and subsidiaries failed to report 280 million yen in income, about $2.4 million at the time. Auditors at the Tokyo Regional Taxation Bureau found that, Kusunoki and his wife, who served as vice president, had also failed to report more than 200 million yen in personal income over a three year period. Kusunoki was also suspected of using part of the affiliate's undeclared expenses as a personal slush fund.[4]

The company was found to have under-reported income by padding travel expenses and Kusunoki, who claimed to be a resident of Switzerland at the time, was deemed to have spent enough time in Japan to owe more taxes than he'd paid as a non-resident. The companies were ordered to pay $1 million yen in fines and back taxes; in a separate case Kusunoki also had to back-pay another $750,000 in personal income tax.

This may seem like just the typical shenanigans of a wealthy businessman, and in dollar terms, with the millions in single digits, far less sensational than the hundreds of millions American executives manage to embezzle But skimming money and stashing it away even as the company disintegrates and workers lose their job security is equally serious regardless of the amount. Students don't get their refunds when branches are closed and lessons ended; teachers and staff are laid off without their final paychecks. When the inevitable collapse of Geos came in 2010, it echoed Nova and ELS: rampant expansion, fiscal irresponsibility and customers left out of pocket; the job market flooded again with stranded teachers.[5] But Kusunoki's old partner Aki had been building his own brand and by now it was as big as Geos. The collapse cleared the way for its sibling rival to flower like a phoenix from the ashes of the eikaiwa crunch. Aeon was free to step in and fill its place.

Like many hopefuls, Andre came to Japan in 2011 to pursue a career in teaching ESL. He worked at various jobs until his early thirties before putting himself through a degree in linguistics and comparative literature. We sat down in Sapporo's bustling outdoor beer gardens in Odori Park one summer evening, to hear Andre relate his experiences. 'I had taught ESL to immigrants in the states, but after dating a Japanese girl in Hawaii, I was curious about the country and its culture. I also wanted to learn the language and thought I'd have a better chance there'. He was attracted by the flash recruitment videos and corporate atmosphere, landing a job with Aeon at a recruiting drive in the US.

Aeon weathered the crash of its sibling rival, eventually rising to 320 branches nationwide and maintaining recruitment centers in New York,

Sydney and Los Angeles. Where other schools have experienced money troubles, Aeon has wisely chosen to keep an account at Mizuho Trust Bank, where 50% of the fees students pay up front are deposited in case the company runs into trouble and cannot pay refunds. The industry has learned from Nova's mistakes. Aeon is also known for paying a decent fixed salary and paying on time, and has largely avoided the kind of labor disputes that have plagued other chains large and small.

Despite being known for paying on time, Aeon, like most large eikaiwa chains, for many years avoided enrolling its workers into the national pension scheme. Though Aeon's website boasts a pedigree dating back to the Amvic days in 1973, it wasn't until 2006 that it extended pension coverage to its foreign teachers.[6] Over a span of thirty-three years, several generations of teachers came and went without so much as a sniff at the honey pot. The General Union website suggests it was union pressure that forced Aeon to cave, yet as mentioned in chapter two, Japan's Social Insurance Agency had also probed rival Nova and threatened to take action against any schools that had not complied with the law.[7]

The national pension and social insurance plans are relatively simple and comprehensive: all full time employees must be enrolled by their companies, with the employee and the company each contributing half of the mandatory payments. The national pension offers retirement benefits from the age of 65 or the option to withdraw earlier for those who wish to make their own retirement savings. The social insurance covers 70 percent of all health costs and hospital visits, as well as hospitalization coverage for invalids and unemployment benefits for those temporarily out of work - a sort of user-pays dole. The rough threshold for such entitlements is a 30-hour work week, which the government recognizes as two-thirds of a full time schedule. Hence the common practice of language schools contracting foreign instructors for, ostensibly, a 29.5 hour week. If thirty hours a week doesn't sound like much work it is because eikaiwa schools count only the time teachers spend in the classroom and disregard most other duties.

Reasons abound as to why schools are unwilling to pay pension obligations. It is certainly an added expense and Japanese employers may see little long term benefit in making such investments in employees who may only stay a year or two. Many teachers see it as just plain discrimination – a foreigner isn't worth it. The most likely explanation lies somewhere in between, and in the devious minds of corporate accountants whose brief is to find efficiency and implement cost-cutting measures for their employers.

When Aeon finally acquiesced and enrolled the foreign instructors it did so with a caveat. Teachers could opt for the old 'part time' contract of 29.5 hours a week, with no pension or insurance; those who wanted more stability were offered a new full time contract for 36 hours a week. In order to get the benefits that another 30 minutes of work per week would entitle them to, these instructors would have to work a further *six and a half hours*. The number of lessons per week was also increased commensurately. Still on paper a 36-hour week doesn't look bad. But that was only on paper. Instructors before and since have found themselves pulling a substantial amount of unpaid overtime: their workload and obligations have been the same as full time Japanese workers, without many of the benefits. Like other schools the teachers are contracted to teach 25-30 hours a week with the remaining five hours or so made up of planning time, usually the ten minute breaks between lessons. Never mind that such a calculation adds up to over eight hours work on top of the teaching time, putting a teacher's day well above the 30-hour or even the 36-hour mark. Andre, who worked at a regional Hokkaido branch for a year, recognized that, 'in eikaiwa, the contract is whatever the company says it is, not the law.'

Though a teacher's hours outside of class are supposedly free, planning lessons of course takes time and there is often extra paperwork such as grading students and completing forms detailing the lessons taught. Teachers are also expected to conduct 'counseling' sessions with the students (more on these later) and even to clean the language center after closing, all of which adds up to considerable non-teaching duties over the course of a week. One Japanese instructor at Aeon affiliate Amnity committed suicide as a result of too much pressure and overtime. The Labor Standards Office investigators in Ishikawa prefecture determined the young woman spent at least twenty hours a week preparing picture cards and other lesson materials for her children's classes. While foreign teachers at Aeon have reported considerably less than this, there was so much overtime that instructors went to the General Union.[9]

One of the stickier Union charges was that branch managers were observed clocking out teachers well before they actually finished work in order to avoid getting billed for overtime. While Andre has never seen such a practice, he was able to confirm charges from the General Union's Aeon page that the company exacts far more than a 29.5 hour work week from its instructors. He recalls, 'Before cleaning the office we had to wait until every student had left. Cleaning itself didn't take long because the branch was a smallish one: a couple of us could vacuum and wipe the boards in twenty minutes while the manager looked busy with her figures for the day.' But some students don't mind lingering after class. 'One

Saturday night, knowing it would take me some time to get out, get changed and head downtown, I arranged to meet my friends at an *izakaya* at eleven. Normally I'd finish my last class at 8:50 and be out by ten, but one student hung around the front chatting to his teacher for two hours, on a Saturday night. Of course I was late for dinner. Every so often, when a wait like this dragged on, the manager felt sorry for us and let us go early.' Magnanimity at its best.

This wouldn't seem so bad if it had been an isolated incident. But teachers have routinely reported at least an hour of unpaid overtime *daily*, as well has having counseling sessions with students or demo lessons with prospective customers slotted in at the end of the work day. Japanese law stipulates that workers must be paid overtime for working out of hours. Aeon's solution was simply not to admit the teachers worked overtime: clocking instructors out before they left at night was one example of how the company tried to sweep overtime under the rug. It is the same tactic employed by other large chains to avoid enrolling staff in the pension plan: don't acknowledge they are full time. This in turn raises the complaint from teachers that if they're not full time, then why are they working so many hours?

A common refrain from management, according to the union website, is that Japanese workers put in long hours as well. This is true; they work some of the longest hours in the world and usually more than English teachers. But Japanese company employees enjoy a raft of benefits from steady salary increases and yearly bonuses to paid vacations and sick leave – all privileges that eikaiwa teachers have had to fight tooth and nail to obtain. English schools exploit a gray area where foreigners are often not equipped with the language, finances or time remaining on their visas to challenge. Thus the teachers are 'part time' when the school needs them to be if it wants to avoid paying pensions, but they are 'full time' when it comes to doing unpaid overtime, the expected norm in a Japanese corporation. Then when it comes to matters of bonuses, profit share and paid leave they are conveniently 'part time' or 'temporary' once again.

In 2008, one Aeon employee struck back. Individually, the instructor took her fight to the labor board and the company partially relented even before the union had a chance to formally demand overtime pay for all members. After a leaflet campaign gave the management a scare, the instructor was initially paid a modest sum to compensate for overtime, but after the union had calculated the real amount owed, and taken the case to the Labor Standards Office (a government regulatory body), the teacher was awarded 150,000 yen (about $1600 in 2008) for three months, or around $530 per month.[10] The union reports that Aeon then made it a policy to encourage teachers to leave the office on time. But apparently the school returned to its old tricks as soon as the heat was off. There has been no large class action payout and the company seems to have learned a mixed lesson. According to Andre, whose experience of unpaid overtime dates from four years later, 'if you don't call them on it, they won't pay'. Perhaps his branch never got the memo.

The typical eikaiwa teacher's understanding of counseling students is seeing them once or twice a year and discussing their progress, assigning a grade and giving a recommendation for future study. To the extent that any attempt to re-sign the student or further motivate them is involved, a gentle encouragement to keep at it will suffice. But Aeon's counseling sessions have a different motive in Andre's opinion. 'They mentioned that we'd have to encourage students to buy some materials but it was only one sentence. I can't say we were lied to.'

James, who interviewed at Aeon in Sydney but wound up working elsewhere, also confirms no mention of sales was made. 'They showed us a video of a typical day at Aeon in order to outline duties. It showed lessons, cleaning the office, maybe mentioned counseling, but said nothing about making sales.' It is possible that different recruitment centers - and recruiters - give varying degrees of information on the matter. Nevertheless, one of the most important roles of an Aeon instructor is to sell: CDs, books, self-study materials. In Andre's words, 'you're not a teacher. You're there to project the company image. There's a corporate culture in every sense.'

That culture is to sell and twice a year the school would hold self-study campaigns. Andre explains, 'This involved offering materials such as CDs, booklets and online products. These were tied in with the counseling weeks, when we would give students an update of their progress, and use the opportunity to plug Aeon's other products.' Counseling thus became a disingenuous affair and teachers had a fairly strict formula to follow: 'We were told to encourage the students a lot, naturally to talk them up. This was to keep them motivated and keep them coming back. But by the same token nobody could be perfect. We had to give two or three good points and one bad point. If we couldn't identify one, we'd have to make one up. The idea was that they could never be ready, the job never finished, because the main goal was to keep them coming back year after year and to buy new materials, not necessarily to improve.'

Andre recalls one student who'd transferred up from Honshu. 'The manager told us to treat him with extra attention because he was such a special customer. The school presented him with a certificate for being a regular student for fifteen years. *Fifteen years?* He should have been fluent by then, he shouldn't have needed lessons anymore. But that's not what Aeon was about.'

Counseling sessions became an opportunity to implore students to improve that one 'weakness' by purchasing self-study materials. Andre feels, 'the reason for the business being there is to make money and they don't let you forget that. There was no direct pressure or a sales target, but we would be told that such-and-such a branch got this many sales and so-and-so was the highest performing instructor in the region. If you didn't meet the targets they let you know in subtle ways. At our branch you'd kind of get the cold shoulder. The manager was passive-aggressive that way'.

All this selling begs the question of what benefit it brings for the salesperson. Andre's branch had four teachers and about 200 students. Instructors taught seven or eight 50-minute lessons per day, plus lobby chat, lesson preparation and cleaning. It's safe to say they weren't booking more students for the pleasure of doing more work. Yet there was no real incentive, no commission and no profit share, in fact the teachers got few basic benefits at all until the unions got on Aeon's case.

The union has not just taken Aeon to task over unpaid overtime. The company has been accused of actually costing teachers money. One of the benefits of joining Aeon as an overseas hire is that the company arranges accommodation. This is no small perk: finding a first apartment in Japan can be expensive and daunting and a lot of foreigners have been turned away by landlords who consider them risky tenants. Aeon rents apartments long term and rotates teachers through them as they come and go. Because the tenant is a corporation and because the apartments rarely go empty this keeps the landlords happy, and makes setting up in Japan a breeze for new teachers.

Yet problems arise when teachers try to leave Aeon accommodation. In theory a teacher has the right to seek an apartment on his or her own and many do move out of their company sponsored flats. But this sometimes creates a tenancy gap. Aeon would like to have teachers finish a contract, move them out, and put their replacements in immediately after, never leaving an apartment unoccupied. If there were a gap of several months, the company would temporarily be paying rent for nothing since it was not in turn making money off any additional occupant. Never mind that the original tenant might still be working at Aeon and generating the same income as before; eikaiwa teachers are overheads, not assets, and an unoccupied flat is wasted rent. Keeping teachers in company accommodation also exerts a certain amount of control. People may be less likely to challenge the company or seek employment elsewhere if it means losing your apartment as well.

The union reports, 'Aeon's written policy on this is vague. The Foreign Teachers' Policy Manual stated that employees could be required to compensate the employer for losses resulting from the employee's decision to change apartments.' Using this clause the company has demanded that teachers keep paying rent after leaving their accommodation, until another tenant is found. Given that rent can be a quarter to a third of a teacher's income, and bearing in mind that even salaried Aeon teachers make just about the yearly average of a Japanese worker, forcing them to rent two places would be prohibitively expensive.

It is also illegal. According to the union the practice violates Japan's housing laws, which are notoriously favorable to tenants, a holdover from the postwar era when housing was scarce and the government needed to protect people from being turned out. In many cases, teachers have simply stayed in company accommodation because Aeon made it too difficult to leave; in at least one case cited on the union website, the company has backed down when a teacher, under union advice, has challenged the policy.

Andre was mostly happy with the apartment he got: a modern single-room studio flat near the middle of town. 'It was within walking distance of the school, the station and the local bar. Everything worked and it looked new. The place came fully furnished.' Yet there was one nagging concern. The monthly rent – deducted from his salary – was ¥75,000. That struck me as a reasonable amount for an 18 square meter flat in downtown Sapporo or Fukuoka - both major cities - or something even smaller in Tokyo or Osaka. But for a somewhat large semi-rural municipality it seemed a little steep. It could be that the landlord smelled extra cash in having a large company as a tenant, or it could be that he was being overcharged. Andre shrugged, 'I suspect Aeon was pocketing about ¥20,000 of that, either to cover the time between teachers when it was vacant, or just because they can.'

Teaching at Aeon was not necessarily a painful experience but in the classroom, the rigid corporate structure again rears its head. Before arriving in Japan, recruits are sent a catalog of dos and don'ts: don't yawn or discuss the politics in class, don't be late - all fairly routine tips to fit in and not to harm the reputation of the company. They are even given some tips on how to deal with racism. Stan recalls, 'The orientation literature told us if a Japanese person gets up and moves away when you sit down next to them on the subway, it's because they're afraid we'll try to make conversation, but I don't think this is true.' Perhaps Aeon at least deserves credit for trying to soften the blow.

The dress code was typically strict: there was even a glossy brochure of suit styles and colors and accompanying shoes that were allowed and not allowed. Andre corroborates this. 'They prescribed every little action and facet of behavior down to the smallest detail.' Like many eikaiwa teachers I've spoken too, Andre has noticed students come with mixed motivations. Some genuinely want to learn English, some are young women trying to fulfill a fantasy; there are children their parents send and there are time wasters who don't seem to know why they're there. With some, Andre says, 'It was like pulling teeth. They turn up to a lesson and they have nothing to talk about and seemingly no interest in the lesson. In some classes they sapped every ounce of strength.'

Yet they were customers and a teacher could not show displeasure or frustration. In eikaiwa, as anywhere in Japan, the customer is always right. The teacher is there to serve, little more. If there were problems in the classroom, with the way the lesson went, it was the foreign instructor's fault: he didn't prepare, he wasn't patient, he doesn't understand Japanese culture.

'I had one kid in class, a twelve year old, a real smart ass,' relates Andre, 'he would be disruptive, talk back, bother the other kids and mouth off at me in Japanese thinking I didn't understand. The whole school knew about it – I'd complained to the office – but nothing was ever done.' Andre pulled him aside and warned the boy that he would tell his mother, but the kid was smart enough to know a foreigner's place in Japan. He told his mother that night that the teacher was singling him out and the mother complained to the school. The teacher was changed but the child's behavior continued to worsen.

'So a few lessons in, he's acting up and my replacement tells him off again. The kid gives him the finger. The teacher pulls him aside and warns him the next time he'll make him leave the lesson. This time the kid's mother calls regional HQ and complains to the manager. In the end the teacher had to apologize formally to the student, with the manager and the mother watching over.' Such antics could be put down to the machinations of a manipulative child and the temperament of a so-called monster parent* but it is also very telling that even a child knows where a foreigner stands.

Many teachers in the eikaiwa industry have related feelings of being lower down the social ladder than the average Japanese person. In the '80s and '90s teachers - even foreign English teachers - had a sort of elevated status. Nowadays, even in public schools there is a growing catalog of unreasonable complaints by monster parents. Eikaiwa however, has been transformed into a mere over-the-counter transaction. As James charged in Chapter Three, changing corporate vocabulary to call students 'customers' elevates them to a status far above that of the 'server' that the teacher is reduced to by default. Yet schools still hire so many amateurs who have done their part to devalue the image and status of foreigners in Japan; after the public scandals and collapses of chains

---

* Nickname for a bossy, demanding parent and increasing nuisance in Japanese education circles.

like Nova, the status of English teachers and the job they do *has* been reduced. One teacher confessed that for a time he was reluctant to be seen in public riding his bike to work and wearing a tie: 'There were only two things I could be – a Mormon or an English teacher, neither of which carries much respect in Japan.' Andre was more direct and personal. 'I'm embarrassed to tell women what I do for a living.'

The incident also highlights how much English instruction has become a retail service. In a country with a declining birthrate, young students, or rather their parents, are an increasingly powerful market. They can demand reductions in fees, putting downward pressure on salaries; lessons can take place at odd hours of the day to suit their schedules, stretching the eikaiwa teacher's day to encompass early mornings and late nights; they can set the content based on preferences and whims rather than accept the guidance of (hopefully) trained professionals with their students' language development goals in mind. At Aeon, Andre confirms, a student can go up a level if she insists she's ready, regardless of whether she is. 'Learning is secondary. The first objective is to keep the customer happy.'

The curriculum itself is geared toward that service. Just as the overarching philosophy is service-oriented, Andres claims, 'The lesson plans are designed to stroke the student's ego, not to expose any weaknesses that need to be remedied.' There are no outside materials or texts – everything is produced by Aeon. The lesson topics are in Andre's words, 'Bullshit. There's no realia, no published language texts and no realistic speaking scenarios. I identified that many students were in serious need of pronunciation help, and when I suggested running specific pronunciation classes I was stonewalled. They told me to leave it to the Japanese teachers, because they could better explain the mouth movements in the students' native language. Yeah, leave the English pronunciation to the Japanese teacher.'

Granted, a regional branch can hardly change corporate policy decided at head office, but only a large eikaiwa chain in Japan could justify such a policy to begin with. Though institutional factors play a part in this small drama it is a common stumbling block to language learning in Japan. James in Sapporo feels, 'like everything they have to filter English through a Japanese prism. In public schools the foreigner is just the ALT - the *assistant* language teacher – a sort of sounding board on which to practice the language point they've learned that week from the 'real' teacher, who can often barely string a sentence together herself. There's this idea that any serious study of a language must be done the *Japanese* way, and that learning with a foreigner is at best just an added extra, at worst light entertainment.'

Andre explains, 'In the states, English teaching is not a joke. You have to teach immigrants and they have to learn real language skills to survive. In Japan it's a hobby, a status symbol.' Andre likens the Japanese approach to foreigners and foreign languages to Edward Said's work *Orientalism,* wherein Westerners have a romanticized image of 'The East' and it is defined by all the things the west is that the east is not: civilized, enlightened, culturally refined, so much so that when Westerners used to venture into Asia and found civilization, they'd often be disappointed that the low expectations of the fantasy they'd hoped to encounter were dashed. 'For the Japanese it's orientalism in reverse. They are conditioned to see themselves as the 'superior' in many ways. They telling themselves, "Our language is difficult to learn" and are even surprised when they see us using chopsticks – a skill they've been brought up to think requires some sort of innate Japanese quality to master. Said wrote that the dichotomy is "I am what you're not." The obvious contrast is that if their language and culture are so difficult then English is therefore comparatively easy. If English is so easy then it must be the teacher's fault if students can't improve their English in one lesson a week.'

In teacher assessments at Aeon, the feedback is much like that given to the students. Lessons are divided up into sections: a few minutes at the start to check homework, a chunk of time spent on the main point, a free conversation section at the end. Just like a fast food chain, the elements are measured down to the minutiae of efficiency and service staff are judged on how well they adhere to the prescribed sequence. 'We'd be told, "You followed the script perfectly but your free talk time was supposed to be fifteen minutes and you did sixteen." This to them was the essence of good English teaching. You can never be perfect. If they admitted you were doing alright they might be obliged to reciprocate.'

Andre's problem was that *he* at least tried to reciprocate. 'I tried to teach, to answer questions, to instill knowledge. I'd stray from the script if it meant I could impart understanding. But the Japanese head instructor would tell us, 'no, you had to show this poster or write that phrase on the board and precisely this point in the lesson and not a minute sooner or later.' There were also contradictions between what the trainers taught and what the head teachers expected. 'The trainer might say leave the poster up, the head teacher would say take it down. I could tell I knew more about teaching than the head instructor ever would, but you just suck it up and get through the day.'

Here then was eikaiwa refined and distilled, the product of two decades of 'development' that has stripped the teacher of all responsibility or creativity and seen presentation eclipse any learning goals. All an instructor need do is stand in front of the class (never sit), follow the steps in the lesson plan (without deviation), avoid crossing his legs (hard enough to do while standing) and God help him if his wardrobe isn't up to scratch. By the second decade of the early twenty-first century, the production line mentality rules supreme in major English school chains. Take burger patty, slap on cheese, add pickle and sauce, place into buns, wrap in paper, put it on the tray. In that order please, we have standards to keep. And don't forget to smile.

Despite the small complaints Andre contends that Aeon wasn't the worst place to work. He was paid on time and never had a pay cut. He acknowledged the things he'd heard from friends at the new Nova under *Jibun Mirai* sounded worse than what he'd had to put up with. He left Aeon because he wanted to move to the big city and there were no vacancies at the larger Sapporo branch, not because of unbearable differences with his employer. Nowadays, he is still happy to have the greater freedom and independence gained from being outside the corporate umbrella and his teaching is much more varied and in depth now, as befits a graduate in comparative literature and linguistics.

Yet after less than three years in the country, Andre is already partially burnt out. 'It's a kind of therapy for them. We might as well lay them down on a sofa. Seeing the foreigner put firmly in his place, in a predetermined role set out for him, is comforting to them. They're terrified of the outside world, and they were supposed to be racially superior, yet they lost the war to us. But in the classroom, the foreigner is manageable and under their individual control. This is why they need blond haired, blue-eyed teacher - that's the image they want to own. It's like auctioning slaves: they check the teeth, slap the butt, they want to see that you're a suitable physical specimen.'

5 Life on Mars

Jason arrived early at the classroom and began to set up. He opened the book and placed it on the desk, plugged in the CD player and took a moment to review his notes. He spent a couple of minutes writing target vocabulary and phrases from the lesson plan, anachronistically on the classroom chalkboard. He brushed pink and blue dust from his suit pants and struck a relaxed pose. He waited for the students to arrive while looking out of the window at the trees and the sky. He had been sent by his language school to a national university to teach post-graduate science majors how to communicate in English like the young professionals they were soon to be. Colleges and universities are increasingly turning to dispatchers and eikaiwa schools to send part time teachers, reducing costs as full time teachers leave, or are not renewed, and are no longer replaced.[1]

'I have a bachelor's degree, ESL certification and years of experience, but normally this would be a job for someone with a master's. I was still confident I could pull it off. We got high caliber students at the school all the time, so this couldn't be any different.' But if high-caliber was what he expected he was in for a rude awakening. 'The room was about twice the size of a normal school classroom. You could easily fit sixty or seventy students in there. The desks were placed side by side in four or five neat rows. The first kid to come in goes and sits in the far right corner. The next one comes in and sits in the bottom left. The third takes a desk down at the bottom right. They were literally sitting as far apart from each other as they could, four or five meters between them. The first thing I did was move them all to the front center and make them sit next to one another. As more came in I had to corral them together. I was expecting them to already have social skills, but we spent the first lesson on ice breakers. It wasn't an English problem: without someone to goad them they wouldn't have spoken to each other even in Japanese.'

It comes as no surprise that science majors might be a little shy. Andre on the other hand, was sent to a lower-end 'university', where the pupils, mostly boys, who couldn't pass their high school finals ended up. Here one should have expected a rowdy bunch of dropouts who spent their time smoking in the halls and chatting up the girls. 'Actually the boys wouldn't even sit with the girls; they sat in groups at opposite sides of the classroom. When I was eighteen you couldn't keep me away. But these guys seemed content to keep their heads in their mobile phones. These kids weren't the best and brightest, okay, but they were at least young adults. They would mope in looking at the floor, mutter to their friends and gaze into their iPhones. They rarely did any homework and really needed prodding to do a class exercise. I'd get them to rehearse a model conversation, and they'd just hurry through the lines and go silent when they were finished. No initiative. One time I had the kids get out their pens and notepads and one guy just sat there. He said he didn't bring a pen. Not that he forgot to, just didn't bring one. They were like surly twelve-year-olds.'

When addressed or asked a question the most common response was to shuffle, mumble or otherwise deflect. Answers to the teacher tended to be single words or lines; questions from students would take an inordinate amount of cajoling to elicit and would invariably be superficial. Andre understood that, 'they really just didn't want to participate. It could be easily dismissed as teenagers acting out, if at eighteen or nineteen, the students weren't already too old.' Students had to make a show of procrastinating when approached by the teacher, as failing to hesitate and showing one could actually do it, would make a student stand out too much from the group.

Teachers at Andre's college reported that after sometimes having to repeat simple questions dozens of times in the classroom, they still wouldn't get a response; students would delay and stammer on purpose, look to their friends or sigh and complain of the difficulty. ALTs have related how students in middle and high school would always make a show of hesitation, turning to their classmates to seek confirmation before answering the teacher, sometimes requiring the whole class to discuss an answer before the speaker responded to the teacher. These are the common responses to basic questions such as occupation and place of birth.

Andre identified a couple of kids who did put in the effort and some who were better at English than they let on, but, 'Japan has this group mentality. Nobody wants to stick out. One guy who always played the fool in class actually had pretty decent conversations with me in the hall, when the others weren't around. A couple of the girls who probably found the class too easy always played dumb so the others wouldn't give them a hard time for being too smart. This wasn't some rough inner-city high school. It was a suburban junior college.'

Even working adults could fall back on juvenile classroom antics when faced with English classes that didn't interest them. 'I was fresh off the boat in 1998,' Jason says, 'and they sent me out to this *suisan*, a fishmonger's warehouse, where they process all the catch for supermarkets and so on. For some reason their management had decreed that even the lowliest cod-gutters needed English lessons though the reason was never communicated to me. Our language school was like that: they'd just get a call and send a teacher, no questions asked. English was just cash to them. So here I was at twenty four and hardly any experience and they've got me in the classroom with these hooligans around my age, who were probably school dropouts. They were the kind who liked drag racing their Nissan Skylines and getting tattoos and hanging out with wannabe gangsters – nothing in common whatsoever. First day in, one punk just sneers, "do you have a big penis?" They didn't just not want to be in my classroom, they didn't want *me* there.'

James recognized Jason's complaint over why some people need lessons at all. 'The school will basically say yes to everyone. They don't even ask why someone wants to learn English and somehow expect us to get it out of them. As head teacher they're always coming to me and asking me to find teachers for this or that new student or new client. They have no interest in what their goals are. It's just, *we need a teacher*. Well how am I supposed to choose the right person if I don't even know what they want? They also tend to nominate the time, even though they know our teachers are working several jobs and can't necessarily say yes. They'll tell me they want a teacher for Tuesday between seven and nine by next week, because they've already said yes to that request. That's the busiest slot of the week. I have to say, no, *I'll* find the teacher and tell *you* the times they can come and you get back to the client and tell them when we actually have a lesson. And while you're at it ask why they want lessons, please.'

As mentioned in Chapter Two, students don't always come because they want to learn English at all. A handful are just trying to get out of the house. They take lessons to socialize, to meet foreigners or because they don't have any friends or hobbies. Duncan reported that often psychologists recommend those with emotional disorders take up such hobbies. Dealing with the quiet or reticent student can be as challenging as the student who acts out. James has seen several students who ran others out of class. 'God bless her,' he said of one. 'She was trying but she just couldn't put two words together and always reverted back to Japanese. After a while her classmates stopped booking lessons with her. At other times the office put observers – potential customers – in with famously quiet students. When you've got someone who just stares at the floor and doesn't answer questions, you don't show them to potential clients. They won't come back if they think they'll see that person again.'

How do 'poor' students end up in mostly voluntary English courses? Michael, who has worked in public education and eikaiwa, says that, 'in a way, they're *all* bad students. It's not their fault. They're educated to hate school and to feel repelled by the classroom. English is a subject forced on them from their early teens, not a language that they learn to use. Unlike their own language, or mathematics, there is no practical use for English outside the classroom or the exam hall. Asking them at that age to learn a subject they *might* need in the future is a tall order.' English in Japanese schools has traditionally been a matter of rote learning grammar rules, translating difficult sentences and reproducing the feat at end-of-term tests. Putting a communicative approach into the lesson has little impact on such habits. 'No matter what strategy was introduced into the classroom, students would focus on memorizing and looking up the meaning of the simplest sentence in the dictionary, word by word, as if deciphering ancient hieroglyphics.' [2]

According to Michael, 'it's basically just like math to them. It's a series of problems to decode not a tool for communication. There's always supposed to be a correct answer to the riddle. When they ask you what's the difference between this word and that – like large and big – and you tell them it's basically the same thing, they don't believe it. There must be a trick to it or a subtle difference which changes the equation. They can't just let it be and feel it.' Students are also discouraged from discourse. 'At school in Japan you don't ask questions, you just follow instructions, and reproduce. The idea that there's more than one way to skin a cat is anathema to them. So many times I've had to ask students to stop, put their pens down and look at me. They've always got their heads in the book because that's where they think the language is.' Andre commented on the notion that the teacher is the keeper of the knowledge and the 'owner' of the language, and if the student doesn't absorb, then the problem must be in the delivery.* 'Participation is a matter of just coming to class,' says James. 'Oh, you can bring them around, but so many at first don't seem to realize that they have to put in some effort and engage their teacher and classmates. So many times, I've walked into a class at the start and everyone is just staring at the floor waiting for the lesson to start. It's an English class. Why not just start speaking with your classmates before the lesson? Surely they're all there for the same goals.'

While students at institutions seem to make a conscious effort to ignore, a certain level of disconnect can still be discerned even among customers who are paying for participatory English lessons. One researcher noted, 'the pretertiary school system has demotivated them to the extent they become unresponsive and display all the signs of burnt out apathy.'[3] While adults returning to commercial English schools will

---

*   See Chapter Four

have had many years to recover, some still surely suffer from that old aversion to the classroom environment. Often with a new student James recounts, 'I've been warned by the counselors that he or she "doesn't like" English. I think, well why are they here? English is not to like or dislike any more than you like pens or notebooks. It's just another communication tool.'

Shyness is a natural excuse. The ubiquitous overuse of surgical masks – once worn only by those with a cold or allergies – is now put down to people simply wanting to withdraw and disengage.[4] The urge to suddenly start communicating with strangers, or even acquaintances such as classmates likely only grabs those with a very bubbly disposition to begin with – it is not considered a normal Japanese trait. Nor apparently is it impolite to simply ignore people you haven't been introduced to yet. Though some might argue in Japan silence is golden, it can be hard for the teacher to break the 'shut up and listen' conditioning students are accustomed to. Another researcher writes, 'in Japan, there exists a strange dichotomy. On the one hand, it is a noisy place: the constant announcements in the train stations and shopping centers, the loud cries of shopkeepers greeting customers to their stores, the hustle and bustle of the busy streets. On the other hand, the Japanese value silence. It might seem odd that silence is valued in a place where such a cacophony exists, but silence in everyday interaction is a vital form of non-verbal communication for the Japanese.'[5] For James, 'Silence is another form of reticence. It's often an excuse for Japanese officials or management to avoid explaining themselves. Everyone else just sort of picks up on it and decides it's better not to say anything at all.'

The culture of silence also often allows officialdom to avoid taking responsibility for policies that are fixed and inflexible. James says,

'They'll do what they're trained to very well, but anything outside that, anything unexpected, and they freeze up. They have to call the manager and the manager has to call Tokyo, and so on up the chain. Nobody can make a practical decision on the spot.' It can also be a way for management to dig its heels in. At Aeon, Andre recognized a need for pronunciation lessons. 'Pronunciation is not part of the curriculum; it's not in the brief or the plan. If a student asks for it you can't spend a couple of minutes digressing from the menu.' He was told to leave it up to the Japanese teachers, doubting if they even offered such lessons or services, but now sure of one thing: that *he* wouldn't be permitted to. This rigidity can leave the foreign teacher frustrated at having his hands tied even when a ready solution is available.

The book by Ethnologist Peter N. Dale, *The Myth of Japanese Uniqueness*, explores the idea of *nihonjinron*, a concept often translated as 'Japaneseness'. Spending any length of time in the country will expose foreigners to many of the cultural myths the Japanese hold about themselves: that their intestines are longer than those of other humans, their brains work 'differently', and that they alone among humanity can communicate with each other with subtle social cues aside from language itself.[6] All can be seen as expressions of the idea the Japanese 'race' is a species distinct from the rest of humanity. In some versions, and popular in the nationalist period up to the Second World War, the Japanese are understood to be descended from a distinct branch of primates.[7] The scientific basis for such claims, for example exactly which branch of primates led to the Japanese, or how much longer the Japanese intestine measures, is never directly explored. It is not supposed to be questioned. Silent acceptance is the expected response.

This fundamental belief in being different - even superior - sours the Japanese relationship with other nationalities. As an amateur observer, James notes. 'Even without *nihonjinro*n, the Japanese are by and large quite convinced they are different, unique and special, possessed of some deep cultural or spiritual level that the west could never comprehend and inferior Asian neighbors can never aspire to. They think they're special simply because they're Japanese and everything they say or do springs from this uniqueness. It's practically their religion.'

Japan is of course an island nation, once isolated by its protective Shogunate and never successfully invaded. Sarah, a Canadian who has taught for some years in Japan, feels that, 'the Japanese consider themselves apart from the world because they are. Few countries are as homogeneous as Japan. But what they don't realize is that all countries are unique in their own way including equally isolated ones like Korea and, I don't know, Bhutan. Yet I've heard them say so many times, "Japan is very unique" that it seems to mark them as something special and maybe better.' Perhaps there is hope in the cliché. The adjective Japanese use to describe themselves as unique – *okashii* – can also be interpreted as 'strange' or 'odd', suggesting a measure of self-deprecating humor built into the notion.

James blames the war, or more importantly the occupation and reconstruction period immediately after. 'Japan was never de-Nazified the way Germany was. They never had a moment when a new guard took over and acknowledged that they were wrong and that the nationalist cult was fundamentally flawed. They simply employed bureaucrats from the old regime and they brought the nationalist ideas into mainstream government and education and subtly perpetuated many of these Japanese fantasies of superiority. Look at the Ministry of Education, Culture, Sports, Science and Technology. There's got to be a conflict of interest between education, science, and cultural superstitions such as *nihonjinron*.'

The subject of Japan's recognition and atonement – or lack thereof – is a volume in itself but the foreigners I've spoken to all feel that the war heavily colors Japan's relations with the world to this day. There are the obvious bones of contention. Japan seems hostage to an official understanding of its attempted conquest of Asia, including atrocities such as the enslavement of comfort women and the Rape of Nanking, that oscillates between hollow apology and outright denial. Highlighting James' conflict of interest, the education ministry continues to this day to censor school textbooks that make mention of sex slaves or Nanking.

The government and media have encouraged the idea that disputes over history are just 'stirring' by China and Korea for so long now, they may have started to believe it themselves. The liberal paper *Asahi Shimbun* was exposed for fabricating some evidence for a story on comfort women in the 1980s: the right wing and even the conservative government under Shinzo Abe roundly seized upon the error to claim that the entire issue of sexual slavery itself was a fabrication.[8] A number of politicians have come out in recent years to deny this and other atrocities. The Abe government even went as far in early 2015, as to send emissaries to US textbook publishers and college professors to ask them to retract their publications discussing the sexual enslavement of women by the Japanese military.[9] The assumption that Japan can reformulate world opinion regarding established history borders on delusional. There are also lingering disputes with China, Taiwan, Korea and Russia over island territory gained or lost in the war, which along with Japan's recalcitrance over war crimes, periodically fuels anger among Japan's Asian neighbors. The response by everyday Japanese varies from regret to hostility, but the idea that Japan can't have been all that bad has a strong mainstream following.

James believes that though there is no over-arching body to oversee the suppression or revision of wartime history, society has been subtly conditioned for the past sixty years. 'It starts with various mantras they learn as youngsters: They're unique, they're peaceful; Japanese are descended from farmers whereas Westerners come from hunters.'

Indeed Japan is a peaceful country now. It boasts among the safest city streets in the world and hasn't gone to war in seventy years. This makes it easy to believe Japan has always been that way and to deny accusations to the contrary. James believes, 'it's a way to shut out the world when they don't want to deal with painful arguments or inconvenient facts. It plays well at home because it leans on Japanese identity and self perception. I suppose it doesn't help that China and Korea keep needling them over it.' Jason pushes a little harder. 'What do Japanese historians and right-wing politicians say? "There's no evidence of atrocities. Don't listen to *them*. Trust us, we're *Japanese*." The entire world has got it wrong and they alone are right.'

The idea that the past can't be viewed separately from the present may stunt any drive toward atonement in Japan. In a separate conversation Hitomi, a middle-aged English student with an interest in historical issues and someone who admits to being 'a little to the right' told me, 'to pour scorn on the war dead is disrespectful to our forbears. They fought for Japan so we have a duty to honor them.' After generations of peace and harmony, most people simply cannot fathom the horrors of war.

There is little in the experience of modern Japanese that can prepare them to confront the atrocities of the past. It cuts to the very heart of Japan's self-perception as different. The flip side is that if Japan is such a uniquely peaceful country, then the rest of the world must by default be warlike. Anyone can just switch on the nightly news for affirmation.

The language of that chaotic, outside world is of course English. James believes, 'they view English differently from say, French or Italian. Those are languages of high culture, music and the arts in faraway, romantic places. But modern English is the language of foreigners *in Japan*; of General MacArthur and the American GIs that still occupy bases in the country. It's not something that they've necessarily sought out for themselves, but something vulgar that globalization has imposed on them; much the same way Admiral Perry forced them to open their ports. It's a form of cultural pollution.'

The fear of 'cultural pollution' extends not just to foreigners entering and living in the country but poses a danger to Japanese who venture abroad as well. Former ECC teacher Sarah recalls, 'I've had these old women in class worried about their grandchildren because their son, or son-in-law is being transferred overseas for a couple of years and is taking the family with him. They're afraid that the children will "forget how to speak Japanese." Never mind that in Bangkok or Singapore, they'll find themselves in a Japanese community, and have Japanese schools and kindergartens and be speaking Japanese at home with their mothers every day. The fear is that their offspring might catch foreign cooties and forget their language, or even their Japanese identity. It's frankly pretty silly.' She wonders why they'd need Japanese schools at all. 'You think they'd jump at the opportunity to get an international education, send them to an all-English school with the other expat kids. But they have to condition the kids for when they return to Japan, for the tests and tests they'll have to do to get into high school or university. The problem isn't that they'll forget Japanese; it's that after several years overseas they still don't speak another language. It's a huge waste, but the Japanese don't see it that way. What's important is that they're ready to come back to Japan, and haven't been deprogrammed while they were away.'

This sense of cultural exclusivity also affects the Japanese approach to English. Studying the language itself could be seen as a cultural taint, too much exposure to 'the other'. Though many students, especially at eikaiwa, have expressed a desire to spread their wings and go abroad, to use English to better their lives or to improve their social standing, there are those who see the language – and perhaps its speakers - as a necessary evil to be kept at arm's length. Though the language is now truly global, spoken by up to a billion people, and only a third of those native speakers, Japanese still want to learn 'authentic' English from a native speaker.

Michael believes, 'it's almost as if they're proud to say, yeah my teacher is a blond. It marks them as having a higher status, like they can afford the higher lesson fees.' While Berlitz and Gaba do indeed charge a premium - up to eighty dollars for a forty-minute private lesson - some Japanese are also turning to the cheaper options and getting a more realistic experience of English. One school in Tokyo is now staffed and run entirely by Indian nationals; the website rarejob.com offers Skype-style lessons from the Philippines at a fraction of the cost of a course at a big eikaiwa chain. But by and large, the traditional image of English persists.

Andre points out, 'the early boom in foreign languages – English and German – was to read foreign manuals and adopt foreign technology. Many of them still see it that way. It's not for two way communication, it's to adapt and copy. It's not to make them more global, but more successful in Japan, better Japanese.' The grammar translation method still taught in schools is a holdover from the days when Japan needed to modernize. Perhaps the stubbornness with which the education system clings to it is because, 'this attitude toward the language (as a code that needed to be mastered to unlock the knowledge of the West) plays a valued role in the development of modern Japan'.[10] For that reason English for communication becomes largely ornamental. The trophy wife on holiday in Hawaii can speak with the locals for her husband's convenience; the salaryman on a business trip can squeeze out a few lines to impress before the translator takes over. The level of communication remains superficial.

As does the level of contact: eikaiwa is the perfect environment in which to get controlled doses of English. The service is delivered by a native speaker, but the machine that backs it up can ensure the service itself remains recognizably Japanese. And eikaiwa isn't the only option. Tourists have long been able to go on packaged vacations abroad, with a Japanese guide and Japanese speaking hotel staff, Japanese menus and pamphlets and a minimum of contact with the environment they're visiting. In the last twenty years however, foreign- themed tourist parks have sprouted up *in* Japan. Now the Japanese traveler can experience a quaint English village or historical Spanish castle without even traveling overseas. The workers hired are typically foreigners who, as in an eikaiwa school, are not permitted to speak any Japanese so as not to lessen the immersion. Here, 'the sights of the world are seen from within the security of one's own culture, which is transported along with the tourist by a means of a highly organized network of commercial services.'[11] Eikaiwa, only outdoors.

Television has taken on board the ornamental English as well. One popular show in the late nineties and the early part of the next decade had a fluent foreigner approaching passersby on the street and getting them to speak a phrase or two in English. Comedy ensued when they inevitably fumbled and subtitles on the screen helped the slower viewers. Most Japanese know their English is poor, so the ritual humiliation of those who made trivial mistakes was a joke the audience and participants could all share in. However such a program, 'kind of makes a joke of English,' according to Jason who watched the show back in its day. 'It's okay to make mistakes yeah, but it also suggests that it's okay to be permanently bad at English, not to pay attention or not to really try. It trivialized the language and sort of reinforced the idea that English isn't important, that it's not an international language but can be a local joke.'

Far more pressing to most English teachers is their treatment compared to Japanese professionals. Many have complained of being viewed as the proverbial bull in a china shop. Many Japanese might argue that the shoe often fits. Yet, while the expected role of the goofy *gaijin*, fumbling his way through Japanese culture, causes offense to many, it is often a requisite in the classroom.

One blogger took aim at newer eikaiwa chain Coco Juku for having its teachers dress up in Halloween and Christmas costumes to entertain the children during the holiday season.[12] James recalls, 'At one job I just refused to wear any get-ups. We got paid half the teaching rate for non-classroom duties and I wasn't playing the clown for anyone, let alone for less money – it's demeaning. I still tell my teachers not to feel pressured into wearing Halloween costumes at all, but a lot of schools force the staff to. Well, the foreign staff. I've never seen the Japanese women dress up in Dracula teeth.'

This 'need' for showmanship, not only in children's classes but adult lessons as well, has become a standard expectation. A common refrain against teachers when it is time to evaluate is that they weren't *genki* or bouncy enough. Another popular TV program is *Basic English for Adults*. In a fifteen minute late night slot – reruns on weekday mornings – the show introduces a 'phrase of the day' via a short story segment following a young Japanese heroine on her travels overseas and a studio analysis by the regular hosts. The roles are clearly defined and strikingly familiar to anyone who has picked up a middle school English text published in Japan. The two main hosts are attractive women – a Japanese starlet playing the struggling learner and an equally appealing *haafu* ('half' – meaning mixed race Japanese) who has fluent Japanese and English.

After guessing at the meaning of idiomatic expressions such as 'Leave it up to me', the hosts call out the token foreigner who bounces onto the screen in flamboyant clothing and apparently high on caffeine and sugar. After playing the human tape recorder for a few lines flailing and gesticulating like the one of the *Wiggles*, the foreign host hands over to a Japanese man sensibly dressed in a jacket and tie and seated calmly at a studio desk. This fourth host plays the role of wise teacher, disseminating and analyzing the components of the phrase in Japanese, with occasional demonstration from the starlets and the energetic foreigner. He is the straight man to the foreigner's comedic presence. In the entire fifteen minutes, there are probably only two to three minutes of actual English.

This is eerily similar to teaching as an ALT in public schools, as James recounts, 'The pupils open the book, the Japanese teacher starts the lesson. The foreigner gives a demonstration of the target language; maybe the students do a little role play or repetition, then the Japanese teacher disseminates in Japanese. That's the way the textbooks are set up. The foreign character in the book is always a blond, big nosed teacher, culturally lost in his first year in Japan, or the Japanese student's pretty home stay sister with freckles and a ponytail, just like Anne of Green Gables.* They want the ALTs to project that image in class.'

The complaint that the teacher wasn't 'bouncy' enough stems from the view that English is a form of entertainment and the foreign teacher must first and foremost be a performer, fitted to a predetermined role. In Andre's experience, 'when they tell you you're good at chopsticks or at speaking Japanese, they're going through three stages of dealing with the foreign "threat". First they belittle the achievement, like telling a little kid she looks grownup in a bridesmaid's dress. Next, they tame the threat: the foreigner is no longer as intimidating if he can do something quintessentially Japanese. Finally they reclaim the act, reassured that this is something at least that they, as Japanese, can still do better. This is how they want their English taught to them, only the English must be tamed into *Japanese* English, so they can still claim to have a better grasp of - it at least for their purposes - than even the native speaker.'

---

* Red-haired Anne, as she is known in Japan, is another staple Western ideal.

Filtering the foreign experience through a Japanese prism is *de rigueur*. The *Basic English for Adults* show dissects English and serves it up it digestible Japanese bites, or in James' words, 'They want their English the same way they take their food – dipped in soy sauce or smothered in *miso* paste, essentially Japanized for the masses. It's like the African dictator in the film *Lord of War*: whenever he is corrected for getting his English idioms wrong he replies, "Thank you, but I think I prefer it my way". For them it's important to do everything, even learning a foreign language, the *Japanese* way.'

As for the portrayal of the foreign teacher, 'He's a clown, an entertainer, not to be taken seriously,' laments James. 'The only way they can interact with us is if we're this soft, comical figure. This is how they put the foreigner in his place.' Until 2012, the card that all foreign residents had to carry was named the 'Alien Registration card'. It has since been changed to the more inclusive 'Resident's Card', but that it took several decades should also remind foreigners of their status. 'We're here at their discretion and for their pleasure,' Andre says. 'They'll only take what they want from us and they're not interested in the rest.'

Modern Japan still sees foreigners as 'aliens'. The *zainichi* Koreans, descendants of WWII era slave laborers, are still not granted citizenship and voting rights after several generations in Japan. They remain essentially stateless. Recently, migrant laborers from China and Southeast Asia, are brought over to work in factories and on farms under a government-subsidized 'trainee' program, often suffering abysmal conditions.[13] These abuses are largely hidden away behind closed doors, and many migrant and trainee workers have little interaction with mainstream Japanese society. When the abuses do come to light they are roundly seized on by local media, but often forgotten in the next news cycle.

Though largely ignored by local news media, perhaps nowhere is the western *gaijin* more outwardly reminded of his 'place' than in the eikaiwa classroom. Large chains have taken this ball and run with it, reducing the teacher to a mere entertainer, and one not paid nearly as well to give the same outlandish performance as the western celebrities on TV. One national chain in particular has lowered the bar so far and so often that the name is synonymous with poor working conditions, low pay and lack of respect for its foreign teachers. If the industry has been sinking for a while, it may just have found rock bottom.

Craig Currie-Robson

6 Gaba Moves the Goalpost

Leaning over a barrel propped up as a table, Michael takes another sip of his beer at an Asakusa corner bar known for its selection of sake, wines and boutique ales. An American, he has recently moved to the suburbs to take up a high school job, but still comes downtown once in a while. Many teachers are worried that I might be a spy for their employers, current or former, and are reluctant to speak about their experiences. It doesn't say much for the industry that it inspires such fear. Michael has the confidence of someone who has found a safe job and doesn't have to worry about looking back. His paranoia is not completely dissolved however: he won't tell me the branch he worked at, and asked that I use only his first name. Those still in the job market in Japan don't need a reputation for critiquing former employers. He worked at a Tokyo branch of Gaba, a rising 'star' in the industry.

Founded in 1995 and headquartered in Tokyo's swanky Shibuya district, Gaba has over forty 'Learning Studios' as it calls them, and over a thousand instructors.[1] With confidence in the eikaiwa industry shaken, students have been increasingly turning away from the well-known language school chains and looking for a more personal experience. Though it is a large chain, Gaba offers one-to-one lessons for most classes, including children's lessons through the Gaba Kids brand. Though Gaba Corporation had been around for some time, it was quick to benefit from the fall of Nova, seeing a healthy expansion after 2007.

Gaba's cryptic name is said to be an acronym for 'Girl's be ambitious, boys be audacious', a play on the exhortations of one Professor Clark of Hokkaido University, who in the 1870s urged pioneering Japanese agriculturalists, 'Boys, be ambitious'. Ironically the school does not operate in Hokkaido. In other telling, the name is a cryptic reference to a favored sports supplement of co-founder Hideki Yoshino. According to the Wikipedia page, four letter acronyms graced the billboards of all the major chains at the time, so it may have just seemed like the thing to do. Some instructors have their own four-letter words for the school.

'One word,' says Michael, 'burnout. This place will work you to the bone then hang you out to dry. There are no rights, there is no respect. You teach ten, twelve, fourteen lessons a day then they spring you with a petty complaint from a client. To them you're nothing, just a machine, and there's always another sucker waiting to take your place if you're not up to the job.'

It was not always so. In the nineties, Gaba founders Karen and Hideki Yoshino recognized the need for a matchmaking service that introduced students to private teachers. Until 1995, when Gaba was established, most people had to go to a school, or find their own teacher on community job boards and through friends. Such agencies are fairly common now and Gaba has moved into a more solid state of booking lessons and providing teachers, but back then it was a fairly novel concept. Matchmaking services do a brisk trade in booking students with teachers. Some of them have premises where the lessons are conducted and others simply let the lesson take place at cafes and other neutral ground, the way private teachers have always taught in Japan. The student pays a membership fee for the service, but the fee for the lesson goes entirely to the teacher. Some say this is a legal gray area that will someday draw the attention of the tax authorities. Whether for this reason or because in-house lessons and handling the money directly was more profitable, Gaba developed its Learning Studios – essentially branch schools - where it could control the financial and academic environment. Gaba learned more than just catchy names from the Big Four.

But it was still a friendly mom-and-pop shop in those days. Things were to change after corporations got their hooks in. The company was sold on twice and went public in 2006. The majority stockholder was merchant bank Daiwa Securities with a 60% share.[2] In 2008 there was a restructuring and Kenji Kamiyama joined as chief of operations. He quickly deposed the CEO and took the post, abolishing his previous post in his wake to ensure the door was firmly shut behind him. His first focus was to reduce 'wasteful spending'. According to Michael, who worked for Gaba in those days, 'We all knew what that meant. The other schools had done it. They were going to go after teacher salaries'.

The defining paradox of the eikaiwa industry, often lamented by grumbling teachers, is that the star players are the ones with the least job security. Like a football team or a Hollywood movie has its favorites, it is the instructors the students come to see and without them you could barely run an English school at all. Yet, in Michael's words, 'we're part timers, with a shitty hourly wage, while the office staff get job security and bonuses. Can you imagine the players on a professional sports team getting less than the secretaries or the office admin staff?'

Michael's cynicism isn't entirely warranted. According to Ian Raines, a General Union official who has represented staff at Nova, Gaba and others, 'The Japanese teachers get even less. Office staff and other employees have low pay and benefits, few holidays and long working hours. Branch managers put in a lot of unpaid overtime.' While it is true that under Kamiyama's predecessor, the company had wasted money on promotional events, rapid expansion and the mandatory plush downtown office space in Shibuya, Tokyo, Gaba was already paying at the low end of the scale when it came to salaries. New teachers received ¥1400 per lesson (now ¥1500 for 40 minutes) and nothing at all if no lesson was booked. Some charge they had to sit in their booths at the learning studio looking busy, or under the manager's direction doing extra unpaid work, but only got paid when there was a student in the room with them.³

There is compensation for lessons canceled late, but some branches have been accused of keeping the teacher there for a whole shift, even if most of the day was spent waiting. In a quick calculation, a fairly busy month could net ¥180,000 - 200,000 for 120 lessons, or as little as ¥120,000 ($1200) if things got quieter at 80 lessons. Though the teachers have flexibility on paper, the studio's opening hours and peak times define the schedule. Managers can also limit a teacher's lessons as a punitive measure against anyone who stands up to the company.

Olivia, who worked at a branch in Saitama came with a hope of using her down time to study for a translating license but, 'the booths at the studio were just partitions so it was pretty noisy, which didn't help. We were allowed to sit in our booths between lessons but the company was strict about behavior. We had to look "professional" for any clients who walked past, even when not teaching. I couldn't really have a bunch of papers and texts spread out on the table. We weren't even allowed to wear headphones or have a drink unless it was in a capped bottle.'

Michael found the company could be very petty about changing schedules. 'Every month we were supposed to mark our availability.

This allowed flexibility for the students and the teachers but in reality once you'd had the same schedule a couple of months running, the counselors didn't want you to change it. When I wanted to change my day off so I could enjoy the weekends better the ISL (Instructor Support Leader) kicked up all sorts of objections: *that will be difficult; so-and-so is used to booking your lessons on that day; you'll lose hours* and so on. He basically threatened me with reduced hours on other days if I didn't keep my original schedule open for them.' He started to think about cutting his hours at Gaba and replacing them with private lessons: 'More money and flexibility, fewer arguments.'

Adrian Ringin is a Gaba teachers' representative at the General Union who has been at the forefront of collective bargaining procedures. The union hasn't dealt with any official complaints that teachers are forced to wait around the studio between lessons, however Adrian does confirm there is some unpaid overtime. 'It is very common for instructors to work for free typing up lesson records after their lessons finish. It is often impossible to get it done during the lesson, or during the five minute break between lessons, so some instructors spend a lot of time afterwards typing up notes.' According to Adrian, those teachers that do put in the work can make good coin. 'The number of lessons that people teach varies widely. Some people just do a few lessons on the side, for others it is their main occupation. People doing it as their main job can make between ¥200,000 to around ¥400,000 per month. But that depends on how much they are booked.'

Nevertheless, most teachers aim for the middle, seeking a balance between work and life. ¥200,000 is below the average wage of Japanese workers.[4] A hundred lessons a month is a grueling schedule requiring a work week of *at least* forty hours if a teacher is to prepare effectively for each lesson. 'Try getting by in Tokyo on that'. Laments Michael, 'We're basically their Mexicans: cheap, disposable foreign labor. Of course without that labor the job couldn't get done. By definition only a foreigner *can* be a native English instructor. But they think somehow they deserve all the profits just for thinking up ad campaigns, while we do the actual work.'

As if ¥1500 per lesson weren't low enough, Gaba lessons cost the students – or 'clients' in company parlance - between ¥5,000 and ¥7,000 per forty-minute slot. This means starting teachers earn only a quarter or less of the fee for each lesson taught. This is even more jarring than the discrepancy between Berlitz fees and wages when, according to Ian Raines of the General Union, 'Berlitz pays into and matches standard employee benefits such as the national pension and social insurance, at least for full time employees.' As Gaba does not pay these, it makes even more money off each lesson than Berlitz and therefore in a sense withholds more from instructors. By Raines' estimate, Gaba teachers earn about 25% less than Berlitz instructors (per lesson) when the missing company contributions to public benefits are factored in.

It *is* possible to make more, and people do. Given that a five-day work week is roughly 22 days a month, in theory a Gaba teacher can make over ¥300,000 teaching grueling ten-lesson days. In practice it often means working split shifts over six days a week to cover the ebb and flow of the peak hours, because they won't get ten lessons every day of the week. Olivia, who worked for several years at Saitama branch, recalls, 'In the beginning I was eager to make as much as I could. When I heard you could make your own schedule, I thought I could work four days at 10-12 hours instead of five 8-hour days, but I ended up working five 12-hour days instead. It was difficult to get a full schedule and fill those hours in the middle of the day.'

In quiet months, teachers reported being barely able to make the rent.[5] Michael chose to teach private lessons outside to supplement his pay. He could earn 2500-3000 tax-free yen for an hour, use whatever materials he and his students agreed upon and fill the quiet hours in the middle of the day, as mornings and evenings were the busy slots at Gaba. Asked if he felt Gaba was underpaying teachers Michael didn't hesitate. 'Definitely. Forty minutes is the better part of an hour anyway. Some smaller schools can still pay in the 2500 range. They've still got the old fashioned notion that they're paying for your expertise rather than simply your labor. If you work in big chains, the smart money is made after hours.' Michael's complaints may be valid, but it's hardly illegal for a company to pay a 'shitty wage'. Japan's minimum wage stands at between ¥650 and ¥850 depending on the district, with Tokyo being at the higher end – around US$11.00 at the time.[6] Japan is finally climbing out of a two-decade economic slump, and general salaries are improving in the major export and financial companies. The consumption tax was raised from 5% to 8% in 2014, with a hike to 10% planned for late 2015. Yet, there's a sense that English teachers will be left behind in the economic recovery as eikaiwa wages have continued to decline even as schools expand. Michael warns, 'they've been gunning for the bottom for some time now, probing for the lowest amount a foreigner will teach for. The excuse of course was the recession. Now the economy is improving, you'll see wages rise and bonuses return for Japanese workers, maybe even the staff at English schools, but not us.' At ¥1500 per 40-minute lesson (over ¥2200 per hour) a Gaba teacher still earns about twice as much a clerk in a convenience store, or as one headline from a satirical website notes, "Working at Gaba provides perfectly suitable alternative to homelessness."[7]

Yet teaching is not a job for grocery clerks. Most teachers are university graduates. They are hired from overseas and qualify as skilled labor or even foreign expertise: the visa most eikaiwa teachers have names them a '*Specialist* in Humanities' and requires a tertiary degree to work as such. Considering that many are also in their late twenties or early thirties, they are surely earning less than their mid-career Japanese counterparts of a similar education and age. A Japanese worker in the offices of a large company – including some major eikaiwa chains - can expect a steady salary, yearly bonuses and paid days off, even if this has been somewhat eroded over the past decade. Such benefits are a distant dream for most English teachers. It is true the Japanese *salaryman* works long hours for his benefits but English teachers aren't even being given the chance to do the same. Michael asserts, 'I would have been more than happy to put in long days knowing there are bonuses and a steady salary and paid holidays. I believe teachers would stay longer and work at being better at their jobs. If we were allowed promotions, I believe branches could be run better by foreign managers because they used to be teachers. These opportunities are closed to us. It's discrimination. There are only so many hours a day, and only so many hours suitable for lessons. If you're getting paid by the hour that is the limit of your income, and you're stuck in that box till you leave.'

How then does Gaba avoid the responsibility of paying teachers benefits, annual leave or even overtime? The secret lies in their status not as employees, but as sub-contractors – *itaku* in Japanese. As a 'self-employed' contractor, the instructor need only be paid for lessons taught, or in the case of late cancellations, because they needn't have turned up at work for nothing (to cut Gaba some slack, some schools don't even pay for lessons that are cancelled at the last minute, or when students don't turn up). According to Michael, 'they like the studio to look full, so it gives the clients an impression that we're all busy. Even at quiet times of the day, we're allowed to go out on breaks, but you get the feeling they'd like us sitting around in the booths, so that the place seems livelier than it really is. But we don't get paid for just being there, so I never saw the point.'

The *itaku* sub-contractor status of Gaba teachers has drawn attention from the industry and the authorities. The industry seems to love it. With more and more schools looking to cut costs, the idea that teachers can be rotated in and out as needed and only paid for the work they do is catching on. It is also another way to avoid paying government-mandated benefits like national pension and health insurance. Schools needn't bother with the pretense that teachers are only part time anymore: now they're not staff at all. This gives employers great freedom to hire and fire, increase or pare down hours as needed and in some cases, to wriggle extra unpaid work out of the instructors. One way is to include lesson preparation and writing up notes in the wording of their contracts as part of the lesson fee, but only paying for time spent in the classroom. Most eikaiwa schools would take issue with teachers using classroom time to write those notes. It is easier to have them doing it as unpaid overtime.

Schools take issue with teachers challenging their absolute word on employment status as well. The Japan Times reported in 2014 that an instructor of 22 years had been dismissed from a Yokohama based school named ICC for challenging his 'subcontractor' status. The union charged that since the school gave him warnings of insubordination, chided him for dress-code violations, and by not complying with workplace guidelines, it was a *de facto* admission that the teacher was indeed an employee The warning letter even referred to the company as the 'employer'. The teacher's crime? Demanding paid holidays afforded employees under Japanese labor law and for joining the General Union. Startlingly the owner of ICC was not even a large Japanese corporation, but a foreign-born entrepreneur.[8]

James in Sapporo fought a losing battle against his school's contract revisions. 'First they all became part time. I think that happened around the time that visa regulations were revised to make it easier to hire part time teachers. Before the year 2000, immigration policy required schools that sponsored foreign teachers to pay a minimum of around ¥250,000 with national pension and health insurance, so most people were on salary. After that it became ¥180,000 or so, making it easier to work part time here and there. Teachers could get their visa and work their main job and still have time to teach privates or another school in their off hours. Hourly pay still ranged from ¥2500-3000 at the time so people still made good money, even if schools could relax on responsibilities such as the pension.'

James' school was quick to take advantage of the potential savings, cutting benefits each year as contracts were renewed. 'Teachers would have a block of minimum guaranteed hours and get paid extra for working over that. Not as good as full time, but not a bad deal in terms of flexibility. The next year the guaranteed hours got longer while the block pay stayed the same and the hourly rate for extra hours decreased. The year after, everyone was reduced to just an hourly rate. Then the number of paid vacation days was cut. Then the hourly rate was reduced again. Basically each year the contract was revised to the disadvantage of the teachers. Then some smart cookie introduced the director to Gaba's practices and his eyes must have gone *ka-ching*! He reduced everyone to 'sub-contractor' status. No paid days off, no benefits at all.'

This should mean greater freedom for teachers, but often foreigners don't have the resources to wade through the tax codes, labor laws and other regulations to find out what their rights are. As self-employed contractors they qualify as a business earning less than ¥10 million per year, so they entitled to more tax write-offs and should be free to charge the client - the company that is - for transportation, preparation time and other expenses; in reality schools decide the rates and whether or not to pay for extras. For their part, schools are obligated to pay subcontractors consumption tax, but few do (Gaba being the exception here at least). Technically a subcontractor could turn up to work any time of the year in casual clothing, since it is her business what she wears to work, but schools still maintain dress codes, some very strictly. If teachers do work on public holidays they get only their contract rate because they're not entitled to the overtime afforded to employees under Japanese labor laws. Theoretically, subcontractors should be able to charge extra for extra work such as report-writing but schools write paperwork into the contract as part of the lesson preparation and teacher responsibilities.

In the case of James' school, subcontractors were contractually forbidden to discuss their employment status, so the company could keep up the pretense that its staff were full time employees. The logic was that the company might look 'weak' if it couldn't even take care of its own staff. 'It was just a way to pay less, but maintain control. The contract stipulated half pay for non-teaching duties, but that the hourly teaching rate included paperwork such as reports. At certain times of the year, reports added up to many hours of extra work in the teachers' own time. Moreover teachers had their lessons taken off them at quiet times and loaded onto James because he was the only one on a full time salary and it could save money, a practice Gaba has also used when advantageous to the company.[9]

In James' opinion, 'the school got all the benefit out of that and still treated the teachers as casual labor rather than anything as respectable as a subcontractor.' In fact with temporary contracts a company doesn't even have to dismiss teachers: it simply doesn't have to offer them any more hours. James says, 'That's one way to get rid of drop kicks, but on the other hand it offers no guarantees to good teachers. After several years, we'd gotten so used to it we'd just roll our eyes and wonder what the company was going to pull next contract. When I asked them about the consumption tax they were supposed to be paying to so-called independent contractors, I was told our contractors are "different" from Gaba's.'

The union's Adrian Ringin dubbed the idea that teachers are not genuine employees, a 'convenient fiction'. At Gaba, and schools that aspire to be like it, the practice is used simply as an excuse to pay less. Companies see only where they might cut costs, disregarding other financial responsibilities that may come with hiring staff. The foreign teachers who are the lifeblood of language schools are regarded as liabilities to be reduced rather than human assets that need to be nurtured.

While James' school modeled its employment practices on Gaba's questionable *itaku* contract, it remained a small regional language center. One benefit to a smaller outfit is that a handful of teachers on shaky contracts lack the strength or willpower to challenge the company. But in a bigger company like Gaba, the body of teachers is large enough to fight back. They have access to all the foreigner-friendly legal and labor consultation services afforded by more international cities like Osaka and Tokyo. The hounds eventually picked up a scent.

The first industrial action came in 2007, shortly after the General Union established a branch at Gaba and started to apply pressure. In April 2008, the base lesson rate was raised from ¥1400 to 1500 and the rate for more experienced instructors also increased. The Union claims this as an early victory but Gaba has maintained the rates were always under consideration. That would make Gaba the only major eikaiwa school to have unilaterally raised teacher salaries in the last decade: the market trend has been to consistently cut pay, as Michael noted, feeling out the minimum that a foreign instructor is willing to work for.[10]

The union has also successfully increased contract lengths. Most contracts at eikaiwa schools run for a year. It is standard practice for a school to review teacher contracts annually and rather than dismiss anyone who under-performs, they may not offer a new contract. It strikes a balance between job security and flexibility: struggling schools can reduce staff when demand goes down and teachers who don't plan to stay in Japan long-term have a yearly chance to review their own circumstances. But while one year is the industry standard, Gaba's contracts were initially only for *four months,* keeping teachers on a precarious ledge dependent on consistently positive student evaluations and good relations with branch managers, because Gaba *does* non-renew.

The union has managed to extend the standard contract to six months, but it can still be reduced to four months as a disciplinary measure. As Michael put it, 'that makes it difficult to make any long-term plans.'

For over a year starting in July 2008, Gaba found itself up in front of the Osaka Labor Relations Commission by the union. Results were mixed. The union claimed that Gaba had not negotiated in good faith, often a tricky charge to make stick. The instructors also wanted to be recognized as employees, not independent subcontractors. They were effectively working part or full time schedules for Gaba at the company's premises, during company business hours and under company guidelines. The commission found that the company had not negotiated in bad faith – a victory for Gaba - but the thirty-five page report also appeared to recognize the union members as employees, rather than outside help. The union has expressed its intention to use this recognition to fight for further rights as employees.[11]

Fearing future action based on the ruling, Gaba sought to remove any suggestion the relationship between the organization and its teachers was one of employer and employees. It is not hard to see what Gaba fears the most. As subcontractors, teachers are not entitled to paid leave, medical coverage or pension. They can be dismissed arbitrarily or by simply not renewing their six-month contracts. Recognizing the instructors as actual staff would not just force the company to treat them with more respect and offer more security. It could open the floodgate for negotiations on a raft of benefits that would cut into Gaba's bottom line. In fact it would undermine the industry's business model which relies on cheap, disposable foreign labor. In October 2010 the Central Labor Commission rejected Gaba's challenge of its finding that teachers were actual staff. Gaba then sued the commission in the Tokyo district court and was struck down again in July 2011.

It is however, easier to take on employees than a government body. In November 2011 Gaba was accused of an attempt at union busting. The chair of the General Union branch at Gaba, Francis Strange, an instructor in good standing who had worked there for over eight years, found his contract mysteriously non-renewed. The only reason could be poor performance or a lack of need, but Strange had received consistently good feedback from the students and managers and the branch was not overstaffed. In fact no reason was given; he was simply not offered another contract. The flimsy contracts perhaps made Gaba feel it could circumvent labor laws that forbid firing staff for union involvement. The union immediately identified this as a decapitation strike and went to work leafleting and picketing Learning Studios in Osaka and Tokyo. The pressure worked. The union negotiated a rehire of Mr. Strange as of February the following year.[12]

Though the union is still a long way from securing standard benefits or even genuine employee status, it has managed to chip away at low pay rates. The main form of incentive at Gaba is its 'belting' system: Higher performing teachers are paid at a higher per lesson rate, all the way up to ¥2,200 per lesson, or about 40% over the base rate, an upper limit which the union has claimed some credit for. The union has also managed to negotiate a ¥200 bonus for teaching at peak morning hours, starting between 7:00 and 8:30am. This is not tied to performance and is purely an incentive for getting up extra early. A teacher at the top end of the pay scale, working an early shift can make ¥2400 per 40-minute lesson, a rate that rivals the *hourly* pay for most other schools. Yet the benefits of belting and working tough hours are fleeting. Teachers can only make the early morning rate for those two hours or so in the morning, a maximum of three potential lessons. Being 'belted' up to a higher hourly pay scale likewise doesn't apply to all lessons: off-peak hours in the afternoon are still paid at the base rate, and these encompass all lessons between 9am and 5pm. Furthermore belting is not a promotion. It is a temporary privilege contingent on a steady stream of good evaluations from the students.

Imagine though, that despite the hefty challenge given them, Gaba teachers pulled together and met, indeed exceeded, such demanding standards. They did just that. Over the years the average evaluation score climbed across the board, resulting in more teachers being belted. If Gaba's incentive system was designed to improve the service, it was working. Rather than congratulating the faculty for a job well done, Gaba responded by raising the average scores needed to be belted upward, once more snatching the opportunity to increase hourly income from many teachers who had been on the verge of greater success.

Despite Gaba's best efforts, the ratio of teachers being moved up to the higher pay rate has consistently outnumbered those being bumped down over the years, but only half of all teachers at Gaba were making more than the base rate of ¥1500 per lesson as of July 2013. Furthermore since Kamiyama took control with an eye toward cost cutting, the actual rate of debeltings has steadily increased, and the rate of teachers being belted up has decreased.[13] Tying performance to customer service goals is not novel or particularly unkind. However, it begs the question of whether Gaba has deliberately set the bar too high or whether there is a conscious fiscal policy to ensure that the company doesn't keep too many teachers on higher pay scales - a cynical excuse to pinch pennies. In Michael's words, 'they grease the pole and tell you to climb it. They don't really want you to succeed.'

Gaba also offers an incentive for the total number of lessons taught in a month. In previous years this meant that instructors who taught above a hundred lessons in a month received a small monthly bonus. Thanks once more to the union, by 2013 the bonus was up to almost ¥16,000. Clearly this was too generous for Gaba: as with the per lesson premium, the rate only applied to *peak* lessons taught - early mornings and evenings after 5pm. In order to earn bonus of about hundred dollars an instructor would need to teach 120-149 lessons, excluding those between 9-5pm; to get that extra $160 or so at the top a teacher would have to perform a staggering 150 lessons or more, all at peak times. Until April 2013 teachers were making only ¥10,000 extra for *over 200 lessons*. In that month only sixty eight out of a thousand teachers – six percent - managed such a feat.[14]

Gaba's recruiting page tells prospective teachers, 'For many, Gaba is their primary source of income. These instructors regularly teach over 200 lessons a month with top performers taking home over 300,000 yen for their efforts.'[15] In comparison, in Melbourne or Auckland a qualified ESL teacher can bring home at least that much teaching a third of the lessons, or twenty five hours a week. Bruce, who returned to the US after four years teaching eikaiwa, now makes over fifty dollars an hour teaching ESL at a community college. The website adds, 'Upon completing Gaba's Initial Certification program, instructors begin teaching. All start at the *competitive* rate of 1,500 yen per 40-minute lesson taught. According to Olivia, the three day 'certification' is an unpaid training seminar and the qualification is merely a rubber stamp to teach Gaba lessons. 'They also have one-day brush up courses that you have to go to once a year, unpaid. They sell it as "career development" but it's compulsory and is required to get belted. It's just another way to avoid paying us.'

The company has yet more ways to ward off the possibility of paying too much in bonuses. Head instructors, known as Instructor Support Leaders, are required now to teach from 40-60 lessons a month in order to cut costs, as their salaries are already paid. This isn't a lot of work, even for a head teacher who should theoretically have other duties. As head instructor at a smaller company, James was required to teach close to 100 hours a month - more than any other teacher at the school: foisting lessons onto salaried staff to avoid paying part timers saves money, but limits the opportunity for contract teachers to rack up lesson totals. At Gaba, this stunts their potential income, including bonuses, and stifles motivation.

An observer could be forgiven for thinking the company was trying to avoid paying incentives or to ensure that as few staff as possible are eligible. Ian Raines of the General Union says, 'We suspect the purpose of switching the incentive requirements to peak lessons only is an effort to move the goalpost. This is one area where we continue to pressure Gaba.' Raines stops short of claiming that increasing incentive targets is a means of cost cutting. 'It directs people to focus on the busiest hours rather than the whole day. Ambitious teachers have to work split shifts, but it ensures they're available when the company needs them most.'

Adrian backs this up. 'It is not just about cheapness on their side, it is about incentivizing instructors to work peak lessons – early mornings, late evenings, and weekends.' He adds however, that while teachers who taught a lot of peak lessons got their incentives, those whose schedules had always been made up of the hours in between saw a reduction in income when they stopped getting bonuses for the total number of lessons they taught. Not only does this mean a potentially hefty workload (CELTA instructors recommend 20-25 hours contact per week at most), but a good portion of lessons taught are *not* counted toward the bonuses. To focus on those peak times, teachers have to work split shifts or, if there are lessons available in the quiet middle of the day, from early morning till late at night.

The teachers haven't been fooled. In a survey run by the General Union, Gaba instructors were asked to rate the new incentive system. Comments included, 'Even though I work 10-12 lessons a day on weekends I find it hard to get the same incentive as before,' 'Thanks to the incentive I'm forced to work extra on weekends and late on weekdays,' and most tellingly, 'Since when was it lawful to make changes to compensation without an employee's consent? Oh right, we're not employees...' In the survey, 86% of instructors wanted all lessons to count towards the incentive, not just peak hours; 82% expressed dissatisfaction with the new system and 73% claimed that their monthly incentive amount had *decreased* under the new plan. Teachers working harder and getting less; from the Gaba's point of view it must have been a resounding success.

Outside of eikaiwa, a teacher can earn ¥2,500-4,000 per-hour in the private lesson market. She would only have to teach a few outside lessons a week to make the same money as she would teaching dozens of extra lessons at Gaba. When just four more private lessons a week could easily net over ¥40,000 a month, tax free, it's a wonder even ten percent of Gaba teachers have put in the effort at all. Adrian Ringin explains that although plenty of teachers do work only part time at Gaba and teach private lessons on the side, plenty still keep Gaba as their sole source of income. 'If people have their visas sponsored by Gaba they have to work a large enough schedule to generate sufficient income to justify visa sponsorship by the school. Also, it can be a lot of work to get and maintain enough private students.' For many foreign teachers it is easier in some respects to go to the big companies: they don't have go out and find students themselves.

According to Adrian, 'working four, five, six or more lessons in a row is standard. There is only a five minute gap between lessons, and usually instructors have less than that because they have to get the student out of the lesson booth. Instructors want to do the best job that we can. But working under such conditions, it is basically impossible to give the effort that the students' high fees justify.' Given that the peak lessons taught bonus is not granted to teachers who have had a couple of negative evaluations, and the extra workload is bound to create more fatigue-related errors, it looks almost as though they've been set up to fail. This keeps teachers on a precarious ledge if they're on a winning streak. Any more than two negative evaluations can see a teacher returned to a lower rate in the following pay cycle.

What constitutes a negative evaluation at Gaba? According to Ian Raines, 'Anything a student doesn't like. No matter how trivial or ridiculous it sounds. One child was intimidated by the use of the word *shark* in a lesson that discussed dangerous animals, and a parent complained because the family had been planning a trip to a beach resort and the child was worried about what might lurk in the water. One adult student wanted to see a wider variety of colors of whiteboard marker used. These evaluations are all saved on file and used not only to deny teachers their peak lesson bonuses, but also as a means of intimidation.' When eikaiwa students can complain about anything from a minor grooming *faux-pas* to 'looking fatigued', this leaves a lot of room for teachers to be penalized. It can be hard for a teacher to stay on a higher pay scale, as it involves constantly navigating the whims of the students to maintain higher evaluation average.

Adrian explains, 'There aren't really meaningful criteria for student evaluations. It is ultimately down to whether a student feels satisfied. Mostly this is fine, but when it comes to unreasonable students this creates a problem. A student could negatively evaluate an instructor for using Japanese in a lesson, or for *not* using Japanese in a lesson; for using the text too much, or not using it enough. Whether students evaluate or not is entirely up to them. Some evaluate every lesson, some never do.' This way the company sets no standards and keeps a free hand to accept any negative evaluation it chooses: so far this appears to be all of them. These negatives needn't be consistent: what works in one class may not work in another and if the student is unhappy, it is always the teacher's fault.

The Gaba union's Facebook page has listed a plethora of student complaints from the ambiguous, 'overused textbook,' to the laughable 'not funny enough,' to the just plain insulting 'adjusted glasses in class'. In one case, a teacher received a negative evaluation on his personal record because a student didn't like the prescribed Gaba textbook. Such small matters would make an amusing anecdote except that every month, teachers who have met or exceeded the number of lessons required for incentives, are denied those incentives under the two strikes rule because they sneezed or took a sip of water in class. Adding insult to injury, these so-called black marks remain on teachers' records and could be used as a stick to beat them with in future disciplinary sessions and at renewal. When asked if the company might be *encouraging* counselors to elicit negative evaluations from clients in order to dodge paying incentives, Ian Raines felt it was a 'strong possibility.'

Adrian Ringin was responsible for collating such complaints. 'Instructors don't like the evaluation system, of course. But the real problem is that the company almost always refuses to remove the negatives if it mentions anything about the instructor. This creates a situation where instructors are always dreading getting a negative. Also, staff at the company almost never recognize a positive evaluation, but as soon as a negative one is filed they jump all over an instructor who receives one.'

Olivia recalls, 'There was an atmosphere at Gaba that made you feel responsible for anything that goes wrong in a lesson. Students would even make unreasonable complaints in order to get free lessons from the company.' Most people who become ESL teachers do not expect the job to be stressful. Those seeking an adrenaline high are usually found on trading room floors or in stunt plane cockpits. But large eikaiwa schools force their instructors to be constantly on guard, adding a level of stress to an otherwise low-impact job that is not detailed on their flashy recruitment websites.

Michael remembers one negative evaluation that he received that still baffles him to this day. 'It was the first one I'd had, so it didn't get me debelted or anything, but I was really offended. My shoelace had come loose and I sat cross-legged in the booth and the client could see it. When I heard she'd complained about my shoelace being untied I thought it was funny at first. I told the counselors, you can't seriously call that a negative complaint. They just shrugged – everything goes in there. If the ISL had just told me to tie my laces to keep up the corporate image the problem could have been solved with a mutual laugh and a roll of the eyes. You can't make a formal complaint about nonsense like that in the real world. At least the company should have enough respect for us not to take it seriously.'

With such arbitrary means of judging performance, it is no wonder that a grievance procedure is on the union's to do list. Such a committee would not only review negative evaluations, but limit the range and scope of evaluations from anything a student pleases, to a more quantifiable and reasonable set of dos and don'ts. At the time of writing, the Gaba union has also had to deal with sexual harassment complaints made by staff against students because there is no formal process in place to deal with such cases, and managers have been reluctant to address them (see Chapter Eight). Raines says, 'Without an agreement they're not obliged to respond to teacher complaints. Using the clunky mechanism of collective bargaining to air a single sexual harassment claim is a waste of time and resources for both sides. These issues can be reviewed far more efficiently by a standing committee that's trained and prepared to deal with them.' As of 2014, the union has finally established two sexual harassment liaison officers at Gaba, in lieu of a company-implemented procedure.

Like all unions, the Gaba branch has a list of future goals, though prefers to introduce them slowly through collective bargaining rather than release them on the website. In the meantime, Gaba keeps the union busy. A November 2013 notice alerted members to the issue of absences during cold and flu season, noting that whether the absence is accepted as 'explained' or taken as 'unexplained' and therefore punishable, seems to vary widely from branch to branch. The Gaba union Facebook page has cataloged complaints of intimidation by managers and ISLs toward teachers who call sick, even those who have been hospitalized.

Another practice that has drawn union attention directly contributed to Olivia becoming a member. A former GU member had overheard a conversation she'd had with her ISL about First Meetings. 'The FM is a kind of promotional lesson for new clients. It takes a full forty minute slot to give the lesson, in which the instructor assesses the student's ability and gives a sample Gaba lesson. The following forty-minute slot is also blocked off because the paperwork and notes are very thorough,' she explains. But in a nice piece of eikaiwa accounting, the teaching block is paid whereas the paperwork block is not.

Not only did this mean an FM-qualified instructor (yes, there's 'training' for that too) can likely have two prime time slots blocked, but only one in which they earn any money. Olivia charges, 'the LS would take away lessons at the last minute from regular instructors and give them to FM-trained ones. This made it impossible for some people to have full schedules because nobody else would likely book them at last minute.' Robbing Peter to pay Paul may work well for the company but often leaves hardworking teachers with lost opportunities to generate income. Teachers are obliged to keep their hours available, but the company reserves the right to pull lessons anytime it suits them.

The courts sometimes side with unions and workers, but are

notoriously supportive of employers. Japan is a society where rocking the boat is frowned upon and paternalistic companies expect unquestioning loyalty. One might argue that in the case of Japanese 'corporate samurai' they get a lot more loyalty in return, but the discipline of corporate culture stands even in eikaiwa. Unions are permitted under law, but frowned upon by a largely anti-socialist business environment. In fact Gaba was taken to task by the Securities and Exchange Surveillance Commission in 2010 for refusing to admit it even *had* a union, fearing a shareholder backlash. Under compliance laws, failure to disclose the existence of a union is a crime, but Gaba was so confident that it even counter-sued the union for ¥58 million in damages and court costs.[16] Raines explains, 'At the time Gaba was up for sale, this is before [medical services giant] *Nichii Gakkan* bought it. Not only would a union possibly scare off potential buyers but there was even union action taking place at the time the company was selling. They were obliged to disclose both these details but kept it quiet, either to guarantee a sale or leverage the price.'

While the Osaka Labor Relations Commission has declared that Gaba workers did indeed fit the description of 'employees', something Gaba's financial statements insisted they are not; enforcement of labor laws is notoriously weak. No agency has stepped forward to pursue employee rights for teachers, leaving it up to the union to keep fighting. The law recognizes workers' right to *form* a union, but they're on their own afterward. The Labor Commission's findings carry no mandatory enforcement and it will take further negotiations and possibly court cases, for the union to secure proper employee benefits at Gaba, if they can do it at all. The ICC case of 2014, opened at the Yokohama district court, could serve as a litmus test. If more courts side with employers, yet more schools will take up the *itaku* excuse. If not, more and more teachers nationwide may challenge the 'subcontractor' system.

The repercussions for teachers are potentially disastrous. Like James' employer, smaller schools across the nation have begun to follow Gaba's lead in paring down contracts and removing the employee status of teachers. They do this to cut costs of course, but also to retain more flexibility in hiring and firing by undermining job security for the teachers because it is an unnecessary stumbling block to profits. This is why rules and regulations are kept vague. The company maintains a free hand to discipline instructors, dock their pay or dismiss them for whatever it chooses to call a reason. As if it were not bad enough that smaller schools across Japan are aping Gaba, the limited success of union action has also emboldened Gaba's large rivals. Nova, no stranger to industrial relations battles, has recently taken ominous steps in the same direction, cutting salaries and reducing staff to part time or 'contractor' status as well as offering 'incentives' on paper that rarely pan out on pay day.[17]

Salary cuts, short contracts, sub-contractor status and union-busting: in the la-la land of eikaiwa, the instructors aren't employees and the union doesn't even exist. For an industry that has already bottomed out in the eyes of many teachers and observers, Gaba has found new lows. Michael cynically muses just how far the company will go. 'It's like Monty Python's *Four Yorkshiremen* skit, where each claim of hardship is more ridiculous than the last. Except here it's real.'

The law is very clear on labor matters. Workers are permitted to unionize. Companies may not interfere with union activities. Staff who are obligated to be at work more than thirty hours a week must be enrolled in pension and health plans. Overtime must be paid. These legal requirements apply to all workers, including foreign nationals. 'The problem,' according to Raines, 'is that the government does not enforce its own laws and companies know this, therefore they feel don't have to follow them.'

Even at relatively benign companies, a union's job is never done, but it doesn't hurt that Big Eikaiwa keeps giving the unions reasons to pick a fight. Olivia complained of compulsory, unpaid parties that instructors were obliged to attend. 'They sell it as networking and improving client relations. It's supposed to be good for your career because if you make a good impression, then more clients will book your lessons. But in reality these parties are just a way to get you to come and entertain the clients for free.' It is because of constant cheap shots like these that the union is always busy. Olivia holds that, 'without unions there wouldn't be weekends, there wouldn't be workplace safety standards or overtime pay. A lot of the things we take for granted in modern companies happened because the unions fought for them.'

This is as true in Japan as it is in most industrialized democracies. In eikaiwa however, workers and unions are starting on the back foot and the process is practically in reverse. Michael feels, 'part of the business model of major schools has been to roll back decades of progress in Japan's labor relations from the very start, because they think foreign staff are not aware of their rights.' Awareness is increasing, but the Gaba union has a long road ahead.

The General Union reported on its Facebook page in February of 2015 that Gaba had tried to intimidate staff who handed out union literature during their breaks. Warnings were handed out even for distributing notices of union events like the Christmas party, and at least one teacher was threatened with dismissal. Since the staff were 'subcontractors' using 'unpaid' break time the union first argued the company had no right to demand they desist. It later found that under the law, union members must not face any company censure for handing out union literature even *during* working hours: It is illegal for companies to interfere with any union activity.[18]

In December 2013, Gaba announced a number of learning studios would be closed for an evening so that the Japanese managers could attend a Christmas party. In another small slap in the face, classes at Gaba can be canceled for company parties. If the party is held for managers, instructors are not invited, but they are forced to lose hours of work, because the branch is closed for an evening. Adrian Ringin points out, 'We don't feel that this is a good reason to cancel lessons, particularly when the company also penalizes instructors who cancel lessons [themselves] for more serious reasons.' When teachers want to cancel lessons for a visit to the doctor, to attend a funeral, a birth, or an appointment with immigration, eikaiwa takes a dim view.

7 Love, Marriage and Charisma Men

One muggy September night in Nagoya, about nine at the cusp of the millennium, Derek from Sheffield was waiting on the train platform to go home. He had just finished an outside course across town for his local eikaiwa. Nagoya is Japan's third largest city and the hub of its automotive industry and his clients were salesmen at a heavy vehicle manufacturer. He was returning home to the British girlfriend he'd come to Japan with, when a woman's voice called out, 'Hi!' from off to his left. 'At first I thought it was someone I knew, a student or someone from the office. I turned and she didn't look familiar. Maybe she was a former student or someone who'd attended a work party. Whoever she was, she was bloody fit.'

The woman was around thirty, fairly tall, leggy, dressed to kill. 'I wasn't sure what to do. Maybe she just wanted to practice her English. Whatever it was I was on board.' She turned out to have a career in cosmetics sales, could speak English well and was definitely interested in Derek. 'After that she would come up to me every Wednesday night for a few weeks till I suggested we go for coffee.'

His relationship was on the rocks anyway. 'We weren't sleeping together anymore. We weren't getting on. She was always angry about something. I started to wonder if she was bi-polar or something. Nothing I did was right, and any excuse to keep me up half the night giving me shit was a good one. I was very passive in the relationship; I'd always been one to just walk away from bullies. I think she sensed that as weakness and it encouraged her to keep needling.'

It didn't help that at twenty six, Derek was surrounded by beautiful Japanese women. 'It was hard to stay faithful when you saw these girls all around, short skirts or tight pants, platform heels, tarted up in makeup and dyed hair. They'd smile as you walk past and you'd catch each other doing a double take. One girl even started talking to me as I was eating breakfast in McDonald's one morning at about 7:30. My girlfriend was good looking enough back home I suppose, but this girl was just gorgeous. I think I spent my whole first year in Japan pretty frustrated. That summer when the subway girl came up to me, I was just about on the end of my rope.'

By the time they went for coffee, she already knew he was in a relationship. 'She didn't seem to mind. Even after I told her, she kept coming up to me same time, same place, so I figured she knew what she was after.' Their second date was at a *yamachan*, a local grilled chicken chain. 'After a few drinks we made out in an alleyway. She wanted to show me her office which was nearby. So we went in at about eleven at night and there was nobody there of course. We did it right there on the boardroom table. In addition to love hotels, we went back to her office a few times after hours and used the sofa in the guest room or her desk in her cubicle. I suppose it was pretty risky because someone might have popped in if they'd forgotten something but she seemed to enjoy the danger of it.'

He carried on with the subway girl for about a year. 'She claimed to be divorced and have a five-year-old son, but she never asked me if I wanted to meet him. She also never stayed the night. She was either not looking for a new man or, I suspected at the time, was not really divorced at all. But whatever, it was there, so I took it.' After his own inevitable breakup, Derek became quite the man about town. 'There was really an endless supply of women. You could talk to just about anyone in a bar, in a coffee shop. The more I tried it, the more confident I got. I'd never considered myself Julio Iglesias before, but for a while I really let my hair down. Sometimes I'd go home with girls from nightclubs, sometimes I'd pursue someone with a few dates first. Sometimes I'd have a girlfriend for a few months, sometimes I'd just keep casual partners. They rarely asked for any commitment. It was heaven for a young guy. The girls were not just more willing, they were so much better looking that what I'd been used to.'

Derek's experience and those of many like him can partly explain why it is mostly young men who come to Japan and stay. It might also explain why so many are willing to suffer the vagaries of a menial eikaiwa job when there is little future in it. Some come with a Japanese woman they have met overseas, others find one after they arrive. Others just sleep around. But the attraction of so many available girls, seemingly interested in foreign men is a big draw for any man. That eikaiwa often selects people for their looks makes it easy for a good-looking guy to meet people.

Some of those fall in love, get married and are determined to stick it out. Often they do advance their careers though usually by working their way out of the eikaiwa industry. Others stay single, determined to play the field long after they might have settled down in their home countries. Derek says, 'You kind of get addicted to it: the job is bearable because you're always looking forward to your next date, or boys' night out. Odds are better than not you'll meet some girls and get a number if you just go out for drinks after work, almost any night of the week.' Or as

Bruce puts it, 'you have zero responsibility. You're surrounded by young, single people and all everyone wants to do is party. It's like being in college again, and during the day all you have to do is turn up to class, even though you're the one standing in front of the whiteboard.'

Around the time of Derek's first Japanese fling, there was a cartoon by Canadian Larry Rodney and his artist friend Glen Schroeder called *Charisma Man*. Originally a comic strip that ran from 1998 in *The Alien**, a Nagoya-based magazine, it follows the exploits of a meek and nerdy white guy, who worked at a burger joint back home, as he becomes a 'somebody' in Japan. For the first time in his life women are drawn to him, just because he's western and they're Japanese. He gets attention from far more attractive girls than any who would bother with him in his own country and naturally it goes to his head. It was a popular cartoon among English teachers in Japan at the time.[1]

The stereotype of the 'loser' foreigner who gets to play Don Juan in Japan, just because his ethnicity gives him a pass is not entirely realistic, but not all fantasy either. Plenty of young foreign men have become veritable playboys here, but given that women all look for fairly similar traits in a partner, even a casual one, it's probably a stretch to say they could only pull it off in Japan. According to Jason who has lived in several international cities, 'you might see the odd 'dweeb' foreign guy with a gorgeous local woman, but the "players" are the kind of guys who would sleep around anywhere they lived. There are meat markets in just about every country and city, and anyone can pick up a one night stand. It's no easier in Japan than anywhere else, if you know the right bar, talk to the right women.'

There are certainly some men who didn't do so well back in the west, but have managed to find a suitable (and even attractive) partner in Japan, but they can hardly be faulted for bettering their romantic circumstances, or following the biological imperative to find a mate. According to Bruce, 'people who say that pretty much assume from the start that this guy shouldn't have a girlfriend, that he doesn't deserve to get attention from women. So who gets to be the judge of that?'

Controversial gaijin columnist and blogger Debito Arudou wonders why critics should, 'Force people back into the inferior positions they managed to escape from?'[2] Even after returning to their home countries it can be hard for so-called Charisma Men to shake the reputation of the loser white guy, deserved or not. Published academic and former ESL teacher Roslyn Appleby notes with apparent schadenfreude, 'their difficulties in pursuing professional success in ELT were not easily resolved by moving to a new educational sector or by moving to other countries.'[3] Is it true though, that men come only to find a mate?

Derek is dismissive of the idea. 'I met a lot of guys who came thinking it would be easy to get into everyone's pants, or at least eas*ier*. But I have never met anyone who came just because he wanted a Japanese girlfriend or to find a wife. People who are social misfits in their home country don't just up and try their luck someplace else, then magically transform from zeroes to heroes. The socially awkward are still the same when they get here, and tend to wrap themselves in their *manga* or whatever hobby it is they have. They do find a partner, but they probably consider themselves lucky just to have met Miss Right at last. I don't think they were expecting it.'

One colleague suggested it was biological. Japan's low birth rate could be due to a dwindling gene pool. After centuries of near total homogeneity, the island nation of 127 million just doesn't have enough variety. A current trend among young Japanese men is the 'herbivore', a passive, somewhat effeminate guy who waits for 'aggressive' women to approach him: this can lead to a lot of waiting since many women will do the same. Any foreign person must look somewhat attractive, on a purely hormonal level, just by dint of being different. It is not only petty to suggest that, like an American high-school drama, a so-called 'geek' who can't find love in his home country doesn't deserve to try his luck elsewhere, it may also be counter-evolutionary. Derek observes, 'the teachers I've met who really slept around were good looking, in shape, had the gift of the gab and would chase women wherever they were, not only in Japan. Usually the meek guy with the pretty girlfriend, hassled for punching above his weight, is just a really nice guy.'

Appleby's paper, published in *TESOL Quarterly* cited cases of the 'Charisma Men' - white male teachers sleeping around among the student body. This does happen, but the vast majority of inter-cultural relationships I've come across are formed outside of work. Appleby speaks smugly of the 'compromised professionalism' of the white Western male, who has escaped an allegedly feminized TESOL industry in his home country only to suffer the, 'emasculating shame eventually attached to classroom teaching in the commercial eikaiwa industry'.[4] Brutal as that may sound, it only echoes Andre's lament that he was embarrassed to tell women what he did for a living.[*]

Yet the industry itself contributes to the promiscuity of male English teachers in Japan and its advertising certainly appears to encourage dalliances. ECC ran a poster on subways and at train stations with an

---

[*] See Chapter 4

attractive young Japanese woman gazing into the eyes of a youthful foreign teacher, a clear blue sky in the backdrop and the caption, *what's next?* Such imagery suggests the target market - young working women - can go on a romantic getaway with the handsome teacher, or perhaps use their new found English skills to meet a tall, blond stranger on their next trip abroad. A poster for Gaba shows another Japanese woman standing side by side with her foreign teacher, handcuffed to him at the wrist: while overworked Gaba teachers may find the handcuff an apt metaphor for their jobs, it also suggests an altogether different kind of fantasy.[5]

James has noticed, 'you always hear from white girls in Asia, anywhere really, and I shouldn't say all of them but enough, how bad we are for dating Asian women. Even guys who aren't sleeping around are assumed to have taken some kind of shortcut they don't deserve by getting a Japanese girlfriend. At first you think they want you to feel guilty just for dating. But if you listen to the vocabulary they use, the arguments, it's not the men they're targeting: *Oh, Japanese women are submissive; they're easy; he can't get a real woman.* It's the girls they really don't like. To Jason as well, 'it's just jealousy. I once had a Scandinavian girlfriend tell me Asian women are dirty. She was tall, attractive, had nothing to be envious of, but that jealousy was there. In the old days it used to be guys who preferred blondes and guys who like brunettes. White women understood those rules and could live with it. They could dye their hair if they wanted to. But you can't fake Asian and that's just too much competition for some of them.'

Sarah, who worked at ECC, says she used to look askance at western guys with Japanese girlfriends because, 'everybody had one. I had female colleagues who'd come over with their partner and he'd leave them for a

Japanese girl. At the start I thought all the girls were just waiting to steal some foreign guy, and anyone could take advantage of that. But I've dated Japanese men and I can't judge. Yes there are guys who think they're studs but most mixed couples I know are just nice boys with nice girls. Some women like tall guys, some like bald guys, some like muscles, others don't. I know girls who only date Latin men, so what if a guy likes Asians? We all have looks we're attracted to. But I still think there are some guys that come over here and think they can get away with a lot more.'

Sarah may have a point. A brief media furor ensued when self-styled 'pick-up artist' Julien Blanc announced a 2014 tour of Japan. Blanc, a paid speaker who peddles his dating techniques to lonely men for exorbitant fees seems to channel the misogynistic life coach played by Tom Cruise in the film *Magnolia*. In YouTube videos, Blanc claims Japanese women are so easy anyone can get into bed with them just by hollering the names of cartoon characters from street corners. He is seen grabbing women by the neck and pushing their faces toward his crotch in the viral clips. After an uproar in Australia, authorities revoked his visa, forcing a cancellation of his speaking tour there. A similar social media campaign was held to have him banned from Japan.[6] But there has to be a market for his pitch to begin with or he wouldn't have bothered to come. It can be hard to remain objective in the face of such aggressive promiscuity. Appleby writes that the question of whether male teachers are simply predators, and whether the female students are victims or willing participants remains 'unsettled'.[7] Yet Japanese women do often come to class seeking romance or a fling and the men who actively harass women are rooted out. What remains is the vast majority of relationships that are mutual and consensual and not in any way the exploitative predation encouraged by the likes of Julien Blanc.

Much has been said over the years about the western man's preference for Asian women, a facet of what Sheridan Prasso termed in her book of the same title, *The Asian Mystique*. Many a western woman teaching English in Japan has decried the 'yellow fever' of her male colleagues when grousing around the water cooler. Conversely, little has been written about the seemingly endless appetite of Japanese women for western men. Mixed couples are a common enough sight in and out of Asia, but perhaps nowhere else in the far east are relationships between Asian women and western men so *mutual*.

We've all heard the typical mail-order bride stories: creepy older, divorced white men marrying young Thai or Filipino women, lifting them out of poverty and into a 'better' life, for the privilege of sleeping with an exotic younger woman. This is not the case in Japan, Korea or Taiwan. Firstly the women are often better off financially than the western men they date, especially if those men are struggling English teachers. While age gaps do sometimes appear, most couples are of a similar age and have similar interests. They meet at barbecues and at parties and other social or sporting events rather than some shady website. They're introduced by friends, hook up at after-work dos or kick off with one night stands after a few too many drinks: the same way a lot of relationships start, like it or not.

Young Japanese women have more free time than their male counterparts and often more disposable income. Once dubbed 'parasite singles' for mooching off their parents until well into their thirties, they live at home, pay little or no rent and spend their salaries on shopping, travel and language lessons. The latter two make women far more likely to come into contact with foreigners than Japanese men, whose university majors rarely include language studies and who are shunted into corporate careers with long hours and few holidays. Overseas study or working holidays are much more common among women. This gives Japanese women a wider international perspective on the world than many men, whose lives and careers must be focused on surviving the rat race at home. Women have more chances to form relationships with foreigners at home or abroad.

An acquaintance in Hong Kong used to snicker at the old expats who'd marry their Filipino housemaids. His line was that they were both marrying up: she for the income and he for the sex. In one sense at least the Japanese woman who prefers foreigners may find herself marrying *down*, especially if her husband plans to stay in Japan for the long term and support a family on an English teacher's meager salary. Marrying a Japanese salaryman working for a big corporation might net a girl a husband with no free time, but at least the couple's economic future is solid. So why do so many Japanese women give that up and fall for foreigners?

Yuki is a former student and we've kept in touch. She is a shade over forty, still single and has been a lifelong traveler, maintaining a keen interest in English and Spanish. She talks freely of the attractions of a foreign boyfriend. 'Marrying a Japanese man carries all sorts of responsibilities. You have to take care of his elderly parents and show deference to your mother in law. You have to become a model housewife and learn to cook the things *he* likes. You have to get up early to make his *bento* (lunchbox) and see him off to work. Basically your life suddenly revolves around him and his family.'

While that may be true of many older couples, younger Japanese men these days are seeking a better work life balance and taking a lot of the pressure off their wives when it comes to child rearing and running a household. They come home earlier, help with chores and have even invaded the kitchen and started cooking, traditionally sole preserve of the woman of the house. Nevertheless committing to a traditional, nuclear family lifestyle when still longing for the open road and far-off climes, is a big turnoff for women like Yuki.

Often women get the best of both worlds, having numerous trysts with foreigners in their younger days before settling down to a serious, financially stable life with a Japanese husband when they reach their thirties. It's not just for the money. Derek thinks, 'even women who enjoy freedom and travel start to feel immense pressure from their mothers and grandmothers as they near a certain age. A Japanese woman in her sixties can feel embarrassed and inadequate if her grown daughter is not married with children, as though she has failed as a parent somehow. One student I taught was very anxious about her daughter who was nearing thirty and single.' In decades past the pressure was even more acute: a woman who hadn't landed a fiancé by age 25 was derided as a 'Christmas Cake' – nobody will buy one after the 25th.

Japanese mothers may have high hopes for their daughter's future spouse but these are inevitably pared down as she crosses the age threshold, leaving parents more willing to settle for an international marriage. Some parents of course are okay with the idea from the start. The daughters themselves are often willing to give up fantasies of true love as their biological clock ticks away and the nagging from relatives gets louder. Many women, finding contentment in filial obligations, settle for a good Japanese match and get down to the business of being a model wife and mother, partly to smooth out family relations. Others ignore the snide remarks about being 'Christmas cakes' or 'parasites' and continue to enjoy their single life and their foreign paramours.

For others still, a foreign boyfriend is a status symbol. Women in their mid twenties to early thirties are considered prime targets for eikaiwa schools precisely because they have an interest in meeting foreign men, hence the suggestive advertising to feed that fantasy. But even those with no prior interest in foreigners can get a boost from walking down the street arm-in-arm with a *gaijin*. Troy, who lived in Tokyo in the early nineties recalls, 'One girl I was dating didn't speak any English, but she liked the idea that strangers would look at us together and think she was well-traveled and probably spoke English fluently. It was an ego thing for her.'

Troy was lucky enough to frequent *Juliana's* near the end of its heyday, the famous dance club in Roppongi that was an epicenter of bubble Japan's nightlife. Here, stockbrokers and 'Office Ladies' (female office clerks and receptionists) mingled on the dance floor. 'The girls wore those little tube dresses while dancing on platforms. You could just talk to girls at the bar or go up and dance in with them on the floor. A lot of chicks didn't mind if you were just a teacher, it was cool to be a foreigner back then. We also had a few bars we'd hang out at in Roppongi or Shinjuku or nearby stations. Girls would just cruise through in pairs or threes or fours, looking to meet foreigners. Sometimes you could walk out with them in twenty minutes. If a girl came in and sat down alone with a cocktail, stayed past the late trains, you knew she wasn't planning on going home alone.'

Though James never matched Troy's claims of twenty-minute

hookups he came close. 'I was in *Booty*, a foreigner-friendly night spot in Sapporo. I arrived after midnight and a friend of mine was talking to some girls as I arrived and just fobbed one off on me, saying it would be a piece of cake. We sat down and talked for about a half hour, I don't even remember if I bought her a drink. Without any making out or touching at all she asked if she could come home with me. I swear I'd been in the place for forty minutes at most and we left.'

Derek recalled the 'ridiculous ease' of hookups at the turn of the millennium and well into the mid noughties. 'One girl I met at a bar was a police cadet, about to be shipped off to the academy. They were celebrating graduating university and her friend was so drunk she was vomiting in the toilet so she had to take care of her. But we met the following Tuesday and had some food and went to Karaoke. After making out in the booth a bit, she asked point blank and without any reservations, if she could stay at my place that night. If her friend hadn't been sick it would have happened the night we met.'

Hookups weren't limited to nightlife. While big schools like Nova maintained famously strict provisions against dating students – at least on paper – not every school had the foresight to write it into teachers' contracts. According to James, 'A lot of women come to class just to meet foreign guys. It's hard to turn it down. I've had several female students suggest socializing outside of class. Some just want to be friends, others want more. Some want to introduce you to a single friend because they think she's curious about foreigners.'

At American Club in the old days, Grant was seeing one student who suggested doing it in the partition, during office hours, because she was an exhibitionist and wanted other students in nearby booths to hear her getting off. Grant demurred. 'Those were the days, but I'm too old now.

These days, working at international schools and colleges, getting involved with students would finish me.'

Such antics recall another school in Sapporo that had bordered on legendary. - *Trendy House*. In Sapporo in the late nineties, James had people telling him not to work there and why. 'Basically it was known that the students were mostly young women there to meet foreign guys. If you were a teacher there you were expected to socialize with students after class. It was a given that male teachers would be sleeping with the students.' James was married at the time and his wife told him there was no way he'd be working there. 'It would have been a dangerous place for a married man with a wandering eye.'

The single man with a wandering eye can get into risky relationships as well. Patrick recalls a teacher he worked with in Tokyo in the nineties who ended up dating a high school student. 'She had come in for what we called promotional lessons, a short sample lesson and level check to see if she would join a class. This girl was in her uniform wearing those fluffy leg-warmer socks they used to have. Well this guy, who was almost thirty, bumped into her in the lift after he was done with her free lesson. He suggested they go for a coffee and they dated for over a year after that.' Another acquaintance, who once worked on the JET program as an assistant teacher in Tochigi prefecture had a similar story. His coworker was carrying on with one of the seniors at the high school where he was assigned. 'Nobody knew it was happening at the time, but when he got her pregnant everyone found out.' Neither JET nor the local education board wanted a fuss. The teacher was quietly dismissed and sent home, and the girl's family made sure she didn't keep the baby.

Families often have a say in relationships even with their adult children. Though not as reputedly strict as Korean or Chinese families, there are some Japanese parents that jealously guard their ethnicity. Others simply know all too well the reputation of foreign men in Japan and don't want their daughters to waste any time with a womanizer who'll dump her for the next adventure. The idea of arranged marriage is not as entrenched in Japan as in India or the Arab world, but there is still a lingering foothold from the feudal days.

It can be used to sabotage relationships with foreigners or with anyone if the parents feel a beau or belle is not up to their standards. Jason dated a Japanese cabin attendant when he worked in the gulf. 'About a year in, her parents suggested she catch up with this Japanese engineer they knew who was working in Qatar. I met him a couple of times and he was okay. It was supposed to be just because he was someone they knew in the town where their daughter was living, a friend away from home, but I started to suspect perhaps the parents were hoping for more. She wasn't interested in him at all that way but occasionally they'd meet for lunch.' Jason's relationship ended after they returned to Japan, and he never found out if his ex had moved on to the Japanese businessman.

Yet every day across the country, even globally, Japanese singles – and their parents – use business and social contacts for the express purpose of landing a suitable spouse. There are various agencies and services that advertise on the internet and arrange matchmaking parties called *gokon*. A 'doctor *gokon*' for example, seeks to match physicians with gold diggers; a 'stewardess *gokon*' caters for successful men seeking a trophy wife. More commonly, informal *gokon* parties arranged by small groups of students or colleagues are a typical flirtatious get-together like a double or triple date. But sometimes a more focused guiding hand is needed in finding the perfect spouse.

I sat down with Nobuhisa Suzuki, a seventy-year-old who has enjoyed studying English for decades. A retired banker, Mr. Suzuki likes gardening, fishing and walking his dog. He is a typical, model retiree. And while not especially conservative or old-fashioned, he believes there is still a place for *Omiai* – formal introductions – for young people who have trouble finding a future spouse on their own. He believes in it so well that one of Mr. Suzuki's hobbies is acting as a *nakōdo* - a traditional matchmaker.

'Friends or relatives ask me if they have a daughter or son who needs to settle down. I've been responsible now for three happy marriages'. The role of *nakōdo* was once a revered position among the Samurai nobility, whose job was to cement the relationship between aristocratic families through marriage. Nowadays it is a less formal role, often filled by men of good standing in the community, such as respected businessmen, not least because they have cultivated a large body of contacts over the years and their judgment is trusted.

Mr. Suzuki explains the process: 'Say someone has a daughter who is over thirty. Maybe she had a couple of bad relationships; maybe she's shy and never had a boyfriend. Perhaps she's not very attractive. But she really wants to get married and her mother won't rest until she's settled. Recently a couple came to me, people I've known for years. They're getting older and don't want to die while their son is still single. So the son is a hard worker at a good company. He's almost forty and hasn't had much luck with women. Both sides want to get married, but neither knows how. That's where the *nakōdo* comes in.'

How does he match the couples? 'First, both parties submit a sort of résumé. They both must come from suitable families, the man should have a stable job; the woman needs a clean history, not working in a hostess bar or *kabakura* ('cabaret club', a euphemism for strip bar or worse). Then we have an initial meeting. I arrange lunch at a nice hotel. The man must wear a suit and the woman has to come in a Kimono. This is the traditional way. There's a sort of supervised introduction and I conduct the discussion. After that it is better if the couple go on a few dates without supervision. If all goes well we meet again for a review. There must be a marriage proposal in two or three months.'

Two or three months sounds like an awfully short courtship. I ask what the hurry is. 'The most important thing is that they're compatible. If they haven't hit it off in three months they probably never will. If they do get along, then the sooner the better.'

And what about true love? 'It's not for everyone. Most people find their own partners. But for those that can't, love isn't as important initially. They feel they have a duty to their families. First comes marriage, then love comes after, if they're compatible in the first place. I wouldn't recommend a couple unless I was absolutely sure they would be happy together.'

Time is often a factor. The couples Mr. Suzuki introduces may already feel they're running out of options; their parents perhaps even more so, when considering their generation married younger and they themselves are in their twilight years. Many people feel a responsibility to be married and settled before their parents die. Perhaps a woman wants to have children and can't wait another five years or risk a failed courtship. Perhaps the man knows he's losing his hair or gaining weight or otherwise slowly sliding out of the market as he approaches early middle age. Perhaps both parties have just been disappointed in love before and don't want to take any chances. Arranged marriage conjures up all sorts of images of forced unions in the west but in Japan is simply another option in the mating game – often a last resort.

Not only Japan. Jason once knew a Korean woman who played the field in her twenties. She'd lived overseas, worked in the Gulf, traveled a lot and, 'more than had her fun'. Yet despite being pretty and sociable and having no shortage of options, as she neared thirty she began to draw on her family and friends back home to find a future husband. He had to be Korean; he had to go to the same church. These were requirements that came ahead of love and passion: marriage was more serious business. Jason feels that, 'people gain fulfillment from fulfilling their perceived roles in society. A large part of that in Asian countries is living up to the parents' expectations. When marrying someone your family approves of and living a respectable life as a housewife is the "thing to do", then you take advantage of every resource available to get it done. A waste though, she was hot.'

James has experienced something similar. His own girlfriend had a grandmother in a northern rural town who frequently pestered her to settle down. 'She doesn't know about the foreign boyfriend or her granddaughter's life in the city. She keeps telling her she can introduce her to a nice local dentist or something of the sort. Perhaps even a fisherman or a farmer. When the old girl was young that's all a woman could aspire to: marriage and motherhood. She must be looking at her granddaughter, good-looking, edging towards thirty and thinking the poor girl is desperate to do the same. She hasn't noticed up there that times have changed.'

But for young western men matchmaking seems hardly necessary. James' adventures started during his first summer in Sapporo in the late nineties. 'It was incredible. Go to a flash bar in Sydney or Melbourne and you'd have to arrive in a Porsche to get that kind of attention. But in those days in Japan, just *being* a foreigner meant you had something they wanted.' The *gaijin* hangout in those days was *Bar Isn't It*, a two-story club built into a renovated grain warehouse from the early twentieth century, in the downtown entertainment district of Susukino. 'I had a mentor of sorts, an American colleague who'd been in town a few years. He'd brag so much about how easy it was to 'score' it was a running joke among the other teachers. I didn't go home with anyone that first night at *Isn't It,* but it wasn't for a lack of chances. I was just so overwhelmed at having so many women come up to me I didn't stay and talk to any one girl long enough.'

European guys weren't the only ones getting attention. The hip hop craze of the late nineties was riding high and Japan had a whole cadre of party girls devoted to African-American fanship, with deep tans and Brazilian curves that appealed less to Japanese men. 'My buddy knew this black guy, buff, shaved head. Looked like a pro football player. The girls were literally lining up to meet him. He'd be chatting to one, a former girlfriend or lover or a new hopeful or whatever, and another would be waiting right there in plain view for her shot at the title. It was the most surreal place.'

The 'mentor' introduced James to other aspects of the Sapporo scene that summer. 'One weekend, we hit the beach a few miles out of town. It was a shitty place, dark sand, cold water, but it had all these cabana bars and shacks along it where they threw beach parties all summer. Chicks in bikinis everywhere, it was heaven. There was this hook-up system where young people drove to the beach car park after dark on Saturday nights; guys in one car, girls in another, all in groups of two to four. The girls would park up and guys would park up next to them and chat them up, then move on and try their luck with another group. If they hit it off they'd go somewhere else or hang out at the beach parties. Some would just go straight to hotels. My buddy and I ended up pulling a couple of girls from one of the beach bars and we went out onto the dunes to make out, it was a laugh. I couldn't speak much Japanese and she didn't speak a word of English, so she had to mime a pair of scissors just to tell me she was a hairdresser. Nothing ever came of it, but it was a story to tell, and we had a lot of those.'

It wasn't as easy the second time around in Japan, a decade later. There was no more *Bar Isn't it*, and the more recent pickup joints didn't have the same vibe, or ease. The heady spirit of the nineties was gone. Or maybe he had changed. 'I was older and knew my game by then too. The girls were older too, a lot in their early to mid thirties, so I guess it evened out.' James has moved in with his girlfriend now and takes it slow. 'I'm too old for it now. I've outgrown it. Sometimes I see a pretty girl and I miss it, but in other ways, I'm glad it's over too. It was actually a lot of hard work.'

Troy's relationships were a mixed bag. Sometimes families opposed. 'One girl was a college student, just coming into her final year. Her dad threatened to stop paying her tuition if she didn't dump me.' It might have been a convenient excuse to get rid of him, or it could have been a genuine case of xenophobia. But not all women or their families were as discriminating. 'Another girl was in her early thirties. She started out as a student, but then I dated her for a few months before I found out she was cheating on her husband. He turned out to be a really nice guy.' After the relationship ended, Troy remained a friend of the family, with the husband none the wiser.

Warren, from New Zealand fell in love with a Japanese colleague in Wellington, and with their baby, the family settled in the picturesque central city of Kanazawa – often dubbed 'little Kyoto'. But their relationship was not all roses. After several years of marriage he found, 'She was bossy and selfish, very demanding and moody. There were many times I thought of leaving her but then I look at my kid and I know why I'm staying.' But if international marriages can be just as rocky as homogeneous ones, responses are surprisingly similar. Warren has had several affairs and credits those too with holding his marriage together. 'It pretty much stops me from strangling anyone.' The first time was an after work party with a young woman who was friend of a student. They got drunk and ended up at an hourly hotel. Later he started an affair with a private student. It lasted a few months until he called it off and they still maintain a healthy client-teacher relationship after the fact, without any romance for old time's sake.

But it was professional courtesy rather than guilt that ended the affair. 'A few times,' Warren tells me, 'I was talking to the mother of one of the kids I taught in the hallway after class. She had pretty good English and I thought I could pick up an extra private student, so we exchanged numbers and went for coffee a couple of times. She was about the same age, early thirties, good-looking and I sensed an interest, but I thought I could exploit that to make some extra cash as a tutor.' The woman lived fairly close to Warren's neighborhood and one evening out on his jogging route she was waiting in her car. She asked him to get in and they talked a while. She told him her husband, a dentist, was having an affair with one of the hygienists at his practice and everyone knew about it. 'After breaking down in tears and getting a sympathy hug, pretty soon we were making out and it just kicked off from there. We were seeing each other for about a year after that.' Warren has since returned to Wellington, his marriage surprisingly intact.

Adultery is perhaps one of Japan's best-kept open secrets. Fox News reported in 2014 that Ashley Madison, the online dating site for married people to hook up anonymously, blew all expectations out of the water with the amount of registered users in Japan after launch: 'The nation that prides itself on conformity and proper appearances reached a million users in eight and a half months, the fastest pace among any of the 37 countries where the adultery site operates.'[8] It also noted that the site provided a greater outlet for married *women* than ever before. They made up more than half the registered users. In even more patriarchal South Korea, the site was initially banned, fearing the damage it would cause to families.[9]

Jason is another teacher who has returned to his home country. I first met him working in the airline business in Dubai and though we had both taught in Japan before that, we'd been in different cities at different times. Now working as a wine salesman and *sommelier*, he once taught at Nova in Sapporo and later at eikaiwa schools in Sendai, Miyagi prefecture and Saitama near Tokyo. I caught up with him in Melbourne and we took a day trip to the Yarra Valley. Sipping Cabernet in the shade of a winery patio on a blistering day, the conversation inevitably landed on an old favorite topic, women. Jason does not fit the profile of a 'charisma man', the geek who struck gold in Japan. He is tall, handsome, in good shape; though last I saw him he was slightly heavier in his late thirties than his 'heyday'. He had an easy smile, a quick wit and was well-read and talkative. He spoke Japanese reasonably well but confessed to being a poor reader. Despite looking like a guy who wouldn't have trouble meeting women anywhere in the world, he says he was shy and unpopular with girls in his school days. Moreover he had never seen himself as a playboy, claiming simply to have fallen into the role. In a ten year span since his late twenties, Jason claims to have bedded dozens of women.

He first came to Japan with a local woman and had only one affair while together. After separating due to personal differences, he wanted to play the field but found himself in a dry spell. 'My single friends had all told me what a blast it would be, but for three or four months after moving out on my own, I just couldn't close the deal. I dated women but I wasn't even getting to first base with them. I had been led to believe it was so easy and looked forward to sleeping around, but I realized I'd have to put the work in.'

So he watched and learned. Within a year he had, 'gone through perhaps eight or ten girls'. Two-timing was par for the course, though none ever ascended to being official girlfriends. He says things took off after moving to Asia and the Middle East. He went through at least as many women again in his first summer in Taiwan, where he worked several years. 'Some were just horny, a couple I suspect were married though I never asked. They never stayed all night. One girl I dated worked at the local fruit vendor. I used to stop in there on my way home and chat her up.'

The first few months of his next job in the gulf netted him a slew of flight attendants. He traveled to Asia, Australia and Europe on a fairly regular basis. 'I met a Japanese girl at the Zoo in Sydney and she stayed the night. There was a friend of a friend in London who sometimes visited Dubai. We'd hook up when I had layovers there, too.' In Bangkok, Jakarta, Singapore, he could meet girls in bars or often line them up on popular pre-Facebook dating sites like *Myspace* and *Friendster*. The internet was convenient because, 'once you'd arranged to meet, sex was almost guaranteed. Some of them already had boyfriends and wanted a fling with someone who wouldn't stick around and get in the way.'

He'd had relationships too. A couple of two or three-year girlfriends but he couldn't stay faithful for long. When he returned to Japan some years later he simply repeated the old pattern: 'Bars, *Izakayas*, barbecues, the *hanami** parties in the park - anywhere I could meet women I'd fish for phone numbers.' Plenty of male teachers in Japan have been just as promiscuous. Accepting an overlap in their target market, there's no reason to believe they couldn't have had as many lovers if they'd been just as dedicated to their trade. 'Of course,' Jason warns, 'A lot of the time you end up sleeping with the same easy girls as the last foreigner to blow through. The Japanese are far less hung up about sex than you'd expect, so there are always girls with a reputation in your local *gaijin* bar.'

Jason has eased up with age as well. 'Two and three-timing can take it out of you, though dry spells are less frequent when you know your game. You get to know your type, the ones you like and the ones that will likely go for you; the ones who will need a date or two and the type

---

* The springtime cherry blossom viewing, often with picnics and barbecues

that are looking for it tonight, you narrow the odds and reduce the chances of striking out. There is no such thing as the guy who can get any girl he wants. It just looks that way because he picks his targets well, and you forget about the times he doesn't.' Jason's story would be hard to swallow if I hadn't met so many others like him. There will always be a number of women curious to enough to date foreigners and enough 'fast' ones to jump into bed with them the first night. Jason thinks, 'it's the same in any country, even back home. Girls go for the foreign guy, the Italian, the Frenchman, the guy with an accent or a tan. Strange as it seems, in Asia, that's us. We're the exotic foreigner. Though it's hard to ever see yourself that way, in a country like Japan we are very, very different.'

The perceived lack of typically 'western' sexual hang ups is often cited. According to Jason, 'they don't suffer from Christian guilt trips. It's pretty much expected that married men will visit *soap-lands** after a few years of marriage when they've stopped sleeping with their wives. A woman with a history is not necessarily a slut'. In Japan, who you slept with in your past life doesn't seem to matter. Even virginity is not such a prize to society: high school girls used to willingly sell theirs for the price of a Gucci bag in the 1990s.[10] And as Jason points out, 'there are no players without loose women. You go to the places where the girls have the same thing on their minds. The ones who want true love won't waste their time on guys like me or on going to those bars.'

On the subject of sex with his students, Jason shuffles uncomfortably. 'Once with a former student. I bumped into her a while after she'd stopped taking lessons and got her number and we dated a few months.' Someone who was *still* a customer? 'Yeah, one of those too. It

---

* The Japanese euphemism for brothels: the service usually includes a bath.

just sort of happened.' At drinks with an acquaintance and his girl one Thursday night, her friend turned up at the bar and happened to be one of Jason's students – a glamorous thirtysomething he had taught just that afternoon. A few drinks and some playful body contact and they were making out in the upstairs bar. They finished the night at a 'love hotel' - gaudy shag palaces where couples can rent a room for a few hours or a night. When asked about the danger of such trysts, Jason shrugged it off. He knew the risks but at the time he was set to leave in a few months and that day couldn't come soon enough. 'There was a sense that what happens in Japan doesn't matter when you leave. It's not part of your real life. Echoing a lot of teachers, Jason adds, 'I thought, when I go back I'll clean up my act'.

Jason gave lie to the *Charisma Man* stereotype. Here was a global player who would sleep around in any country and didn't need to be in Japan to do it. He is still a committed bachelor. 'I don't want kids, and most women do. That pretty much rules me out. The older you get the more used to your own company you become.' Asked how he could have devoted such time and resources to chasing exotic women, Jason didn't have to think. He had already done the soul searching. 'We certainly punched above our weight there. One reason men work hard and try to succeed is to make them more attractive and land a suitable mate. Up to a point, Japan is a shortcut to that goal: you can get straight to the women and skip the success. I think it's why so many guys stay past their prime, when they know they should be doing something else.'

It should come as no surprise in a country with fewer sexual hang-ups, that Japanese men can be equally caddish. Former Geos teacher Jennifer moved from Osaka to Nagano, home of the 1998 Winter Olympics, partly because her Japanese boyfriend was into snowboarding. 'I wanted to experience a different part of Japan and he insisted on snow, so we chose there.' Over the winter she lived in town while he worked as an instructor at a nearby mountain resort.

'One day a Japanese girl found me on Facebook. She was planning a surprise party for her fiancé and was contacting his friends. Well, it turns out her 'fiancé' was my boyfriend and she had just found me on his friends list without suspecting anything. She was looking for people to join the party.' There was more than that to it. The other woman was already pregnant, hence the engagement. 'He tried to explain his way out of it, but I was done with him after that.'

Yet while liaisons between Japanese women and foreign men are commonplace, relationships with a blonde, blue eyed foreign girl often seem like an impossible dream for Japanese men. Not only are few available – far more western men than women work in Japan – generally Japanese men feel that foreign women find them unattractive. They could be forgiven for being bitter about the comparative success foreign men have had with the local girls, and wonder why they can't do the same. Perhaps more darkly, they also tend to objectify foreign women based on historical and media stereotypes - ideals that have little to do with realistic expectations. While plenty of western women have entered into happy and stable relationships with Japanese men, for the single foreign woman in Japan there is also a singular threat.

8 Stalkers, Gropers and Serial Masturbators

On March 26, 2007 a cluster of plainclothes police officers congregated around a drab apartment building in Tokyo. Earlier in the Day Nova had reported one of its teachers, a young British woman named Lindsay-Ann Hawker, had been absent from work for several days and her roommates had not seen her. The roommates knew she had been scheduled to meet a private student at a cafe on the 24th, a young man by the name of Tatsuya Ichihashi. What the police knew that neither Nova nor Hawker's friends knew was that Ichihashi had been arrested before for stalking and assaulting a woman. That case had been settled out of court, but it made him a person of interest.

Ichihashi was not a large man, but was wiry and fit – a keen martial artist and cyclist. He also had a yen for violent *manga* comics graphically depicting underage sex, rape and bestiality.[1] The police were not allowed to enter without probable cause, and at this stage they were only seeking an interview. They loitered several hours outside. Ichihashi, not suspecting anything untoward, left his apartment in the evening, carrying a gym bag and curiously, not wearing any shoes. The first group of officers on the fourth floor tried to apprehend him but he was athletic, nimble and slipped their grasp. Without radios on hand they were too slow to notify the officers downstairs, and Ichihashi managed to evade them too. He would go on the lam for two and a half years.

With more than enough reason now to search the place, the police entered the flat. Inside the apartment, there were signs of a violent struggle and Hawker's belongings and items of clothing were strewn about. On the balcony they found a bathtub filled with sand and compost. Underneath a thin layer was the 22-year-old Briton. She had been beaten badly, sexually assaulted and strangled to death. The bathtub was an attempt to decompose the body. One hand was slightly hanging out. The neighbors appeared not to have noticed.

Japan is an exceedingly safe country, but violent crime has increased in recent years. Hawker had taken all reasonable precautions, short of not following Ichihashi into his flat: she had notified friends of who she would be seeing and the young man was known to them. They had his phone number and email address. It was not a well-planned murder on his part. Indeed after he was finally apprehended in Osaka in November 2009, boarding a ferry to Okinawa, Ichihashi insisted he had not planned to kill her at all. He admitted he *had* intended to rape her, but she had been suffocated in the struggle. He cannot have expected to get away with rape either: Hawker's friends knew who she had planned to meet that day, and Ichihashi himself can't have forgotten his earlier brush with the law. Even in patriarchal Japan, had the victim survived, it would be hard to argue she had consented to sex with his history and her bodily injuries, and Japanese courts give short shrift for crimes against the person. Hawker had been naively trusting; Ichihashi had been brutally careless.

Though Hawker's killer had been a private student, not one of her Nova clients, the incident underscores the dangers a young woman can face overseas, even in a country touted for its safety. In the early nineties an acquaintance rolled his eyes and recounted cynically that every white woman in Japan has a story about how someone stared at her breasts on the subway. Unfortunately it is well known that western women are indeed leered at; Japanese women have to suffer so much groping on the subway, the language even has a word for perpetrators of that specific offense: *chikan*. Comics and pornographic films glamorize the crime in the same way they showcase sex with women dressed as schoolgirls or the violation of unwilling housewives by tentacled space creatures.

Gary, who has worked in eikaiwa and dispatch says, 'Japan is an advanced country technologically, but socially it lags behind. There's still a massive gender imbalance and an equality gap in the workplace and society. One student had a guy at the gym slap her bum, and she talked about it like it's to be expected. A woman doctor told me harassment is rampant in hospitals, especially of female doctors because the males feel threatened and have to put them in their place, as they see it. Men and women aren't equal and won't be for a good long while.'

In the eikaiwa classroom it is not unknown for foreign men to come onto students. At James' school, one teacher was dismissed after multiple complaints from female students that he was constantly haranguing them for dates. Grant recounts how at one eikaiwa where he worked, a married man was slipping his phone number to teenage girls. After several rumblings and complaints, 'the head instructor basically raided the classroom and caught him red handed passing a note to a fifteen-year-old, in her school uniform and all. He sacked the teacher on the spot.'

Yet, while eikaiwa is quick to jump on offending teachers for harassment cases, and rightly so, there have been many disturbing complaints from the faculty that have been handled with varying degrees of indifference, nonchalance and even hostility by their employers. If ever there were an area where an English school should take the side of its instructors it would be in cases where their personal safety is in jeopardy. Yet when sexual harassment claims are made the reaction is to dismiss the problem or blame the teacher. Seldom is firm action taken against the student. In Japan, the saying goes, the customer is God.

Samuel from the UK had a sticky student. A divorcée in her early forties slowly became friendlier as each private lesson went by. She had originally come for business English lessons but over time, began to slip hints. 'I was on a tricky spot,' Samuel recounts. 'I didn't want to offend her and being a part timer, I needed the regular student. But if I'd said anything to the front desk or she'd gone to them with a counter claim, I would probably be the one who got blamed.' After several months the student finally confessed her love for him and he had to explain to her very gently that it wasn't that sort of a relationship. A week later she'd pared down her offer to mere sexual liaisons 'as a start', but Samuel still demurred. 'It took a meal and a long chat to set her straight and after that she went back to being a normal student again. But the fear was always there that she could accuse me of something so I had to tread carefully.'

With genders reversed, amorous advances can be more intimidating. Female teachers have been touched in the classroom, and subjected to suggestive comments, even followed home by students. Women teaching in Japan find themselves with a dilemma that has largely disappeared in Western countries where proper procedures are in place: what to do when harassed at work. Refusing to teach an offending student can make the teacher look lazy, uncooperative or overly sensitive in the company's eyes. Complaining about sexual harassment is still often viewed as the victim's fault.

Raised in California, Stephanie had always wanted to live overseas and her family had a history in Asia, through business and the military. 'I majored in Japanese studies at college. The course covered culture, history and modern literature. I felt It was the natural next step for me to go to Japan.'

After graduation, Stephanie applied for the JET program and was waitlisted for some months, due to the large number of applicants. In the meantime, she found work at a winery management company. The organization bottled and marketed wine produced at various smaller wineries in her home state, as well as managing their brands for them. Stephanie performed well: the company even offered to pay her way through a master's degree to prepare her for greater responsibilities, but she was not interested in wine all that much. 'Finally, I got the call from JET. They wanted me to leave fairly soon. It was difficult to do. There were new wineries opening everywhere and opportunities were expanding. But JET said, "Here's your start date, take it or leave it." I decided I still wanted to go to Japan.'

Japan Exchange and Teaching is a government program that sends over four thousand assistant teachers every year to public schools up and down the country. Yet when she arrived at Kansai International Airport in the fall of 2005, Stephanie had no idea yet even where she would be posted. The JET program knew, but they only drip-fed information to her. 'A handler met me at the airport and shunted me onto a train to the town of Shin Kobe. It was surreal. I had no idea where I was going, I only knew I was to get off at that station and someone else would be waiting for me. When I got there, they took me to a hotel and told me to be up at 6am, then met me there the next morning with staff from the local education board. They drove me to this small country town, two hours from anywhere.' The cloak and dagger start was soon softened by the serenity of Stephanie's new surroundings. 'There were trees, hills, beautiful rice paddies, and the trains only came once an hour.'

The school was a technical high school, in Stephanie's words, 'a bit rough'. She later heard rumors among other JET teachers that the *yakuza*, Japan's organized crime rings, had a presence in the town and that many of the school pupils were mafia kids. In any case they were not the finest young minds Japan had to offer and liberal disciplines such as English took a back seat to machinery, crafting, farming and the ubiquitous test-cramming that dominates the lives of high-schoolers across Japan. There were plenty more practical skills than English on offer that would prepare the pupils for their future careers devoid of any direct international contact.

'The previous teacher had left for health reasons. She was later diagnosed with cancer and had to return to the US for treatment. But she basically warned me before she left that I was in for a dull assignment. The kids weren't really interested in learning English and the school wasn't particularly motivated to teach it.' As far as being the foreign teacher went there were always reminders that you were different. Stephanie, a lifelong football enthusiast, recalls joining the kids after school soccer club, but, soon got tired of it because nobody ever passed her the ball.

Some teachers report being made to feel extremely welcome and others report a miserable lonely existence. James in Hokkaido remembers one country school he was sent to each Friday by his eikaiwa. 'One day I turned up to find that they'd forgot to warn me the lessons were canceled because it was a day of sports activities. It was the middle of winter and the grounds were snowed under, but they invited me to join them in the gym. I taught the kids the basics of cricket, which they loved because it was so similar to baseball [Japan's national sport], but they couldn't resist the urge to throw the bat away whenever they started running.' Others remember being completely left out of the loop. David, who was a JET in Kanagawa prefecture recalled, 'They were always nice to me but never saw fit to tell me what was going on. I would come to the staff room to find everyone was at assembly, turn up to class to find the kids were already in the gym, that sort of thing. The response from the Japanese staff was just, "Oh sorry, we forgot to tell you."'

Stephanie's experience was somewhere in the middle, but there was definitely a sense that the kids didn't see her as one of the faculty. The foreign teacher is often treated as an object of curiosity or even a sort of challenge to be faced down. 'The girls would giggle hellos at me in the corridor, the boys would mutter, "I love you," stuff like that. They were interested in me, not as a teacher, or a person, but as a kind of exhibit.'

This is one of the ways Japanese adolescents 'tame' the foreign threat. They're not just hazing the new teacher, but in a way pretending they are not intimidated by this tall, self-confident woman thrust into their midst. Almost any foreigner can relate stories of smartass schoolboys calling out 'Hello' or 'Nice to meet you' on the street, just to show their friends they're not threatened by the idea of a stranger in their homogeneous world. In this environment, contact with the students remained superficial and somewhat distant for Stephanie. 'The lessons were basic and centered around the textbook. The Japanese teacher would set up the lesson, then the ALT provided the human tape recorder. I never really conducted a lesson myself.'

It seemed Stephanie was set for a typically mediocre JET experience. There were regional gatherings of the other nearby JETs, but otherwise life would be a ho-hum affair at a quiet country school where her efforts and input were destined to make little if any impact. One of the charges often leveled by JET teachers is they are simply used as a prop, or even forgotten about. Direct hire ALTs at local education boards find their schools, their students and by extension themselves, much more motivated, the powers that be having made a conscious decision to pursue a more serious approach to English communication. In the case of many JETs however, they are simply fulfilling an education ministry requirement, whether the school feels it needs them or not.

This quiet drudgery however took a nasty turn for Stephanie. 'One day, quite unexpectedly, one of the boys groped me in the common room. I was shocked; I'd never been physically accosted before.' The boy himself had never caused her any trouble before. 'Like the others he was a bit of a slacker, but he had never bothered me directly. He was shy more than cheeky and had certainly never shown any signs of aggression.' The response from the Japanese staff was weak. 'I immediately reported the incident but the principal and other teachers only reassured me, but I didn't want him to be loose in the school anymore, and I no longer felt safe in the halls.'

The school seemed less interested in dealing with the problem than sweeping it under the carpet. 'I handed in my notice and stayed for the notice period. I don't recall if the boy was disciplined or punished at all. I didn't see him after that so he may have been off school, but then a lot of the kids were absent for long stretches, it was that kind of school. Nobody told me if anything had been officially done.' Stephanie emailed her coordinator at the JET program, the regional supervisor for teachers in her district, but didn't get much more than sympathy. 'They never gave me a straight answer on whether the school would take action or

JET would. There were also no positions open for me to transfer, so there wasn't much left for me to do but resign from JET.' When asked if this was a cover up, whether JET refused to transfer her because they didn't want her story getting out and scaring away other teachers, she shrugged. 'There are enough hardship stories out there anyway. There is such a high demand for positions at JET that losing one teacher is not a big deal. If there was nowhere else to put me, they had no real incentive to keep me.'

Olivia first came to Japan from the United States in 2006. 'I did a double major in Asian Studies and Japanese Language and Culture. I'd been teaching English for three years before coming to work at Gaba, though it was my first eikaiwa job. I was on the JET program for two years in junior high schools and then did a similar program in Korea for one year in an elementary school.'

A former coworker had been working at Gaba and the flexible schedule and one-to-one classes appealed to Olivia. But there were financial tradeoffs to working part time while starting over in a new country. 'The schedule was more difficult than I'd anticipated. I didn't get a paycheck for almost two months after starting because each month is paid in arrears on the 25th, and I started at the beginning of the month. I had to borrow money to make ends meet and even spent the first month without any appliances at all, which meant I had to go to the grocery store every day and wash my clothes in the bathtub.'

The 'flexible' schedule was really only flexible for the company. Due to the demand for as many peak lesson teachers as possible and the need to keep lesson slots open in case a client booked, Olivia soon found herself working five twelve-hour days. But the money was finally coming in and she didn't experience any real problems despite the schedule being harder than anticipated. 'I was hopeful as a new employee. I thought things would get much easier once I'd established myself. I was starting to form friendships with other instructors, which was a really positive part of the job.'

Yet as with most large eikaiwa chains, teachers start to see the cracks as time goes by. Olivia saw several supervisors come and go (called Instructor Support Leaders at Gaba) and they could be a mixed bag. 'I soon realized the first one was a bit of a bully. He complained when I started to shorten my hours, even though I told him it was because I didn't feel safe going home alone at ten every night. He observed a lot of lessons and was always quick to tear down the instructors and their teaching methods without offering any advice for improvement. He badgered me about my success rate at trial lessons for prospective students. He asked me about things like why I was more successful with men than women. He offended all of the instructors on a regular basis and treated the counselors very disrespectfully, even in front of clients.' Olivia's next ISL never forgave her when she complained of harassment by a student.

'The client wore an extremely small, extremely tight pair of red shorts to his first lesson with me,' explains Olivia. 'They were so small that they looked like they were probably meant for a child. I was worried his genitals would actually fall out during the lesson. I was embarrassed to repeat that to anyone, but I did talk to the ISL about the lesson. I asked if there was any dress code for clients, and he just laughed and said no. I explained the situation, asking if there was something he could do. His response was "Well, no one's likely to want to talk to him about something like that." It stands in contrast to the strict business dress codes enforced on teachers in eikaiwa schools, often even denying them the increasingly common Japanese practice of 'cool biz' - going without neckties in the hot summer months.

The client also had a skin condition and the disconcerting habit of picking at his scabs and leaving the flakes on the table during the lesson. Olivia raised this problem with her ISL, specifically the danger of blood borne diseases, but her concerns were dismissed with a mild expression of disgust. In addition the student had often been confrontational and on numerous occasions even reached across her body, close enough to brush against her, to retrieve pens and other items from the table. In one instance, he even flung a pen violently down on the table when he was done with it. All of these actions suggest a person with hygiene issues and social problems, yet in the eikaiwa world day in, day out, teachers are forced into the classroom with 'customers' who make them feel uncomfortable or gross them out. If only it had ended there.

'The lesson took place in February, 2012,' explains Olivia. 'In our warm-up, he wanted to talk about how he didn't like cold weather because he has to wear more clothes. He repeated several times that he didn't like to wear clothes. I assumed he meant layers of clothes and tried to coach him on that point. He was wearing something like track pants with insulation. I was doing a review lesson with him and, as usual, he didn't really make any progress. He had his chair pulled all the way up to the desk and I could hear him moving quickly against the fabric of his pants. It put me on edge, but I tried to ignore it. I assumed that he was probably scratching again and tried to remain focused on the lesson.'

But towards the end, the client pushed his chair back and turned to

Olivia. 'He had a visible erection through his pants and was stroking it with one hand. I was so shocked I didn't know what to do. I felt paralyzed and trapped. He was between me and the door, so I backed up into the corner as much as I could and continued to teach, hoping the last few minutes of the lesson would pass quickly. He started touching himself with both hands, running his palms along the sides of his erection.'

Olivia wasn't even sure she could leave the booth without being fired, an example of the perennially weak position the teachers find themselves in at large chains like Gaba. Even when their health and safety may be threatened, they feel obliged to see their duties through. 'When the bell rang to signal the end of the lesson, I stood up immediately, positioned my chair between us, and waited for him to leave. Another instructor saw my face over the booth walls and noticed I was upset. He showed concern but couldn't ask what was wrong since we both still had clients in our booths. In what remained of the 5 minute break, I tried to explain to the concerned instructors, cried and disinfected my table and the pens he'd touched. In the next lesson, I kept crying. I tried to tell the next student it was just allergies but she never booked me again.'

Olivia's fight was only beginning however. Having been stripped of her dignity in the classroom, Gaba corporation was determined not to give an ounce of it back if that meant jeopardizing its clients in any way. Olivia emailed her ISL and the area manager an eloquent but forceful letter outlining her ordeal and finishing with a firm, sensible recommendation: *I wouldn't wish him on anyone, but I really feel that no woman in particular (instructor or counselor) should ever have to be in a booth with this man.*

'The area manager expressed sympathy that it had happened but, 'rather than blocking the client from my schedule immediately, he merely told me that he would have the ISL interview other instructors and counselors about the client, but that since they'd never received any prior complaints, they wouldn't do anything yet. He said it was unlikely that I would have to see the client in the meantime because he tended to book flexible lessons and it was more likely his lessons would end up in the hands of another teacher in the pool.' Pointedly, manager did not assure her that she would not have to teach the student again, *period*. About a week after her complaint this step was finally taken, but she had spent a tense week worried that the student would be foisted onto her schedule again and that refusal would mean disciplinary action.

At first Olivia was assured that only male teachers would get the student from then on, but after a while that rule was forgotten and he started to appear on the schedules of all teachers except her, including other women. His harassment continued regardless. 'I still had to see him in the hallways or waiting room for the remainder of my employment. In addition, he sometimes waited in the train station after his lessons. One night he tried to barge into me as I was walking through to go home, though I saw him and jumped out of his way. On another night someone smashed into me and walked away before I could see his face, though it certainly looked like him from the back.'

Gaba dealt with this in a manner that would be considered substandard by international norms. Olivia feels, 'the action they took was literally the least they possibly could have done for me. The way they handled it implied that they thought it was my fault and I spent a week checking and rechecking my schedule to make sure I wouldn't have to face him again. I thought the way the ISL treated me was very unfair and I was incredibly uncomfortable with still having to see the client at work. It was especially bad if he passed my booth or had a lesson nearby while I was waiting for my own client. It was an awful sensation to have to keep smiling and acting professionally while face-to-face with someone who'd taken advantage of private lessons to force his sexuality on me.'

That might have been the disappointing end to it, but eighteen months later, in the booth with another middle-aged male student, Olivia was exposed to exactly the same kind of harassment a second time. 'As the lesson continued, he made me feel uncomfortable by sitting too close and reaching across my body. Before long, I noticed that he had cupped both hands over his crotch and was swiveling them both forward and back. He stopped occasionally to pull his shirt over his pants, but would start up again immediately. I was in shock that it was happening again. With this man I didn't feel intimidated, just disgusted. Even so, I was worried about being penalized for doing anything the company might consider unacceptable, like ending the lesson or telling him directly to stop.'

With harassment so commonplace in Japan, women teachers have no shortage of stories to trade or tips on how to dodge it in the classroom. Olivia elaborates, 'we can't just stand up for ourselves because we're not taken seriously, get blamed for bringing it on ourselves or are treated like trouble makers so we have to find creative ways to deal with harassment. I can't tell how many times I've had similar conversations with women, sharing ideas about how to protect ourselves or avoid danger.' As one of this student's goals was to learn business etiquette, Olivia used it as an excuse to tell him it was more polite in a business context to keep his hands on the table where she could see them. 'I asked him several times in slower, simpler language and again demonstrated a few times.'

This was one of the strategies Olivia and other teachers had developed to deal with harassment in the classroom, but the deflection didn't work this time. 'It seemed to me that he was intentionally disregarding my requests, knowing that I was uncomfortable with it. Nothing I did made any difference.' She then tried to botch the lesson so that he would request not to be taught by her again. She spoke too quickly, trying to distract him with the speed, but he took no notice and continued touching himself. 'I had one more lesson after that. I don't know how I got through it, but afterward, as I was writing up all my lesson records I broke down again, sobbing at my desk.'

By this time Olivia was a member of the union. Its representatives were helpful and willing to challenge the company directly on her behalf. The ISL was about to take several days off, but forwarded her complaint to the area manager. 'On the ISL's next day at work, he was able to tell me that the client had already been blocked and that they would move his lessons from my schedule as soon as they were able to inform him. It was taken care of much more quickly than the previous time and without interviewing other people in the learning studio.' Olivia holds that union involvement made Gaba sit up and listen this time.

Yet crucially, in neither case was the offending student struck off the books. 'No one wanted to have such a conversation or to make the client uncomfortable by spelling it out. In the second case, they met to agree that *I* was uncomfortable in the lesson and that he would no longer be able to take my lessons. I was told he seemed confused, which shocked me because of how bold he was in the booth. Again, this man willfully behaved in a way he knew to be inappropriate. I saw him in the LS later as well, and he acted upset when he saw me.

Despite quicker action, the resolution again fell short of Olivia's expectations, and no doubt those of her supporters. Not only did the area manager give her the cold shoulder thereafter, probably she surmises, 'because he just didn't want to deal with it', but the fact that the offenders were allowed to remain at Gaba and even to be taught by other female teachers was something of a slap in the face. It certainly did not send them the message that *their* behavior had been wrong. 'Why would they want to turn away income? I know the ISLs get bonuses for exceeding their quotas but I don't know how much.'

'A lot of people like to talk about how harshly sexual harassment and groping are punished in Japan, but it's far from true. The truth is that no one wants to face the problem at all, and victims are faced with roadblocks the entire way. People like to trot out the 99% prosecution rate in Japan, but most [harassment] cases never come anywhere near being examined because of how many people are determined to make it go away quietly. This problem certainly isn't unique to Gaba, but by consistently handling it inadequately, they are ensuring that the problem remains. From what I understand, other eikaiwa companies like Berlitz have policies to handle it and, I believe, have less trouble with it.'

While violent assaults are not frequent, harassment happens very often: groping strangers on the subway may be illegal, but is encouraged via pornographic movies, and *hentai* (deviant) comics. In the greater Tokyo area, over 2,100 cases were reported in 2008 alone and this may be only the tip of the iceberg: in 2004, 64% of young women claimed they had been groped, but only 2% have ever reported the incident. About 1,800 men are apprehended every year for the offense.[2] Whereas most western countries restrict the depiction of sex in mainstream pornography to consensual acts between legal adults, Japanese fare routinely includes fantasies of torture, rape, incest and sex with minors. Unsolicited fondling on public transport that then turns into 'consensual' sex is a popular fantasy in adult videos, and the general theme is of the unwilling female participant and the dominant male. Even though the authorities in major cities have clamped down on the ubiquitous subway gropers in recent years, the *chikan* culture has had several decades' head start, allowing the practice to take a foothold in the sexual psyche of generations of Japanese men. It is even common, Olivia reminds me, to see men reading *hentai* comics in public, such as on commuter trains or buses. These are displayed on convenience store shelves in full view of children.

Olivia partly blames western media. 'I think it's that in Japan people don't discuss sex. When they see movies with nude scenes and people talking freely about sex, maybe - and this is a lot of speculation - they think that attitudes towards sex are so free in the West that there doesn't need to be much of a relationship. American movies and TV shows portray an image of hypersexual women, who are always ready for it, as if we're all nymphos who want it all the time. They don't realize movies are just movies.'

Olivia thinks it may also have something to do with the sex trade, where Russian or Southeast Asian prostitutes or hostesses color the image Japanese men have of foreign women. 'Women from certain countries or backgrounds are sometimes fetishized in Japan much the way Asian women can be fetishized in the West. How many *me so horny* jokes have you heard? Both ways, women are being dehumanized so they can be used, and often the "other" culture is trivialized or dismissed in the process.' Indeed, popular shows such as *Sex and the City,* freely available on DVD rental shelves, portray an image of promiscuous American women more hyperbolic than merely frank. It stands in stark contrast to the chaste Japanese heroines of popular homegrown television. When shed of social strictures on brazenly approaching local women, the Japanese male may feel he can live out his fantasies with an 'easy' foreign one. Or at least, he may surmise, she won't object to him touching his privates in the classroom.

'I once saw a guy playing with himself in traffic,' recalls Olivia. 'I was sitting in the bus and could see down into his car window. Everyone else was just pretending not to see. A certain amount of sexual deviance seems to be excused. The same way they do with alcohol abuse, they say, "Poor men, this is how they get release because they work so hard." Nobody wants to talk about the problem. It's the way they handle a lot of things: if they ignore it, it will just go away. It's similar to their understanding of the war – just sweep it under the rug.'

Sexism is both institutional and societal. When a group of male students at the prestigious Waseda university found themselves up on multiple gang-rape charges in 2003, cabinet minister Seiichi Ota, praised them for being 'vigorous', whatever that meant. Chief Cabinet secretary Yasuo Fukuda complained that his own comments on the case were taken out of context when he was quoted saying, 'There are women who look like they are saying, "do it to me".'[3] Women in Japan still face an uphill battle against entrenched misogyny, and gender-related violence is still very much a subject that society is reluctant to discuss openly.

Sweeping sexual harassment under the rug seems to be par for the course in eikaiwa, too. A union source at Nova, where students can now take online lessons from home via a Skype-like video-phone, reports one woman instructor was faced with a high school boy whose hand was moving in an equally suspicious manner to his rapid breathing. 'The details were out of view of the webcam but his red face was telling. The teacher left the computer classroom and had a Japanese manager come in and talk to the boy. He broke down in tears, afraid that his mother would find out what he'd been up to and that the lesson had been canceled because of it.' To save the boy's reputation, and no doubt, keep the student, Nova agreed to keep it a secret from the boy's parents. 'He was told to carry on as if the lesson were still in progress, even though the teacher would no longer be on the other end.' At other schools, teachers have been touched, propositioned, even followed home by students, raising deep concerns for their safety that their employers did not want to deal with at all.

As far as Olivia is concerned, Gaba did not really try to resolve her harassment complaint. 'Their position was that the procedures in place are good enough. Go to your ISL, who in turn goes to the manager and head office decides what to do. This is not nearly adequate. At another branch, the school had a student who was autistic or some sort of savant. He kept asking the female teachers for oral sex. Everyone had blocked him from their schedules. When told of the problem, the management simply shrugged and said he can't help it or he doesn't know it's wrong. Well then somebody should *tell* him.'

Even after experiencing harassment twice, Olivia was forced to deal with the amorous attentions of later clients in the booth. Like many language schools, Gaba has strict standards when it comes to the possibility of offending a client in the classroom. 'In training, they tell us what we can't discuss: all the standard stuff like sex, religion, whales, the war and so on, but there's no training what to do if the client brings one of these up. It's uncomfortable but every job has uncomfortable parts. It shouldn't be just our job to deal with it. Especially when you can be debelted or non-renewed for anything that goes wrong.'

She likens the eikaiwa response to harassment to gas-lighting, a term coined after the 1940's film *Gaslight*, where a husband tries to drive his wife to suicide by convincing her the house is haunted and she's going mad. 'They do everything first to convince you it's all in your imagination. They ask if you're sure, they ask what you were wearing, then tell you it can't have been what you thought. Whatever it is you must be making it up or imagining things or overly sensitive. It can't have been the clients fault.' This is among the reasons why Olivia didn't report the incidences of intimidation to the police. 'Non-Japanese women especially are disenfranchised in Japan. If it's an issue of his word against hers, who will the police believe? Especially with this myth of innocent men's lives being ruined so often by vengeful women who lie about assault, it's not hard to see.'

There was also fear of retribution - not from the offender but from Gaba itself. When asked why she didn't just file a police complaint after the first student had stalked her to the station, Olivia cited fear of dismissal. 'They were very strict about confidentiality. A teacher can be disciplined even for writing a student's name on a piece of note paper for reference. If I had reported him that would be in breach of Gaba's confidentiality policy, its agreement never to disclose information about a client. Just the fear of being fired is enough to stop you going to the police.'

While the company takes strict steps to ensure customer confidentiality, the reception staff at Olivia's learning studio still felt obliged to accommodate a student with a crush on her, even after her harassment ordeals. 'This was another middle aged man, unmarried. He was a hard worker and really didn't have any hobbies. He always asked for my lessons exclusively. A counselor had told him I was to be leaving soon, and he brought it up at the beginning of the lesson and cried; he could hardly speak, he was so upset. In their remaining lessons, the client's behavior changed. 'He had offered to show me around Tokyo once before and I said no, but now he was inviting me out in almost every lesson. He said he would drive us to [historical sites] Nikko or Hakone, and I always told him I didn't have the time. He gave me all his contact information - three phone numbers, his email address and his home address - and asked me to get in touch if I wanted to go. He even invited me to hiking in the mountains together.' He did not say whether she would need to bring her own shovel.

On Olivia's last day, the client waited around the LS and though the counselors had told him it wouldn't be appropriate, he insisted he would not leave until he'd said goodbye. His final gift to her was a *kokeshi* doll. The *kokeshi* is a traditional Japanese gift – an elaborately carved and lacquered rolling-pin shaped wooden doll. 'Later, one of the counselors asked me to open it so she could see the doll. When I did, she was impressed with how expensive it looked. It came with a small wooden sign about an award the design had won. She said it must have been worth hundreds of dollars. In his letter, he again wrote all his contact information and asked me to get in touch. Some of the other instructors joked that I should check for hidden cameras before taking it home. One instructor pointed out that *kokeshi* is sometimes used as a slang word for a dildo, because of the similar shape. I don't know if the client had been aware of this or not, but I couldn't help but wonder if he had meant something by choosing that as my parting gift.'

In late 2013, The General Union set up two case officers, one male and one female, to deal with sexual harassment claims. The GU sexual harassment web page posted the results of its industry-wide survey in early 2014. Schools large and small were canvassed and a staggering 57% of female teachers reported some form of harassment (men stood at 48%). Just as tellingly, a further 30% of women and 9% of male teachers thought that 'perhaps' they had experienced some form of harassment. This adds up to more than 80% of women and over half of men who've been made to feel uncomfortable in some way at the eikaiwa workplace. Worse, the same survey tracked the responses of those teachers' employers. When women complained, they were taken seriously in only 45% of cases, with the normal company reaction to ignore the case, delay action or make the teacher feel she was to blame herself. In only 15% of cases was any action taken and only 5% of offenders were removed from the teacher's schedule.[4]

The survey shows that men have not been spared unwanted attention, and not only from female admirers among the student body. Some have experienced harassment from male students and one General Union source even cited a case at another large chain where a gay teacher was constantly teased by a female student for his sexual orientation. Only 8%

of male teachers' complaints have been taken seriously and as far as the poll stands at the time of writing, not once has an offending student ever been removed from a male teacher's lessons for sexual harassment. Moreover, the rate of active complaints is very low. Most teachers are too afraid to lodge a claim or they do not believe the company will be responsive. Only 45% of women and 38% of men spoke to management or lodged a complaint when they felt harassed. Most felt the company would be unhelpful or dismissive. The union states, 'With no official procedure in place, or even an adequate definition of sexual harassment, it is very difficult to ensure that the person who suffers harassment feels safe and protected from ever having the same experience again.'[5]

In the summer of 2014, The Japan Times ran an article on the handling of harassment in eikaiwa. In addition to Olivia's story and the Nova online lesson incident, it outlined a litany of complaints by instructors at Gaba. Teachers have been subjected to inappropriate questions of a personal nature on numerous occasions, but complaints have been brushed off by management at some branches. One student tried to hug a teacher during a mild earthquake and also once told her he wanted to drink her breast milk; the teacher's supervisor suggested it was her fault for being too nice. In another example, the student with mild autism was reported to have tried to initiate bodily contact with almost every female teacher he had been in the booth with. Not only was he never reprimanded, as Olivia attests, but because so many instructors refused to teach him, he was moved from branch to branch in the area until he became famous among the female staff for his antics. Gaba willfully shared this problem student with as many teachers as possible because it didn't want to address any of their complaints.[6]

As outlined in Chapter Six, Gaba's evaluation system wields

inordinate power over the careers of teachers and the progress of individual learning studios. Managers and ISLs are under a lot of pressure to make sales, keep student numbers up and reach targets. Likewise teachers fear the dreaded negative evaluations that unhappy students can send their way. 'Negatives' can be used to debelt instructors and give them a pay cut, or as an excuse to non-renew them. One teacher reported having only two negatives out of 6,000 lessons taught in her whole career – both from men she'd refused to date.[7] Not only did the studio not question the clients' reasons for dissatisfaction, but these evaluations remain on her record permanently, a weapon for Gaba should it ever need to reprimand her.

Women teachers at Gaba have developed a variety of strategies to deal with harassment. In addition to swapping stories as Olivia described, to craft the best deflection techniques, many leave code-words and phrases on the student records of problem clients, a warning to other female instructors of what to expect. It is telling that rather than address harassment openly, risking the ire of the company, they have been forced underground to deal with the problem as best they can without attracting retribution from management. Teachers reported calling sick - and forfeiting a day's pay or risking non-renewal - because they just could not deal with a serial harasser on their schedule. The company's insistence that teachers who claim they have been harassed continue to leave their schedule open for the harassers until an investigation is completed causes such absences and undermines its own commitment to promise clients a lesson whenever they please.

Though some ISLs and managers have been sympathetic, many have been dismissive, or reluctant to act. Counselors have insisted that teachers who have complained continue to teach the client who has harassed them because the customer has paid for the lesson. Teachers have fired back that the 1,500 yen a lesson they receive does not cover the stress and humiliation. Gaba's default position is to protect the client at all costs, at least until the teachers and the union kick up a storm and force the company to take action. Yet it bears repeating that when a student makes the slightest complaint about a teacher's performance, attitude or grooming, this is recorded, logged and can be used to dock her pay or non-renew her contract in future.

With large eikaiwa schools still issuing teacher contracts that forbid contact with students, and maintaining policies that punish consensual liaisons with anything up to and including dismissal, one has to wonder why they'd bend over backwards to protect the honor of stalkers, gropers and serial masturbators. When it comes to sex, the contempt for foreign women seems almost biblical, as if they are temptresses who have corrupted the otherwise stoic Japanese male. This cocktail of gender and racial discrimination leads Big Eikaiwa to protect its client base and cover up any scandals at the cost of the dignity of foreign instructors. It can actually put them in physical danger as well.

Craig Currie-Robson

9 ECC - Appetite for Compromise

Sarah graduated from business school in Ontario with a minor in language studies. She had always had an interest in Asia and imagined that whatever her career was, it would have her bridging gaps between east and west. 'I took classes in Japanese and Mandarin, but really was pretty open to working anywhere. At first I heard about ECC in Thailand and then found out it was affiliated to a Japanese company. When I heard they had offices in Toronto I thought, *right, this is me*. Though newly-hired ECC teachers have to fund their own plane ticket and start up costs, the company is helpful when it comes to getting set up in Japan. 'Both on the website and at the recruiting they told us we'd need to bring some cash to get started: the more the better, but at least a few thousand. Training lasted two weeks and covered the bases – how to manage a class full of kids, what to wear and what not to say, that sort of thing. It was exciting in the beginning. I felt like I was stepping into something bigger than me. Well, it was my first real job.'

ECC stands for *Education through Communication for the Community*, which doesn't sound any smoother in Japanese. Started in Osaka in 1962, the chain operates 171 schools, most in the regions around Osaka, Nagoya and Tokyo, covering Japan's three largest cities and their bedroom communities. There are over 650 foreign teachers, mostly of English, and a large number of franchise holders who conduct small local suburban classrooms. Branches are heavily concentrated in populated urban centers - ECC has over 370,000 students on its books –

and it has also benefited from the gap in the market left by the collapses of Nova and Geos.[1]

Instructors are almost entirely hired in overseas recruiting campaigns from the usual Anglophone countries. Sarah was posted to a branch in Osaka and her week consisted of afternoon and evening classes. Sometimes she worked Saturdays, but she almost always had two days off per week. Though the classes were fun, they could be 'exhausting, especially with the little kids'. She was struck not only by how different the working environment could be in a Japanese company but how different teaching in Japan was from her expectations.

'Often we were sent out to the franchise classrooms in our neighborhood. These were run at malls, and department stores where the school rented rooms, or held at the Japanese teacher's house. The Japanese teachers were mostly women who didn't have children or whose own kids were grown. We would team-teach children from the area; there was a lot of singing and flashing picture cards. What baffled me is that these women worked really hard to build a relationship with the students and parents, but were only paid a part time wage. In many ways they were the bread and butter of the kids division and they did a lot of work outside class, but they only got paid when they were in the classroom.'

One researcher I spoke to was working on a paper that compared the benefits of the eikaiwa system's insistence on native English teachers to the possibility of hiring non-native, but fluent Japanese speakers of English. He felt that there should be no reason a fluent Japanese person couldn't teach just as well. I was reminded of the business model of ECC and Berlitz parent Benesse, wherein small local children's classrooms were run by semi-professional teachers, mostly housewives. Indeed

Japan probably has more than enough fluent non-native speakers of English to replace the ten or fifteen thousand foreigners working in eikaiwa and dispatch at any given time. In a country of 127 million there may be twice that number.

Sarah speaks from experience. 'Firstly the majority of these talented speakers will be women. It is women who tend to take language courses and study English abroad, and this is usually because they are not expecting to have a career in engineering or finance. Because Japanese women have been traditionally conditioned to seek marriage and motherhood, they are not looking for careers in teaching English either. Schools can be chauvinistic. Women who do teach in eikaiwa may not be encouraged to develop their careers, especially once they have children of their own. Precisely because they're not expected to be full time workers, even talented speakers aren't on the front line, and are shunted into small side businesses.'

Sarah also saw a problem with language learning goals, from her later experience at other schools. 'In Japanese education, the target is rarely English fluency. Even with a teacher fluent in both languages and properly trained, if the goal is simply to pass Japanese standardized English tests, then the teacher won't be called upon to share her full knowledge of the language: the idea is to teach to the test and get a score, not to learn a language for the purposes of communication. Without a shift in curriculum, it doesn't matter whether the teacher is a native speaker, a fluent non-native speaker, or just has passable English. The teacher's actual language ability is secondary, as long as she's better than her students.'

Sarah feels the need for foreigners is still a necessary marketing gimmick. 'They want authenticity. You have to have the look. I know

Asian colleagues who have had parents request another teacher be sent after they took one look at them and didn't see the poster child they were expecting. But we didn't go to every branch every week. Some kids only got to see the native teacher only once in a while. You have to ask how much good our supposedly awesome native command of English can do, or how much it matters what we look like, when we hardly spend any time in the classroom – it's lip service.'

Though she enjoyed teaching children, both at her ECC branch and outside classrooms, she did find the focus on edutainment somewhat grating. 'I didn't mind at first, but every Halloween we were "asked" to put on costumes for the kids. It was expected of us really, and sold as a piece of cultural input, but in reality a few teachers found it demeaning. I was tempted to ask why the Japanese teachers weren't expected to dress up and play the clown. In my third year I just told them I didn't want to wear a costume that year and they were disappointed but nobody forced the issue.'

The charge that teachers have to embarrass themselves in such a manner has also been leveled at Coco Juku, where one blogger posted pictures of rather forlorn looking teachers in costumes standing over a classroom of children.[2] The General Union's ECC branch took up the issue in 2013, demanding that if the company insisted teachers wear Halloween costumes, then they should provide an allowance to the teachers for purchases. In a union survey, 82% of the teachers wanted the company to pay for costumes.[3] ECC now keeps costumes on the premises for teachers to use when the need arises.

While the health and safety of the children were of paramount importance to ECC, the company's policies in that regard sometimes sent mixed messages to the teachers. When a Typhoon struck her region and many schools and businesses were closed for the day, ECC announced it would do the same, exhorting kids and parents to stay home for their own safety. Nevertheless teachers still had to show up for work. Though not a union member at the time, Sarah agreed when the union took issue with the company asking teachers to turn up for work, regardless. 'I get the Japanese work ethic. But classes are closed and there's nothing for us to do. If it was so dangerous for students to come to the school why was it okay for teachers to battle our way out there in a typhoon? They didn't seem to care that much for our safety.'

At least some attention was paid to teachers' safety, when one teacher at another branch was knocked off his bicycle on the way to work. 'We heard that one guy had been hit by a car and injured, of course he had to take some days off. They told us we were not to ride our bikes to work, that we had to take the subway or bus, because that's what we received transportation money for. But for a lot of people cycling to work could be quicker than public transport. If you only lived three stops away it was much better than walking to the station and waiting for a train. I'm not sure if they were more worried about our well being, insurance claims, or someone not turning up at the classroom because of an accident.'

Sarah has few serious complaints about her time teaching in Japan, though rare is the English teacher with nothing at all to grouse about. On the whole she says, 'They treated me fairly. I had no real run-ins and the students and my coworkers were mostly great.' So how does an eikaiwa school, one of the big chains no less, score such high marks on employee satisfaction? It certainly goes against the trend over the past decade or more. Yet ECC has a comparatively cleaner record than most of its competitors, at least when it comes to labor relations.

With a generally satisfied faculty of teachers and a robust union, ECC has had many years to develop its responses to staff demands. The union doesn't always get everything it wants; neither does ECC. But they have found ways to accommodate one another that puts other major schools to shame. Among the conditions the union has won at ECC are flexible paid leave, a grievance procedure, to avoid the kind of arbitrary complaints that Gaba teachers receive and to have a forum of their own, and, the holy grail for other union chapters, health and pension coverage. None of these was achieved without multiple rounds of collective bargaining and some have even required limited industrial action, but ECC has generally been willing to listen rather than to dig in its heels.

Yet every silver lining has a cloud. Some union achievements, such as getting mandatory training and meetings listed as paid working hours or overtime, hint at previous skullduggery by the company. Eikaiwa schools up and down Japan have long tried to coerce or cajole teachers into unpaid work duties outside of lesson time.

Liam has lived and worked in Japan for over fifteen years, in and out of eikaiwa. His long involvement in the ECC union began shortly after he joined the company. 'One of the foreign teachers' union's strengths was that the Japanese staff had already operated one for decades,' Liam says. While the full time employees or *seishain* always had a union, ECC was 'still somewhat shocked' when the teachers organized in 1997. Not everyone is a member and Liam is reluctant to disclose numbers, but in a chain with over 600 foreign teachers, the union is clearly large enough to have made a difference and to have bargained on behalf of everyone. It was important for the foreign teachers to open their own branch of the General Union, because joining the existing one can be a double edged sword. 'An in-house union makes it easy for a company to follow labor union laws, but could also be used to keep the workers in a weak position if they don't know their rights.'

In Sarah's opinion, 'There's this sense I think in Japanese companies, that the foreigners are not entitled to a voice. They're offended when we organize. There's this feeling that we're here only by the good graces of the company and we shouldn't bite the hand that feeds us, so when a union of foreign teachers is formed, or really when we ask for anything, the default position is that we should shut up and do as we're told.' There would not be much point in joining a union that served only to rubber stamp management decisions. The teachers had to organize.

At ECC, the union started as a response to growing discontent among the ranks. 'Working conditions were getting tougher, teaching hours were getting longer. According to a history of the chapter posted on its website, teachers first began actively unionizing back in autumn 1995 when ECC announced its intentions to enact the "Beyond Borders" project. Beyond Borders was a plan to recruit university students from overseas on 40 hour per week contracts. This was a busier arrangement than the current teachers were getting and they worried it was an attempt to truck in cheaper labor in order to squeeze them out, or to reset the teachers' working week by stealth. The website states, 'Teachers were generally concerned with the declining working conditions at ECC and decided to join the General Union for support.'[4]

The union subsequently bargained for, and won, the 'right' to be consulted before any unilateral changes were made to working conditions. This was already a condition of the labor standards law that the company should have been following in the first place. As with Gaba and Berlitz, it takes pressure just to make the company stick to its preexisting legal obligations, and it is not just the eikaiwa business: the Japan Times reported that in 2013, the labor ministry found almost 4,200 Japanese firms in violation of regulations regarding forced and unpaid overtime. This is probably just the tip of the iceberg.[5] Sarah is suspicious. 'English schools have been up to this for a long time and the authorities only really started to notice when it affected Japanese workers in other industries.'

The next fight was over paid holidays, which at ECC were all fixed to summer and winter vacation seasons, when the school was closed anyway. This is fairly common practice in eikaiwa schools, assuming they close for the holidays and offer paid leave at all. But if teachers called sick just before or just after these periods, they would have pay docked from their vacation days, as automatic punishment for stretching of the holidays.

When a business is closed for the weekend, New Year or on national holidays, salaried employees still get their monthly rate. But many Japanese organizations still insist that workers take leave only at the company's discretion. At an English school this amounts to a shortening of paid leave days, as the ten or more statutory leave days effectively disappear, swallowed up by the school holidays. Now ECC teachers can ask to take their leave outside of school holidays if they wish. The two weeks or so in summer and winter when the school is closed remain simply days off on the schedule. This allows the recruiting site to boast that ECC offers a lot more paid holidays than other schools, and this is true, thanks to the union.

Sarah encountered resistance to this flexibility at the branch level.

'When I went to my supervisor with holiday requests, I got a lot of mumbling and foot-shuffling. They were pretty reluctant at my center to let anyone go when the place was open at all. Even though they had roaming substitute teachers, you had to negotiate carefully, compromise, and do make up lessons, but it was possible to get the dates you wanted.' Though it is arguable in a language school, getting time off is by necessity a negotiation, it opens the question of how much has changed on the ground. Moreover, under Japanese labor laws, businesses are obliged to pay workers 60% of their wages during furlough (such as when a school is closed for the mid-term break) if this is a normal part of business operations. By insisting teachers take their 'paid leave' when the school is closed anyway, most eikaiwas avoid this responsibility.[6]

In a more recent agreement, the union has scored a protection clause against non-renewals, one of eikaiwa's most convenient ways of getting rid of foreign teachers when times are tough. Language schools sometimes need to let instructors go this way for genuine reasons such as a poor attitude or frequent absences, but it has also been used to break up unions, reduce staff numbers when enrollments are down or most commonly to circumvent labor laws that allow staff to demand full time employment after a set period. Liam explains 'So many times in collective bargaining rounds, ECC stated they renew everyone except under exceptional circumstances. We said, okay let's put that in writing, but they resisted. Why resist unless hoping to keep the option open to non-renew at their discretion?'

Following a change in Japan's labor laws, companies must now accept part time staff as full time employees after five years: if a part time or temporary worker has renewed five yearly contracts with a company, on the sixth she is entitled to full time status.[7] Following this law would shake up not only the eikaiwa trade, which relies on disposable part timers for two-thirds of its teachers, but many industries across Japan, where over a quarter of the active workforce is now defined as part time. Major trade unions and many politicians have been pushing for such worker protection for years, but business has resisted. But the change has been something of a Pyrrhic victory: the law kicked in on April 1, 2013, but does not apply to any contracts from previous years. For anyone seeking full time employment, the clock has been reset to zero, and they will have to wait a further five years before they get their chance at a full time slot. By that time the law could well have been changed again, and a lot of employees non-renewed in the meantime. Given eikaiwa's record of ignoring the law, it is unlikely that any of the large chains will comply. How did the government manage to draft a law that seems designed to be ineffective? Liam shrugs, 'the business lobby is that strong.'

Nothing so far done by ECC seems as egregious as the antics at a Gaba or a Nova, and in union bargaining the industry leader also leads by example, with a remarkable appetite for compromise. But being simply the best of a bad bunch is not a glowing report card either. When asked what was the company's worst offense, Liam had to struggle for a moment. It seemed almost to have slipped his mind. '29.5 hours. That was their idea. ECC started that.'

The 29.5 hour work week has become the excuse that eikaiwas large and small have used for the past two decades to drive down staffing costs and limit the professional development of teachers. Without such a precedent, some of the major players in the industry today would not be able to operate at such profitable levels because the cost of hiring and maintaining foreign teachers would be 20-30% higher. Nor would companies such as Berlitz and Interac have faced such prolonged union battles had they chosen not to adopt the practice. According to Chris Flynn at the Fukuoka branch of the General Union, 'The figure of 29.5 hours was always just an internal guideline for labor ministry auditors. If they found workers doing more than that then they would ask why the company hadn't enrolled them in the national pension and social insurance. English schools have seized on this and use it as a get out of jail card even though the law states that anyone working roughly 30 hours a week should be enrolled. The union believes 29.5 equals roughly thirty.'

Sarah worked at least that much. 'Sure, I *taught* less than thirty hours a week. But I was *at work* from twelve till eight or one till nine, sometimes longer. There were class records and evaluations and other bits of paperwork. There was commuting time when I was sent to home classrooms. I taught fewer lessons those days but it can hardly be called time off work when I'm going from the school to another branch on their time. Nobody believed the line that we were part time, and it's not like we could say, oh look, my 29.5 hours are up, I'm done for the week and sorry about the paperwork.'

Effecting change wasn't as simple as just marching up to management and demanding full time recognition. The union had to show it was willing to play hardball. 'We went to the labor standards office and complained for a number of reasons,' Liam explains. 'For example any workplace with more than ten employees has to have workplace rules on the notice board. We also complained that part timers didn't have a full time option.' The workplace rules are simply a set of regulations. These could cover break times, smoking rooms, the dress code, and any number of mundane points. But under the Labor Standards Law, these rules must be displayed at the workplace. Whether on a wall poster, notice board or online, the regulations must be accessible to all employees. Companies are also obliged to undertake a workplace agreement with the staff. This agreement underpins the regulations and must be agreed upon by staff members, whether they're unionized or not. It includes fixing holidays, defining lunch breaks or allowing overtime. It must also be posted for all staff to see. In both cases ECC had not complied. A lot of companies don't, and it wasn't an especially important issue for the union, but it was a good way to get the labor department's attention.

'Normally you lodge a complaint, the inspector calls company and announces an audit, gives company time to prepare,' Liam explains. 'In this case the inspector popped in during Golden Week (Japan's annual spring vacation), when government offices are supposed to be closed and the ECC head office was shut. There was a surprise inspection at one branch and when managers couldn't produce the workplace regulations and agreement, they knew they were in trouble. It was a shot across the bow, to make them sit up and listen.'

But according to Liam, the Labor standards office is too short-staffed and overworked to audit companies regularly. Spot checks do occur, like the raid on ECC, and the labor ministry is looking to create a blacklist of companies with high staff turnover. But they can't be everywhere at once. Usually, it takes a change in circumstances to alert auditors, for example when companies or workers stop paying social insurance contributions. For eikaiwa teachers who have never been enrolled in the social insurance program in the first place, it is easy to be overlooked.

One might hope that with high-profile union battles and court cases going on over this very issue at large eikaiwa companies today, some government officials might take it upon themselves to investigate. However, with general workforce complaints on the rise, foreign teachers could be forgiven for thinking that Japanese society is not too worried about their plight.

Sarah has heard tales of the good old days. 'There was a time, maybe twenty years ago, before I got here, when English teachers made good money. Even ten years ago you could get 5000 yen for some private lessons. But even though teacher salaries have gone down twenty, thirty percent, there's still a perception that English teachers make good money. It doesn't help that school fees have only gone down five or ten percent so students are still paying a lot. They just don't know teachers are seeing less of that money these days. There doesn't seem to be any general sympathy because they think we have it pretty good.'

But foreigners are not completely powerless. With schedules heavy on children's classes, ECC teachers may have found that eikaiwa's emphasis on customer service and loyalty has strengthened their bargaining position. Sarah points out, 'other schools can fire strikers, or bring in strike busters. Adult students don't mind a change of face so much. Some schools even see it as beneficial to have a high turnover.' But children are less fickle. Usually it takes them a while to get comfortable with a new teacher. Parents and kids come to depend on teachers who are good at their job and popular with youngsters. 'Sometimes a good, stable teacher moving on can be the catalyst for parents who were thinking of pulling their kids out at the close of the semester. ECC is probably more willing to bargain with the union because it doesn't want to upset the parents with strikes and people quitting.'

The battle to get *shakai hokken* and the national pension saw strikes in 2005 and 2006. Liam says, 'Every few years the union has to reassert. Big companies like Gaba rely on the 20% savings they make on teacher salaries to grow the business. Nova's expansion was paid for by the *shakai hokken* that its teachers should have been getting instead. But all the corner cutting forces the good teachers out. Dispatchers [agencies sending teachers to public schools] are another example. The Osaka board of education has gone back to hiring its English teachers directly because dispatchers couldn't provide reliable teachers. The poor pay and conditions invited slackers and caused good teachers to leave mid-term.'

The combined pressure from the labor standards bureau and industrial action finally netted results. ECC was forced to recognize that 29.5 hours was indeed 'roughly thirty' and agreed to allow regular teachers to apply for the national health and pension benefits from 2006. This was a big win for the union as it amounted in effect to a pay increase: the company would have to match employee contributions to both the health and insurance plans. The national pension can make for a helpful nest egg even for short term teachers, as they can pull out their combined contributions after three years.[8]

It is telling though, this is not offered as part of the base package: the pension contributions are optional - not offered on arrival - and new hires are still brought in expecting a 'part time' work week of under thirty hours. Teachers have to find out for themselves how, but at least the option to join the national pension program is there, and this is more than the other major chains are willing to offer. At the company that instituted the 29.5 hour shortcut, the decision was finally overturned, but many large eikaiwa schools still use it to avoid employer obligations.

Sarah muses, 'If ECC hadn't led the way would it be the industry standard it is today? Yeah, somebody else would have thought of it.'

It is one of the great ironies for eikaiwa teachers, that while they personify the product, and are the prime requirement to meet the goals and needs of customers who wish to learn English, they remain at the lowest rung of the ladder. ECC has come to recognize the essential relationship between teacher and student (or parent) that keeps customers coming back. Whereas other large chains are quick to discipline or even dismiss staff who challenge their bottom-rung status, ECC has grasped the importance of keeping its instructors happy as well.

Not too happy of course, and unpaid overtime remains a bone of contention. In most eikaiwa schools, the teacher's work does not begin and end with the lesson. There is preparation, and sometimes a lot of it. Even at the cookie-cutter chains with ready made lessons, there are at least student information cards to check off and other papers to file. At ECC, teachers would often be caught up with a backlog of between-lesson paperwork at the end of the day. Being good workers, they'd 'touch out' using their staff cards at the time they left (seemingly an anachronism, the labor ministry insists that companies keep a record of employee hours for various purposes, from assessing taxes to gauging overtime).

'When the Labor Standards Department looked at the time cards, they saw a lot of people doing a lot of unpaid overtime,' Liam explains. 'ECC added a 19-minute warning to the system so that teachers touching out 20 minutes after the end of the work day would be flagged.' This encouraged teachers to get their paperwork done more efficiently, or at least to get out the door more quickly regardless. However it seems to have led to some misunderstanding between the teachers and the company. The flagging showed up as a system error, which meant only that the company needed to review whether the teacher needed to be paid overtime. The Union web page warns that 'This does not mean that overtime under 20 minutes should not be paid'.

At ECC, getting the recognition that teachers were in effect full time was the greatest battle the union has had to fight, but there is a laundry list of future targets. Being a full time English teacher is not the same as a permanent company employee. Contracts still last only a year and whereas Japanese office staff get bonuses and other perks, the company has so far refused to offer such incentives to the foreign staff. How do teachers get on the gravy train?

The union fought and 'won' the right for teachers to be promoted to *seishain*, or full time company employees, yet as of 2013 only two foreign staff out of more than six-hundred had been promoted.[9] These two were in management or training positions at head office, not teachers, and neither was a union member. Liam concedes that 'Japanese employment practices are difficult to fit to the teacher model. They'd have to work longer hours, and there's the chance of being transferred. Twenty teachers were asked but on balance they felt they had a better deal already and that the company needn't become their primary commitment. Such a change in circumstances forces teachers to decide how long they intend to stay in Japan.' Full time office staff might have to work the notoriously long days of Japanese office workers, and teachers can't do twelve hours of contact time. The company would have to find other work for them to do that would be perceived as useful or valuable, perhaps a hard thing to do for someone hired solely as a teacher and never expected to be needed for anything else.

Despite the small number of initial candidates, there may be more teachers interested in attaining full time employee status, but conditions of a permanent employee may not be just difficult to fit to the teacher model – they may be prohibitive. While company workers with a long term future are used to being moved around in Japan, English teachers are used to staying put. Those with families, relationships and other roots in their adopted towns are unlikely to want to move. ECC may find it convenient that the fear of transfer limits the number of applicants. While some teachers I've spoken to said they would be happy to work as hard as a Japanese salaryman if only they were compensated, that might not translate so well to eikaiwa. Large chains rarely see foreigners as good for anything but teaching and are unlikely to nurture their careers towards management, marketing or R&D. In order to get its money's worth an eikaiwa school would likely want to see the permanent foreign employee in the classroom as much as possible. If working a typical Japanese twelve hour day meant nine or ten in the classroom, quality would certainly suffer.

In addition, the procedure for becoming *seishain* at ECC is convoluted. It requires a letter of recommendation from a branch manager so the managers have to take an active interest in the career development of their teachers, assuming they haven't been instructed to put as few names forward as possible. A common defense for not giving eikaiwa teachers full time status is because they won't be around forever like Japanese staff. Though that sounds like a 'loyalty' issue, it also sounds a lot like they're not given these benefits pointedly because they're *not* Japanese. The lack of future prospects in turn drives the teachers to leave, making it another of eikaiwa's self-fulfilling prophecies.

Even the nominal title of permanent employee might come with a different understanding when applied to a foreigner. In 2012 the General Union took up the cause of a teacher at language school Epion Mabuchi. The teacher, who was well-liked and had received consistently good evaluations for over a decade at the company. He had become *seishain* in 2005, under that company's very progressive terms: the rest of the industry's drive toward part timers and subcontractors was in full swing by this time. Then a change of management brought in a new guard eager to cut costs and perhaps curious as to why foreigners should be treated as well as Japanese staff.

After his colleagues were gradually shunted out, the teacher found himself the only remaining permanent non-Japanese employee. Despite positive evaluations from students, the company suddenly concocted negative assessments and used them to dock his pay. He was told that he was a poor teacher, despite still being called upon to train newer (cheaper) foreign instructors. Daily meetings were held in which he was consistently reminded of his faults. He was assigned to menial tasks at the head office and kept out of the classroom.[10] The union saw this as a form of hazing to force him to quit. Recently married and about to become a father, his family's future was crumbling before his eyes.

With union help the Epion teacher was allowed to keep his job, but many teachers in the industry have not been so lucky. In eikaiwa, a permanent position may seem like the proverbial pot of gold at the end of the rainbow, but for bonus chasing vice-presidents and CFOs, the foreigners who surely don't really belong in Japan anyway must make an inviting target. A change in management or a corporate buyout can be the difference between a steady job and a part time one; part time and subcontractor status; a subcontractor job or no job at all.

ECC has posted increasing profits over the past few years but teacher salaries have risen only in tiny increments. The union cites figures found on a national business database, one of the benefits of ECC being a publicly listed company. At the industry's nadir in 2009, the company made no net profit and salaries remained flat. In 2010, there was a 4% jump coinciding with the Geos collapse, and those teachers who fulfilled the service length requirements got a 1.5% raise. But as the business bounced back the teachers saw no benefit. In 2012 net profit stood at 114% while the average pay increase among teachers was only 4.5%, much of those standard increments after the first or second year of service.[11]

On the heels of such good business, average summer bonus for Japanese *seishain* at ECC was ¥855,000 in 2013. This is more than three times the monthly salary of the foreign teachers, who got no bonus at all. *Seishain* get two bonuses per year, even at the graduate entry level.[12]   If an English teacher at ECC got even half of that average bonus, just once per year, it would amount to a hefty 13% pay rise. How can an eikaiwa school be so generous to its native Japanese staff in the office, but so cheap when it comes to its front line teachers?

Sarah reminds us, 'it's an *English* school. Its main business is providing English lessons taught by native speakers. It can't operate without them. If the company has made such huge profits it's because of the efforts of its *teachers*. It can't be despite us. We're the ones driving the bus.' It is fair to say if the teachers were all Japanese, ECC wouldn't have as many students or be such a successful chain, since using native speakers is the model for all major eikaiwas. Regardless of whether a foreign teacher will be a loyal lifetime employee, surely it is only fair they deserve a proportionate cut of the profits accrued while they work there. When a school's success is heavily dependent on its teachers not being Japanese, it is hard to imagine why they should be penalized for it. The union is pushing for a modest ¥100,000 contract renewal bonus each year. So far the answer is, 'Not yet.' On the heels of a profit revival, the Japanese office staff get three month's wages in performance bonuses; the foreign staff apparently don't even deserve enough for plane ticket home.

Liam recalls for a time union membership was on the wane. 'From the late nineties, ECC shifted recruitment overseas, whereas before it had predominantly hired locally. This affected union numbers for a while as new hires were not really aware there was a union. However when conditions worsened again, new members started signing up.' Hiring overseas remains the preferred method of most large eikaiwa chains and dispatchers. Outsiders don't know the conditions, or their rights. They are not jaded by previous disappointments in Japan. They are fresh meat for English schools.

Despite ongoing demands, the ECC union has won an impressive list of concessions. The company officially 'recognizes' the union's right to strike – a no-brainer enshrined in labor laws that other schools have violated. Previously unpaid workshops and training sessions are now paid. Maternity and childcare leave are also guaranteed under Japanese law and government workers can be pretty sure they'll get a fair shake. However in the private sector, companies continue to subvert the law and the phrase *mata-hara* (maternity harassment) is used to describe the bullying employed to push mothers out of the workplace.[13] The union has gained provisions for childcare leave at ECC. Teachers can now be sure they can return to their old position after a stint away for childcare, which has proven a stumbling block for foreign teachers elsewhere.*

Another union victory was over 'special leave'. According to Liam, 'Working conditions unique to Japan are often hidden and not offered to foreign workers. There were highly detailed regulations for special leave for occasions such as funerals and illnesses in the family, for taking care of elderly relatives and so on. These were for the Japanese staff, not us. It took several years of negotiating, and a deadlock, even mediation at the prefectural labor relations commission, but we finally got recognition of the same rights in April 2012.' Not quite the same. For the foreign teachers such leave remains unpaid.

But small victories ECC far ahead of other eikaiwa schools in terms of both worker's rights and employer responsibility. Yet it is worth pointing out again that not only did ECC try to avoid granting special leave to its foreign teachers at first, but the company had always offered it gladly to its Japanese staff. ECC knows what teachers are up against and where it stands in the job market. The company makes no wild promises on its recruiting website. It rather meekly encourages candidates to 'Enjoy Japan with the most progressive employment package in the business.'[14] Compared to the competition, this is sadly

---

* In March 2015, the union asked to have ECC's child care leave policy translated. The company flatly refused and the union had to wring it out of them via collective bargaining.

true. However nothing in this 'progressive package' was given willingly: click on the link to the benefits page, and the contract package is practically a mirror image of the union's list of victories on its own site.

The fight is not over. On May 31, 2014, ECC teachers went on strike in Osaka, pursuing the union demand for better pay. They asked for a 5% increase in salary, noting that consumption tax had just increased by three percent and was slated to climb another two. They reminded ECC that the base rate had not been raised in fifteen years, despite company profits. They requested a contract completion or renewal bonus of up to a thousand dollars. They demanded the option to become permanent employees after five years, following the recent change in labor laws. It was enough to bring ECC back to the table and collective bargaining has resumed.

In an industry where non-renewals and insecure paychecks are the norm, where no excuse to take time off work is a good one, and where intimidation and union busting are the go-to tools in labor relations, ECC shows what can happen when eikaiwa schools, however grudgingly, try and listen to their teachers. Far fewer come away citing their time at ECC as a negative experience, or feeling they've been cheated out of a decent living altogether. In Sarah's words, 'if you just keep your head down and do the job, and make sure the union has got your back, it's not a bad place to work. Not compared to the horror stories I've heard from other schools.' It's as close to a glowing reference as an eikaiwa school might get.

10 Interac's Phantom Jobs

Michael Collison was not in the habit of leaving his mobile phone switched on in class, but today was the one exception. He was teaching as a dispatch ALT (Assistant Language Teacher) at a public school in Kanagawa, near Tokyo, doing well at work, the father of a one-year-old and about to become a father again. His wife was in hospital due to late pregnancy complications and he was anxiously awaiting word from the doctors. When the phone rang he excused himself from the lesson. It was the call he had been dreading: now he needed to leave school early to be by his wife's side. They had lost the baby.

His reason for asking to leave school early that day was obvious: it was a medical emergency. The response from his employer was unsympathetic. In a phone call the following day from the Yokohama office, a Japanese staffer told him the company required one week's advance warning of a medical emergency. Apparently emergencies unfold very slowly in Japan. Dealing with the tragedy - and handling matters pertaining to the deceased infant - required a few more days off, for which Collison gave adequate notice.

Collison was by all accounts an exemplary teacher. The Hiratsuka district education board, to whose schools he'd been dispatched to teach, praised him for his efforts. His employer, the dispatch service sent him a letter of commendation in December of 2008, stating that 'The feedback from your school was particularly good.' It went on to assure him he could, 'let this letter of commendation serve to show our gratitude for your hard work.' Yet several months later, after the death of his child, and when it came time to renew his contract, Collison's supervisors told him that he would no longer have a job in the coming semester. They were non-renewing his contract.

He protested the decision; one he felt was based entirely on his absence during his bereavement. In a high-tension meeting at the office with a foreign coordinator and another Japanese staff member, the company tried to pressure him into signing a letter of resignation, effectively waiving any responsibilities it might have as an employer dismissing an employee. Collison took it up with the General Union and English language newspaper, The Japan Times; he sent an eloquent and moving account of his ordeal to author, blogger and foreigner rights crusader, Debito Arudou.[1] After posting the story, Debito's blog was flooded with responses from former dispatch teachers with similar stories of intimidation when it came time to sign their 'resignations', often for absences due to a sickness or death in the family. Japanese and foreign company hacks refused to let them leave the room, grew heated and flustered, coerced and bullied until teachers relented. In at least one instance, a foreign supervisor ripped off his necktie and paced the room like a scene from a bad cop movie.

Debito (otherwise known as David Schofill) sought and received a response from the dispatcher. Though it was rare to see an English provider face the foreign press over allegations of wrongdoing, the response was still tepid. The company insisted that Collison's dismissal had nothing to do with the medical emergency, but it was unable to provide an alternative reason, citing 'privacy' concerns. The email weakly promised to ensure such 'miscommunication' would not occur in future, but notably did not mention how. It was not signed off by a company representative, and nobody's name appeared on the document at all. It ended with a simple, 'Thank you for your support, Interac.'

Teaching at a public school has traditionally not been considered a tough assignment for foreigners in Japan. Even with cultural misunderstandings or in whatever passes for rough neighborhoods, few hardship stories have come out of working for the government. An English teacher at a public school can look forward to a light work schedule, weekends off, long holidays and at least back in the day, a fatter salary than eikaiwa. For many years, boards of education have relied heavily on the government-sponsored Japan Exchange and Teaching program (JET), which recruits graduates abroad and brings them over for up to three years. In addition to a famously easy schedule, JETs, as they are known, receive a salary above the national average, national pension, health and unemployment coverage.

Even for those not lucky enough to get into the JET program, teaching as an ALT (Assistant Language Teacher) for a local school board as a direct hire has been a traditional refuge from eikaiwa. The perks - back in the day again – made eikaiwa teachers drool or even seethe. ALTs made 20-30% more; they had long school holidays; some had health insurance and pension plans, and completion bonuses. Most had comparatively light teaching schedules. But the double whammy of an economic crunch and declining birthrate has seen government schools cut costs, with many smaller country or suburban schools closing altogether and being amalgamated into larger neighboring ones. This has led school boards to reduce the use of foreign teachers - or at least the direct employment of them - even though the education ministry makes repeated calls every few years to improve the level of English in public education. With the cushy direct employment option for ALTs dwindling, schools have increasingly turned to dispatch services, temp agencies that hoard pools of foreign teachers and send them all over the country on assignment. According to the Ministry of Education, the number of JET program ALTs dropped by about 15 percent from 2002-2006, while non-JET ALTs doubled.[2] Enter Interac and a host of other dispatch agencies who have stepped up in the past decade to dominate the ALT trade.

The International Education Research and Analysis Company sounds more like a think tank than a teacher dispatch service. Interac's original brief was teaching 'business English', that hazy corner of the industry that promises to improve students' business communication skills, regardless of their actual level of English, but it has since moved into the dispatch business. With over 2,500 ALTs on the books and an expanding network, Interac is now the largest dispatcher by far. The company was founded in 1972 and has another division called IGS offering recruitment services for the education industry. Teachers from Interac's corporate training department are also dispatched to private sector companies and non-profit organizations such as JICA*. According to government figures almost one in six public school pupils in Japan is serviced by an Interac ALT.[3]

Dispatch agencies have therefore managed to choke an avenue of escape for under-appreciated eikaiwa teachers. Experienced teachers used to move to public schools because they paid better and offered easier hours. Now, most ALTs are hired through a third party: any level of experience will do and the money is just the same as working at a language center, or less. JETs earn over $40,000 a year; by sending their instructors in bulk, and offering lower pay and benefits dispatch agencies can charge around $30,000 per year and keep a third of that. The ALT receives a mediocre eikaiwa-style salary of around $2,300 a month before taxes. To Gary the reason is simple: 'The meaning is all in the name – *Assistant* Language Teacher. We are the assistants teaching our own language under the supervision of a Japanese teacher of English.'

The 'assistant' label is not necessarily an effort to be crafty or undercut the status and salary of native English speakers. Under Japanese education laws, in order for a teacher to have sole control of the classroom, she must carry a Japanese teaching license. This requires rigorous study and examination in Japanese. There are non-Japanese who carry the license so it is not impossible, but the level of Japanese required to pass a government examination is beyond the reach of most foreign teachers. The way around it of course is to have assistant teachers (and in Japan there are many such unlicensed teachers of all subjects) and this has provided an 'in' for many foreigners.

Being an assistant teacher didn't always mean a low salary, but with the torch passing to eikaiwa-style dispatch agencies, downgrading was inevitable. Employing economies of scale and adhering to the 'McPrinciples' of the eikaiwa industry, these agencies can afford to pay less and waive benefits by sending teachers en masse insisting they are working less than a thirty-hour week. Once again that magic number of 29.5 serves to undercut salaries and limit career development. In some cases, they simply wave the wand and declare teachers 'subcontractors'. The policy may not be entirely disingenuous: ALTs still work a notoriously easy week – commuting to school and teaching three to five classes a day, usually finishing in the afternoon and often having weekends off. Gary gladly took a pay cut to leave eikaiwa for the relative ease of Interac. 'Working till nine on weeknights and most of the day Saturday didn't leave me with time for hobbies. At a public school you get off work and it's still light. You can go to the gym or do some cooking. You don't feel like cooking when you come home exhausted late at night.'

ALTs may be at school around thirty hours a week, but none faces the grueling lesson schedule of eikaiwa teachers. Many are paid less in the summer and at new-year holidays when school is out, but at least they *get* paid holidays. They are also free in the evenings and most Saturdays to teach private lessons or pursue other interests. Nevertheless the teachers' brief - or the school's expectation - often requires them to be at work seven or eight hours a day and the law is very clear on the responsibilities that entails for employers. As with most eikaiwa schools, Interac does not meet these responsibilities.

Interac's web site states, 'As a regular Interac ALT, you will most likely qualify for a gross salary of between 230,000 and 250,000 yen per calendar month. If you are employed on a part time contract the salary terms will be determined by the specification of each position. National income tax and employment insurance is automatically deducted each month; however, city tax and health insurance are not. National income tax is less than 10% of your monthly salary.'[4] This is all comfortably above board, and on paper at least, a fixed salary is more than most eikaiwa schools offer. But in line with the eikaiwa industry that Interac bases itself on, the devil is in the details. Few teachers have seen their salary paid at the promised level, and the conditions of working at a dispatcher skirt legality. Interac has not been able to avoid attention from the union or the authorities.

Chris Flynn, a tall Australian with salt and pepper hair, has been in Japan for over two decades. He is a university lecturer, accredited Japanese translator and a General Union representative. A lifelong rugby union man, he coaches teenagers and even still plays for the over-fifties side of his local team. Flynn first arrived in Fukuoka in 1988 when he worked at an *izakaya* pub while completing his studies. He also worked as a radio DJ no less, for five years at an English language station targeting the foreign community. It was at the station he had his first experience of union procedures.

'The station was in debt so it tried to sack the foreign staff. They claimed that the foreign DJs and producers were all *itaku* – independent subcontractors, and as such could be summarily dismissed if there were no longer a need for them.' The idea that in a business where the foreigners are the star players, yet sit at the lowest rung on the ladder is not limited the English teaching world. A quick and hopefully painless removal of the foreign tumor seems to be common practice in many struggling businesses, from the lowliest local language school to corporations such as global camera giant Olympus, which fired its British born CEO when he went to the board with evidence of financial cover-ups taking place.[5]

Flynn recalls, 'We had all misplaced our original contracts that we'd signed five years before. So we set about digging up copies because we were sure that we'd been listed as employees. We managed to get our hands on the company's archived copies of our contracts and got in touch with the union. Sure enough they named us as employees. When we took this to the management we were told, "That's what it says, but it doesn't actually mean that".' Again this is a familiar refrain. The rules, Japanese companies will tell you, are "different" for foreigners. The Fukuoka Union website warns, 'don't let anybody tell you that conditions are different because you are a 'gaijin'. This is irrelevant.'[6]

After a stint back home in Australia, Flynn returned to Japan, with a wife and a one-year-old child, ready to start over. He worked for a time in eikaiwa before getting a master's degree and landing a job at a junior college. This was back in the days when eikaiwa still offered stable, full time employment and teachers could afford to pursue postgraduate studies. The college eventually became an accredited university and he has lectured there ever since, some seventeen years. As a union official himself, Flynn has represented teachers from schools large and small, including nationwide chains such as Nova, and dispatchers like Interac.

There have been numerous complaints against such services, including unpaid leave, phantom contracts, summary dismissal and unexplained deductions from teacher salaries. Nevertheless fighting through the unions rather than going to court often turns out to net the best results for both plaintiff and employer, though employers might see it as a net loss. According to Flynn, 'going through the courts is an Everest to climb. It costs a lot of time and money for the company and they risk an unfavorable verdict. What normally happens is after the first hearing, a judge recommends an out of court settlement and it's usually cheaper. The threat of going to court is usually enough to make a company listen.'

This is not to say teachers get what they want all the time. Those without union representation are often left hanging. 'Many teachers are unaware there's a union, don't want to fight the system or think they can't make a difference. A lot don't plan to stay long enough. There's a good deal of apathy towards the union and we have to work hard to convince people of the value.' There may even be, in many dispatch companies, an active program to discourage foreign staff from joining a union. The Fukuoka branch's FAQ page details a litany of hurdles an employee might come across when the topic of unions is broached at work: *my employer has been saying that the union is corrupt; they're just after dues money; joining a union isn't the Japanese way; the company would close down if the union came in.* Flynn argues, 'these are all just excuses to avoid empowering the workers. No company has ever gone out of business because it was forced to give its workers a better deal.'

In the dispatch arena, the Fukuoka General Union has identified a number of 'scams' that aspiring ALTs might fall prey to. These are listed on the union web page and Flynn took the time to explain in detail over several Skype sessions. 'Every time we identify and challenge one bad practice, the dispatch companies change tack or substitute it with another. It's like playing snakes and ladders. Whenever we stamp out one dodgy practice, another one pops up elsewhere. If the union manages to improve the conditions and get the teachers up a ladder, the company slips in a snake and they slide right back down.'

First among the scams Flynn cites is the general condition under which ALTs are hired and dispatched to local schools. It is this scam that largely makes all the others possible: the convenient fiction that the teachers are not even genuine employees. In the dispatch business, the presence of the ALT is deemed a service. There are two variations of this service – a dispatch contract or a service subcontract. These have two very different names in Japanese (*haken* contracts and *gyomu itaku* contracts respectively), and carry different obligations under labor laws and education ministry directives. Notably very few ALTs are on direct employment contracts. This is the privilege of JET teachers and the lucky few who have managed to secure a job with a local board of education that does not use dispatch services.

Under the dispatch (*haken*) contract, the dispatch company inks an agreement with the BOE to send a teacher to provide English instruction at its schools. While the ALT is employed by the agency, she is under the direction of the BOE, and therefore the school, in her day to day schedule. Under Japanese labor laws, a dispatch worker has the right to seek full employment directly from the board of education after a period of 1-3 years. This is not the preferred outcome for BOEs, who find it cheaper to take dispatch ALTs, or for the dispatch company, which wants to lose neither teachers nor BOE clients as a result of turning to direct hire.

According to the subcontracting service (*gyomu itaku*) contract conditions, an ALT cannot seek direct employment at a BOE even after working there for a number of years. The ALT works under the direction of the dispatch company, which is her employer and crucially, neither the school nor the BOE is permitted to give directions to or assess the performance of the ALT. This would be a breach of education ministry regulations and education law. Though the union claims that schools certainly have a moral obligation to do so, they cannot directly negotiate with teachers or with the unions on a teacher's behalf. This is the contract preferred by large dispatch companies such as Interac, as it allows them to hold all the cards, though exceptions are made depending on arrangements with the education board and often, the rules are not enforced in the classroom.

The union holds that in practice, the use of a subcontractor in the classroom is illegal. By the very definition of the job, an *assistant* language teacher must work under the direction of the licensed Japanese teacher in the classroom. However to take any direction from a BOE employee would be against the conditions of the *itaku* contract. On the other hand, if an ALT were given a free hand to run the class as she (or her dispatch agency) sees fit, this would be in breach of education laws, as only a teacher who holds a Japanese teaching license is permitted to conduct a class in full.

Just how an assistant teacher is supposed to teach *without* direction from the school she works at remains an open question, or as Flynn puts it, 'they just file that in the Too Hard Basket.' Because few foreigners are certified teachers in Japan, and because directly hiring JETs and ALTs is too costly for BOEs, most local and regional authorities turn to dispatch agencies to provide wide-eyed foreigners to entertain their classrooms on the cheap. It excuses the schools from paying benefits and managing the careers of native English teachers. It allows the dispatch companies to pass them off as part timers who spend most of their time out on contract work and who are not entitled to the benefits of a full time employee. It allows them to dismiss teachers, reassign them or rotate them with a minimum of fuss. One complaint from students and parents, aired in a TV exposé on such practices by news station *Nihon Terebi,* was that teachers were replaced up to seven times in a school year.[7]

Flynn explains, 'The education ministry has issued directives over the years, indicating that it would prefer local boards to directly hire their ALTs, but nothing has been done on the ground. The Fukuoka Prefectural Board of Education has gone back to JETs because the high turnover of dispatch ALTs was unacceptable. Kitakyushu is the only one where ALTs are full time employees with national health and pension benefits.' Perhaps even more interesting, some Kitakyushu ALTs are supplied by Interac. Interac sends most of its ALTS as dispatch or subcontract workers, yet it offers full time contracts to those sent to Kitakyushu. This is because that city has stipulated in its contract that the teachers must be at the school eight hours a day and be considered full time employees. Interac's recruitment page states about 10% of teachers will have full time contracts, though it doesn't mention which of the handful of BOE contracts require it, and few Interac ALTs will be lucky enough to be sent to Kitakyushu. For BOEs that have lesser requirements, or want ALTs on the cheap, Interac will tailor its bid for the contract. Usually that means the cheaper the better and those cuts come from the teachers' pay.

This is not to say the BOE is playing it completely straight. Though dispatch teachers working in the district do get the proper legal insurance coverage, they only get it for a little over half the year. Like many dispatch teachers, the ALTs are employed on contracts between the holidays: six weeks from June through July and about six months from September to February. The rest of the year they are technically unemployed and must enrol themselves in the public health program if they wish to remain covered. This was uncovered after the Fukuoka union went over the contracts carefully. Flynn adds, 'Kitakyushu shares the haken (dispatch) contracts around with Interac, OWLS and KBS.'

Not only do agencies offer different rates to different candidates, depending on which contract needs filling, but those rates can change even after the contract has been signed - another of the scams posted on the union website. In a YouTube video posted by the union, Flynn outlines a case in which a teacher ended up getting a pay cut after he had started work, because his dispatcher had since negotiated a lower bid with the BOE he'd been sent to. The teacher was offered ¥245,000 per month in the initial contract - ¥230,000 as a basic salary and ¥15,000 to cover public transportation. In September, when he returned to class after summer holidays, the teacher noticed that his pay packet was suddenly ¥15,000 lighter. After the union looked into it they found that the school had asked the dispatcher to cut the transportation fee. The dispatcher had started docking it directly from the teacher's pay to cover its own losses. Lawyers for the company argued mendaciously that the amount of pay specified in the contract was not legally binding.[8]

For teachers who have to commute from a company sponsored apartment in a nearby city to various country schools, the bill for subways, trains and buses can be as much as $200 a month. Dispatch agencies have been known to pay for transportation, or not pay, depending on the contract awarded by the BOEs. If they need to bid lower in order to get the contract, they'll do so. If they must waive the transportation fee, so be it. The cost of course, is passed onto the teachers.

Moreover an offer of ¥250,000 a month is not always what it seems. 'We've seen cases where the monthly figure is only stated for eleven months, not twelve. Interac will claim it offers paid holidays but doesn't actually pay at all for the month or so in summer when school is out.' How is this done? The company simply spreads that ¥250,000 'per month' over the whole year, minus one month. So in the summer, the teachers still get paid, but the actual salary over twelve months is about ¥230,000 – about $200 less per month than what was promised.

Gary did well in the sales business before leaving Christchurch, New Zealand in search of adventure overseas. 'I had a company car, steady pay increases. I bought a house, renovated and sold it. I was making good money but I was also overworked, smoking and drinking too much, gaining weight. I decided to chuck it in and see the world.'

The overseas experience or 'Big OE' is a milestone in the lives of many young New Zealanders. There pervades in the island nation at the bottom corner of the world, the idea that you have to get out and experience something more before you get too old. Young kiwis fresh out of university or in their mid to late twenties can be found in all kinds of exotic places: backpacking around Thailand, working bars in London, crewing Gulf airlines such as Emirates and Qatar, or teaching in Japan, China and Korea.

'I was going to go to Europe and had it all planned out. I was going to visit the Parthenon, Dublin, Dubrovnik. I was going to see the Coliseum and run with the bulls in Pamplona, all the standard stuff.' But a friend had already wound up in Japan and lured Gary with tales of hard partying, beautiful women, and powder snow. 'I already knew what Europe was going to be like, I already knew everything I was going to do there, but Japan was a mystery to me so I decided to give that a go instead.'

So after traveling through Asia, Gary found himself in Sapporo in summer of 2008. He quickly managed to secure an interview at an eikaiwa chain and it wasn't a challenge to get the job. 'They just happened to be holding interviews the day I went in to drop off my résumé. My first day at work, when I went in for training, the head teacher said he had a favor to ask. Several teachers were on strike and I was told I may be needed to teach. I'd never taught English before or ever received any training, but there I was on my first day a strike buster.' After the branch he was at closed in 2009, Gary moved to another regional eikaiwa school. 'At the time they were merging their brand with a national chain and the classes were all getting mixed up. We had thirteen-year-olds in with sixty-five-year-olds: people who had nothing in common and often their levels didn't match. The student records got mixed up all the time, it was Monkeyville.' By the time a couple of years had passed, Gary was somewhat burned out and looking for a change. 'Eikaiwa isn't that bad for a young guy in Japan. We could go out partying all night, get home at eight in the morning. Work doesn't start till twelve or one. You can go snowboarding for three hours before turning up to your "full time" job. No preparation, nothing to think about when you leave the office. It was easy money in that respect.'

Yet Gary also wanted to better connect with his students. 'In eikaiwa they didn't seem serious. You'd get old ladies coming in who just wanted to get away from their husbands, sick of looking after their in-laws. I had one spend a half hour talking about how she makes pickles. People who wanted to come and experience foreigners, without getting to know them. They wanted to be entertained, to see the guy telling the joke or a funny story. I wanted to move away from all that.' Being at ALT paid a little less, but salaries in eikaiwa were dropping by the year anyway. Despite a small pay cut, moving to high schools would also free up evenings and weekends. Gary put in with Interac.

Gary never had his transport money cut, but like the teacher who did, he also had to sign two contracts a year. He recalls he got 60% of his regular salary during the summer break and 70% in winter, but there was no pay for the month of April when the first contract was finished: those who re-signed to start again in May got a small signing bonus of ¥60,000, not something offered to every teacher in every district. But why offer *two* contracts to cover just one school year at all?

Under national laws covering dispatch workers, a dispatched teacher can request employment at the BOE after a year's service, which they are obliged to consider. After three years running with one board, the authority is obliged to offer regular employment to the teacher. Of course dispatchers do what they can to avoid teachers staying in one place that long. In Flynn's words, 'the BOEs and Interac work hand in hand to sack the teachers before they get too demanding. Their contracts end on February 28th then start again March 1[st.] This is a stand-down period to ensure that the contract doesn't roll over. The next contract is a new one, not a continuation. Therefore they could argue that even if a teacher has done three contracts, he hasn't worked three years running.'

Of course this was a little cheeky and the union could easily fire back that three days short of a year was as good as a whole year. A labor court might even agree. It also left open the question of what happened in all the down time, those long school holidays when the teacher was not needed at all. Spreading an eleven-month contract over a whole year was all well and good, but what happened when teachers didn't even work that much? Typically summer holidays run the entire month of August, winter holidays for several weeks over new year, and a short spring break to prepare for exams in late April. BOEs were under pressure to cut costs and dispatchers certainly didn't want to pay foreign teachers to sit around all summer. First Interac simply didn't pay over the summer break, but Japanese law requires that workers are paid at least 60% of their regular monthly salary when on furlough and the union forced Interac to comply. In response, Interac started offering split contracts. One ran from June through July, as the local boards found the students were too busy for English lessons at the start of the semester in April (a low priority it seems), and there were too many days off in May. The second contract started in September and ran until the end of the year.

Together, these effectively ensured the ALT got only eight months' work out of a year and was unemployed in the spring and over the summer. Now for the furlough periods, these teachers, ostensibly employees of Interac, didn't legally have a job at all. This had benefits for everyone but the teachers. Firstly, Interac could save several months of pay and lower the bid (or simply pocket the difference). Secondly, because the dispatch law stipulates that if a yearly contract has a gap of three months or more, the clock gets reset on the countdown to regular employment. Teachers were now on shaky contracts of two months and six months respectively, and would find it hard to claim at any point that they had put in a year's work at the BOE they were assigned to.

Short term contracts are not only used keep the ALT in a weak position when it comes to bargaining, or to shave off holiday pay wherever possible. The flimsiness of both the dispatched worker status and that of the service subcontractor make it easy for schools and dispatchers to chop and change teachers wherever they deem necessary. Flynn adds, 'Schools needn't take any responsibility for the teacher or the quality of the lesson. If they don't like the work, they just call the dispatcher and ask for the teacher to be replaced.' The idea that a school need only complain that the robot they were sent is broken, and they'd like another, has led in some cases to what Flynn calls, 'A game of musical chairs'. If a teacher isn't up to scratch, the dispatcher simply reassigns him to another BOE or school and brings in a teacher from somewhere else. He adds, 'it's hard to terminate a teacher mid contract. They'd basically have to be deemed unfit under labor laws - three days absent without notice, sexual harassment, theft, that sort of thing. In one case, an ALT at OWLS who was still serving a suspended sentence for drug possession in Japan, stole two computers from the school he was assigned. That's what it takes to get fired'. It is also a testament to how thoroughly some dispatchers vet their new hires.

While dispatch companies would probably like to fire more teachers on the spot and wash their hands of any troublemakers – real or perceived – it is much easier simply to non-renew them when their contracts are up. This has happened to several union members. Moreover it can be problematic to change horse mid-race if there aren't enough staff on hand to step in as replacements. The main recruiting season is at the start of the year. In order to win a BOE's contract, the company has to have enough teachers available to show it can meet the requirements outlined in the tender. As discussed later, this can create its own problems, but generally speaking, the agency hires its staff for the year at this time. Big dispatchers like Interac keep roaming substitute teachers in each region, who will be sent to cover whenever a gap opens up. They don't want to keep recruiting people all year.

Another scam, and a potential source of classroom tension, is the gulf between the expectations of the foreign ALT and the host school. The ALT's contract normally states they work 29.5 hours a week - the eikaiwa standard used to avoid paying pensions and health insurance. This is further elaborated by a specific number of teaching hours per day, usually four to six, but well under the eight-hour day a full time Japanese teacher is expected to put in. Breaks are not paid and teachers may have been led to believe their time is their own when not in the classroom.

At the schools however, the teachers and principals expect to get the most out of their ALTs. They have not been told the details of the teacher's individual contract with the dispatcher and often erroneously believe they're dealing with a full time employee. They are also unlikely to be aware of how low an ALT's pay is – sometimes as little as ¥180,000 per month, or half the salary of a typical Japanese teacher. Like their Japanese counterparts, ALTs are often encouraged to join after school club activities with the children such as archery, calligraphy or band practice. They are expected to sit in with a class during lunchtime (curiously this is a duty that Japanese teachers are excused from above sixth grade). They may even be asked to participate in after school cleaning of the classrooms, as the students and teachers all pitch in at a typical Japanese school. They can be expected to remain at the school for the full eight hour day, even though they have long breaks between classes.

When it came to the classroom, Gary found this disparity created mixed results. 'Since we were on "service subcontractor" contracts we were officially quite limited in what we could do. Some schools or teachers were aware of this, others weren't. Some wanted to use us to the best possible benefit to the students, others just wanted us to stick to the script so they could keep control of their classroom.' There was no real formula or standard procedure because Interac's main goal was to please the school or the BOE and make them think they'd gotten the right teacher based on their requirements. These varied from assignment to assignment. 'How well you performed in the classroom depended a lot on how much they elected to use you. The school was the customer; not the students.'

Students could be a mixed bag too. Gary worked mostly junior high school where, 'First graders weren't sick of it yet; second graders were lazy, just cruising, going through puberty; third grade had to study harder. They had to meet attendance requirements in order to appeal to good high schools. They had to sit their exams though, so had less interest in English as a language.'

Though he had to be at the school at least seven hours a day, Gary was only paid based on the number of hours he had to teach. Sometimes just two or three lessons a day. There was no question of challenging this alleged part time status. 'Non renewal was used as a tool. They had a never-ending supply of fresh graduates so it was easy to let a troublemaker go at the end of the contract.' In addition, Interac teachers were made to sign a clause in the contract stipulating they would not seek employment with the same BOE they had been dispatched to for at least two years, another tactic of questionable legality. 'There was no way to enforce such a rule; it was just intimidation – exploiting our lack of awareness.'

Flynn explains, 'Interac has it as a standard condition. They could sue for damages if the teacher tried to break the rule, but the settlement wouldn't be significant. Mostly, it's there to intimidate them.' In 2005, the MOE directed local boards to hire ALTs directly, but Interac still muscles its ALTs into signing off on their temporary status.

The General Union has also accused Dispatch of duping teachers into signing resignation papers when they were no longer needed. In Japan most workers pay into the unemployment insurance scheme, and are eligible for some kind of unemployment benefit - usually three to six months at 80% of the previous salary - should they be laid off, fired or simply non-renewed. By strong-arming teachers into signing resignation papers where no job existed anyway, Interac eliminates their chances of collecting a benefit and denied them crucial government protection while they search for a new job.[9] It also likely masked the fact that the company had hired people it could not employ, as resignations look a lot better on paper than layoffs.

In yet another source of tension, Interac teachers were asked to block some holidays as standby days. On these they could be called up in an 'emergency'. Interac supervisors would call the ALTs up and if they had made other plans or couldn't get into the office they had their pay docked. The practice was suspected to be a cost-cutting measure: even if the teachers were not needed the company could save a few bucks by making a phone call.

When teachers did go into the regional office during holidays, it was usually for several wasteful meetings and so-called training seminars per year. 'Once a year they just gave us a forty-five minute lecture on drug and alcohol abuse. It was like being in high school. Another time we were all asked to take drug tests. They took saliva swabs from everyone. They weren't really serious about it, they just wanted to show BOEs that the "dirty gaijin" weren't using. The test kits they used were these cheap ones you could buy over the internet. It was amateur hour.'

As with Nova of course, it was only the foreign staff who were tested. One could argue that it is doubly important for teachers working public schools to be drug-free. But while all teachers - ALTs and Japanese – are supposed to be tested for communicable diseases such as TB, Japanese public school teachers are not forced to take drug tests. Private companies such as Interac are not legally allowed to force workers to take drug tests at all. Refusal however, at least on an individual basis, would lead to dismissal one way or another. The Tokyo General Union branch of Interac has taken up this issue in the past. In an open letter demanding emergency collective bargaining on the matter in 2012, the union stated:

> The need for drug testing is not accepted for an ordinary employment relationship and drug testing of employees in general is accepted only in extreme circumstances. We strongly oppose your casual testing of employees also in light of recent requirements to protect individual privacy, including the passage of Individual Information Law.[10]

As with ECC and its 'bicycle ban', transportation rules have raised a few hackles among dispatch teachers as well. A typical day was at least seven hours, according to Gary. 'I had to be there from 8:30 to 3:30, though I was technically only paid for four or five hours teaching. In many cases it took over an hour to get there. They had a policy that no teachers were allowed to drive to work, but there were ways around it. My supervisor told me where to get free parking at a store near the school. If I went in my own car it took thirty minutes. If I took public transport that was ninety minutes by subway and bus.'

In many cases companies fear liability if a teacher is injured or has an accident en route to work. One eikaiwa teacher in Sapporo was instructed to take two modes of public transport to a kindergarten after having a minor car accident: the trip increased from about twenty minutes by car to over an hour by subway and bus. There is no law that allows companies to *insist* on the transportation methods used to get to and from work; it is another area in which the lack of bargaining power among foreign staff is widely exploited.

Gary continued to drive to work whenever the school assignment was in a distant suburb on the edge of town. 'At one place I used to park at a supermarket a few minutes down the road from the school. I took care when returning to the car that no students saw me. Once or twice when I arrived at the car park some of the kids from school passed through it. I pretended to be ducking into the store for something or other till they'd left.' It was unlikely that the students would mention it to their teachers. It was also not likely the teachers knew Interac's transport policy or if they did, would bother reporting Gary. But it is illustrative not only of the discrimination that pervades the industry - schoolteachers can drive to work and use the school car park but foreign ALTs cannot – but it also demonstrates the common fear in eikaiwa and dispatch of being 'dobbed in'. Many teachers have reported the feeling that everyone is watching, just waiting for a chance to pounce. Gary laments, 'it grated on you as a human.'

Perhaps none of the schedule or transportation requirements could be termed asking *too much*, but when an ALT pops down the street to buy lunch, or kill time at a cafe between lessons, his Japanese colleagues or the school principal may perceive this as laziness or disinterest. They don't realize that the ALT is off the clock at these times. In most cases, the ALT sucks it up and does the school's bidding for the sake of harmony, knowing that trouble with the dispatcher is only a phone call away. Teachers sent to country schools may have nowhere to go between lessons in any case. So in effect the teachers end up on duty for well over thirty hours a week. However since they are not actually in the classroom, they're not paid by the dispatchers for every hour they are at work.

When asked if a teacher had ever challenged the practice, such as saying that no, they were off duty and could go home early or take their breaks as they saw fit, Flynn gives one example. 'One Interac ALT found on the union website that he didn't have to work during breaks and when other duties came up, he told the school that contractually he was not obligated to carry them out because it was unpaid overtime. Of course the school complained to the company and he was sequestered to the office. Rather than explain it to the school or getting into a fight with the union over unfair dismissal, they opted to pay the teacher to stay home.'

A Fukuoka teacher was removed from his assigned school at the principal's request, and found out just how far Interac is able to push the envelope when a teacher pushes back with union help. The ALT wasn't getting along too well with the Japanese teacher: whether it was a personality clash or a professional disagreement, he certainly had not faced any specific complaints about his performance. After hearing from the school, Interac pulled him out and told him to stay home until they found him other work. He went to the union when he found out they were not going to pay him while he was off duty. Flynn elaborates, 'the teacher was on salary, and there was nothing in the contract about not paying him just because he wasn't teaching lessons. The company hadn't fired him – they'd have to pay him out if they did that. Since he was still officially employed, we got involved.'

When challenged on the details of the teacher's reassignment, Interac could offer no specifics. There weren't any. The customer was simply not satisfied with the 'product'. When asked how the teacher's work was assessed as 'substandard', Interac replied that was the opinion of the Japanese teacher at the school. 'We reminded them that under the subcontracting law, the teachers could not in fact evaluate the ALT. They claimed then they felt he could not complete the service, in their words. However there was no memo, no record of a disciplinary procedure, no talk of retraining, just an automatic reassignment of the teacher. They were still even sending him out to substitute for other teachers at other schools, so Interac had clearly not deemed him unfit to teach.'

The teacher was given work to do in the office for a time, but then everyone else just sort of forgot about him. He ended up sitting out his contract, and still getting paid, for the final six months: perhaps the dream of many an ALT or eikaiwa teacher fed up with the long hours and small rewards. Without union help, he could just as well have been fired or sent home with no pay, neither of which would have been legal. Flynn adds, 'often they come to us when it's too late, and they've already got the sack. Apathy makes recruitment hard among current teachers.'

Having a child can be just as bad for your career at Interac as losing one. One foreign teacher was non-renewed when she became pregnant, and Interac realized the birth would fall in the middle of the school year. This was despite a sterling record at the schools where she had taught, and more importantly, despite a raft of Japanese labor laws that ban the practice of firing women just because they're mothers-to-be. Once the union got involved, the ALT was granted a generous settlement, though she was unable to get her job back because a replacement had already been hired.[11] There were no repercussions from the regional board of education, nor was there any censure of the company from the labor or education ministries.

The union argues that ALT dispatch contracts are incompatible with education laws and regulations, hence illegal. The education ministry has instructed boards of education not to use dispatched teachers and instead to hire their own teachers directly or through the JET program. The union has known of this since at least 2005, when it challenged Interac on the practice.[12] Eight years on, no changes have been made on the ground. Indeed, the number of dispatch ALTs nationwide has ballooned, the number of direct hires has dwindled, and the contracts and pay for ALTs has become less and less competitive.

In the next scam, dispatchers such as Interac shift company tax and insurance burdens onto the employee. The magic figure of 29.5 hours a week is used to dodge the legal responsibility employers in Japan have to enroll staff in the national pension and social insurance schemes and match their contributions. According to the Tokyo General Union however, even 29.5 hours is not necessarily an upper limit, and that an employee can be enrolled no matter how few hours he or she works.

The union has sought clarification from the labor ministry and 30 hours is reckoned as ¾ of a full time, 40-hour week. But it is only an internal administrative guideline that the ministry uses to determine who to crack down on (the same way that a police officer might not pull over some one for going a couple of miles over the speed limit but will definitely pull someone over for going 10 miles over). There is actually no specific number under which a worker would be disqualified from coverage, because there is no minimum requirement for a worker to join.¹³ Dispatch services and the eikaiwa industry have simply seized on this benchmark as an excuse to cut costs, rather like a motorist will slow down only where he knows there is a speed trap.

To 'compensate' for the lack of public health insurance, Interac has offered teachers the choice of joining its own private insurance scheme. The sales pitch is insidious. New hires are told they can join the *shakai hokken* or social insurance at a cost of about ¥30,000 a month, the more limited *kokumin kenko hokke*n or public health insurance at about 10% of their salary or ¥20,000 a month, or they can take the private health insurance plan with InterGlobal for a mere five to seven thousand. Most don't expect to fall ill or spend long in Japan and they choose the cheapest option. Furthermore Interac even asks teachers to sign a disclaimer, stating they will be responsible for their own healthcare, a document of questionable validity under Japanese laws, in light of the fact that every employee is supposed to be enrolled.¹⁴ Flynn elaborates, 'What they don't tell you is that they'll be obligated to pay half if you join the social insurance, and that both the social insurance and public health insurance pay 70% of medical costs, even for pre-existing conditions, something private insurers do not cover.' And if the private plan provider InterGlobal sounds a lot like Interac, the similarity is not lost on the union. Insurance premiums are directly debited from the teachers' pay, 'making us suspect there was a business relationship and that there was some skimming.'

Yet under Japanese law, workers *must be* enrolled one or another of the national schemes. Private plans are for the self-employed or those who need additional coverage. In 2009, the immigration authorities began to insist that foreign workers seeking visa renewal be enrolled in the public health plan. The problem for teachers is that under the law, a foreign worker must be enrolled from when he starts working in Japan. Flynn points out that, 'most teachers had never been enrolled. To get into the system they'd be obligated to back-pay up to several years of missed premiums, depending how long they'd been in Japan.'

Because of the cost - roughly ten percent of a worker's monthly salary, calculated from the tax year before - many foreigners in Japan forgo the public health insurance. They do so at their peril, but some rely on traveler's insurance or agencies offered up by the likes of Interac or Nova that provide limited private plans. With income tax at about ten percent, resident's tax at five, many young, fit English teachers would be loath to give up another ten percent for insurance they may never need. And, as the rates are calculated on the previous year's income, the two thirds of all English teachers who work part time might find themselves paying out *more than* ten percent of their current income when a lean year follows a good one, or when an employer cuts their pay.

As in the West, private insurance offers less coverage. There is no help for pre-existing conditions. Sports injuries are often not included. Patients must pay the cost up front at the hospital then claim from the insurance company, which may or may not pay out after reviewing the case. Under either of the national health plans, the government pays 70% of health related costs up front, without question and pre-existing conditions are included. The patient is charged 30% at the doctor and the rest of the bill is charged to the government via their insurance cards. It couldn't be much easier and for struggling English teachers who suddenly come down with food poisoning, or crack a rib in a skiing accident, and would be a welcome safety net, especially if their employers fronted half the premiums. Many Japanese companies, including eikaiwas and dispatchers, do this for their Japanese staff.

But for foreigners, the burden of local and national taxes, public insurance and pension plans can be crippling. With a below average salary to begin with nobody wants to see a full quarter go to the government. The notion that they'd have to back-pay a year or two threatened many teachers with bankruptcy. Few English teachers have several thousand dollars sitting around, much less several thousand they'd be willing to give back to Japan after struggling so hard to squeeze even that much in savings out of the place. When fears were high in the eikaiwa community in 2009, many teachers were ready to simply leave the country if the government decided to come knocking. That would be the point where the salary earned simply no longer justified the cost of living in Japan. Cutting and running would for many teachers be the best decision for their long term financial futures.

To warn its teachers about the potential changes, Interac issued a letter, encouraging foreign staff to enroll in public health insurance on their own. It estimated the cost would be as much as ￥20,000 a month for some. Naturally the company was in no position to assist because, 'for most of you, as your working hours are limited to 29.5 hours per week, *shakai hokken* is not applicable...If you were to find yourself in the situation of having to make back payments it is normally possible to discuss a monthly repayment schedule that is affordable for you with the city office.'[15] While Interac offered an email and phone number that teachers could use to seek advice, the message was clear: you're on your own.

Even having private insurance does not necessarily save teachers money if the authorities decide to crack down. Flynn outlines the case of one English teacher who got a bill for health insurance backdated two years, which had been the current length of his stay. 'When he didn't pay it he had money seized from his bank account. After cleaning out his bank account, the city then went on to seize his salary. Nothing happened to the company.' All this while the teacher thought he was covered under the company's private plan. Flynn estimates Interac saves up to $250 per teacher per month by avoiding health coverage.

Not content to merely dodge health insurance and pension costs, or to make money off staff by peddling its own private insurance, Interac has also been accused of costing its ALTs more in taxes. For teachers listed as contractors, the company is obliged to pay a 5% consumption tax, as the teacher is technically a small business earning less than ¥10 Million per year. Though an added cost, it is a lot cheaper than matching social insurance and pension payments. In effect this means that ALTs are double taxed. They pay income tax from their salary and consumption tax is taken out on top of that. The costs are slated to rise: the conservative government under Prime Minister Shinzo Abe announced plans in 2013 to raise the consumption tax to 8% in 2014 and 10% a year or two later. This could mean that by 2016 the average ALT will not only make less money than the average Japanese teacher, but will be taxed twice as hard.

Perhaps the greatest scam of all is the existence of dispatch jobs at all. In most districts there are several dispatch companies vying for the education board contract every year. Each spring the BOEs put out the tender for their ALT contracts and Interac must dive into the mosh pit and elbow out some space. There are other players: WING, Borderlink,

OWLS and Maxceed, which is a sister-company of Interac's under the same parent and offers competing bids for the same contracts, ensuring a better chance one of them will get it.[16] In each district board there can be only one winner.

Competition raises the standards, but it also encourages dirty tricks. Not only do some companies bid under two names, like Maxceed/Interac, but they must demonstrate, among other conditions, that they have the requisite number of teachers before they get the contract. This leads to dispatchers promising work to potentially hundreds of new foreign instructors before they know if they even have the work to offer in the first place. Gary shudders, 'every spring you're waiting on tenterhooks. You don't know if you've still got your job till two or three weeks before the semester starts.'

This instability led to institutional problems in the way the dispatcher delivered its services. 'Because the tenders are only for a year, there are no long-term structural improvements,' Gary says. 'The company isn't thinking of how it can improve English education in general, how it can best use its teachers or how to create a valuable service that the schools will keep coming back to. They're only thinking about how to get the contract for one more year.' That of course meant bidding lower and offering more teachers than the competition. It was quantity over quality – all about putting as many foreigners in the classrooms as cheaply as they could.

The schedule is tight. BOEs usually make a public call for tender in early February. By this time the dispatchers are already hiring furiously or have selected their candidates. The deadline for a proposal submission is early March, by which time the dispatcher must have 'hired' enough candidates because the proposal needs to demonstrate to a

BOE that the candidate has enough teachers to fill the job. Some BOEs require as much as 20-30 ALTs each year to cover all their district schools. As little as a week later – and a week or so before the school year begins in April - the bids are closed, and the successful candidates are asked to submit a quote. A few days later the winner is chosen. The lowest bidder usually wins. Not only does Interac double bid under the Maxceed name, but dispatch companies are allowed to submit multiple quotes. Flynn found that, 'They're not told how much or how little the education board will pay, or what the competition has offered, but they're allowed to keep cutting the price till they hit the right number.'

This leads to two problems: as in the case of the teacher who had his transport money cut, new hires may find their actual salary lower than what was promised. If the price remains open to negotiation they may also see further cuts after the summer holidays. More glaringly, what happens to all those ALTs who were hired by the dispatcher in order to get the contract, when the contract is awarded to someone else? Also, what happens to teachers already working at one BOE when their dispatcher loses the contract for the coming year?

Another New Zealander, Matt, found out the hard way. He worked for Heart Inc, a dispatcher that had held the Sapporo Board of Education contract for a year. Naturally the bid was low: the salary was only around ¥220,000 per month, before tax, and there was of course no pension or public health coverage. Furthermore, he had to cover his own transport costs which could run as high as ¥20,000 per month – Sapporo is a spread out city with far flung suburbs that can only be reached by bus or JR train. He estimates that on payday he only netted about ¥180,000 per month.

Yet at the close of the school year in early 2009, Matt suddenly found himself out of a job. Heart had lost the bid to Interac and he only found out a week before the new term. Dozens of teachers in fact were now unemployed, covering schools all over the city. Ironically, Heart had toppled Interac the year before because it had undercut the bid, leaving Interac's crop at the time without jobs that April. Yet in order to sell themselves so cheaply Heart had cut teacher pay so much that it simply couldn't keep them. Teachers were leaving in the middle of the semester and everyone was running around trying to cover each other. The BOE retreated to the relative security of Interac. In Osaka, the education board has given up on dispatchers altogether and gone back to hiring direct.

Laying off workers comes with responsibilities. According to page 40, 'Barring disaster a company may not dismiss workers without giving 30 days' notice.'[17] Yet every year dispatchers do just that as a matter of procedure, announcing just before the start of the semester that there are no jobs available and contracts will not be renewed. According to the Tokyo General Union's Interac web page, the dispatcher simply forces teachers to resign just before contract renewal. This not only washes the company's hands of the problem, but denies the employee a chance to collect on national unemployment insurance, which for many is deducted automatically from their paychecks each month. Dispatchers, like eikaiwa schools exploit foreigners' lack of knowledge to undermine their responsibilities under Japanese labor laws.[18]

Interac also dodges responsibility by offering the job, but not the contract. Teachers only receive their contract after a successful bid by the dispatcher. This opens the door to further chicanery. Between being chosen for the job and receiving the contract, all manner of changes might have taken place between the dispatcher and the BOE without the new teacher's knowledge. The transport allowance could have been reduced or waived; the overall price of the winning bid could have been cut, causing the dispatcher to pass that loss onto the staff with a reduction spread out over all the contracts. Teachers may find that while they were told they'd be paid for five hours of lessons per day, the schedule has been reduced to four, but they'll still be stuck at school all day. In the end they could find themselves suddenly asked to resign because the dispatcher has lost the contract altogether.

According to Flynn, ALTs are the only teachers hired by tender. This cattle auction for foreigners serves to underscore their low value. As long as a dispatcher can supply the requisite number of ALTs on paper when it makes the bid, any foreigners will do. The French fries at one chain after all, taste much the same as those at another. 'We challenged the Fukuoka BOE, and asked them why they put only the role of assistant English teachers up for tender, and not that of other assistant teachers. They replied that ALT contracts were not the only contracts public school boards secured by tender. The security guards and the cleaners were also selected that way.'

Gary muses, 'If the dispatchers offered a good, professional service, it would be more palatable. But they're just in for the money and it shows. Their indifference rubs off on the teachers and quality drops as a result. Dispatch ALTs will never be great for the students because the dispatchers and the BOEs only have budgets in mind. The board is the client, not the learners.' Gary didn't have a terrible experience overall as an ALT, but when he saw a better opportunity career-wise he grabbed it:

a friend worked at a private junior high school in the city. The friend was leaving mid-semester due to family reasons and so he was asked to suggest his own replacement.

But leaving a dispatcher carries its own risks. The Japan times reported a case in early 2008 of a teacher who had fought to get her unpaid holidays from Interac the previous November. Forced to take two weeks off due to illness, the company informed her that she had to use up her allotted seven days of annual leave to cover the days she was sick.[19] Yet the law requires workers are given ten days, not seven, with an additional day for every year in service. This teacher was entitled to twelve. Nowhere does it state that annual leave days *must* be used for sick-calls either: this is fairly common practice in Japanese companies, but it is not the letter of the law.

Because of widespread knowledge of cases like these, Gary followed the lead of other teachers and sought union advice when it was his turn to resign. Though Gary was not a member, the General Union in Osaka was happy to let him know what his rights were. 'The Hokkaido office never mentioned unused leave. Basically I told them that I had a record of how many unused days were still owed to me and that the General Union told me I was entitled to have these paid out to me when I left.' Whether due to the threat of union attention or because the Hokkaido office was in the habit of playing straight with teachers when they left, Gary got his paid leave in the end, added to his notice period so that he could shorten the time before leaving.

He lasted about eight months at the new job and when his contract came up for renewal the school began casting about for a new teacher. 'I hadn't performed badly, but I had only ever been a stop-gap teacher and they could afford to be picky and what they really wanted was a qualified schoolteacher. They found a better-qualified candidate and let me go at the end of the school year.' Gary is freelancing now. He teaches at several companies and small schools and keeps his weekends relatively free. He expects to stay in Japan for another five years or so and may get a master's degree for a high school or university job. He can't imagine returning to eikaiwa or dispatch. 'For people who want to have a laugh right out of university it's good,' he says. 'You get set up and accommodation assistance with a lot of them. You get a lot of free time and you can experience a new country. But it's not forever and just don't expect high standards.'

One cool October morning in 2011 in Sendai, Miyagi prefecture, a lone union representative stood outside an Interac training venue handing out flyers to trainees as they arrived. The leaflet explained that health and pension benefits, paid vacation time and protection from summary dismissal are all mandatory under the law, and urged the future ALTs to know their rights. When Interac staff came out and asked him to leave, the union rep politely explained that he was breaking no laws by handing out flyers in a public space. Interac then called the police. Upon arrival, officers agreed the rep was within his rights and explained they were unable to interfere. The company resorted to springing for pizza to keep the trainees indoors during lunch. Many still received the flyers when they left in the evening. Some of those staff may later have joined the union to fight for their legal rights as employees.

It would be wise to. BOEs and dispatchers are both well aware of an ALT's rights under the law. Many tricks have been used in the past to hide these rights, from simply keeping mum on employer obligations to active disinformation and discouragement. Employers have also been dogged by the unions for several years and, as mentioned, have even received bad press even in the Japanese language media: the *Nihon Terebi* story gave a layman's breakdown of the different contracts and offered a comparison between the job satisfaction enjoyed by a direct-hire ALT and the financial and contractual hardships endured by teachers under dispatch and service contracts.

But rather than embrace their legal responsibilities, dispatchers and education boards continue to circumvent the law and hobble teachers' job security to this day. In a recent development, the government changed the *Shakai Hokken* law effective October 2016. From that date onward, all companies with more than 500 employees will be obliged to enroll those who work more than twenty hours a week into the public health and pension schemes. This should be a major coup for teachers working for large eikaiwa chains and dispatchers as practically all of them are working at least that much, even when only classroom hours are counted..

Always one step ahead, Interac has already made moves to avoid this obligation. In late 2015 the company announced it would split into at least half a dozen 'subsidiaries' to cover different regions and 'position ourselves to manage growth in the market'.[20] This will ensure that Interac's more than 3,000 employees, most of whom are ALTs, are working for smaller companies that do not meet the threshold requirements. The law will not affect smaller firms for the foreseeable future: these are slated to comply at an unspecified date, so for the time being Interac will be able to dodge that bullet – one that would have markedly improved the working conditions of its core staff. The house wins again.

11 How Does Eikaiwa get away with it?

The Tokyo Metropolitan Government's Labor Consultation Office has issued a handbook in English with legal advice for foreign workers. It is freely available on the internet in PDF form.[1] The Foreign Worker Guidebook draws directly from labor laws and regulations to explain the rights of workers in Japan, just in case their employers haven't told them. In the case of eikaiwa schools and dispatchers, they usually haven't. Flicking through the chapters it is hard to find labor regulations that have not been routinely violated by Big Eikaiwa.

The first principle of the guidebook is that, 'Japanese laws concerning labor apply to all employees in Japan, regardless of nationality.' On its website, the General Union in Fukuoka has identified instances of employers telling their staff that the rules do not apply to foreign workers. This is not true. Article 3 of the Labor Standards law stipulates that, 'The employer shall not engage in discriminatory treatment with respect to wages, working hours or other working conditions.' Major English schools do so nevertheless. Savvy organizations such as Gaba and more recently Nova and Interac, reduce their teachers to *itaku*, or 'subcontractor' status to avoid their responsibilities as employers. Smaller schools simply cut straight to the 'avoiding responsibilities' part.

The chapter on labor contracts also informs readers that working conditions must be stated clearly. At many schools there is no concrete list of do's and don'ts for the teachers, giving the company a free hand to discipline or dismiss teachers over any indiscretion or complaint, real or perceived. 'Matters pertaining to separation (including reasons for dismissal)' must be clearly outlined. Nor can an employee be 'fined' by the company for any offense, unless it has directly caused a loss to the company. Yet Gaba reduces bonuses for subjective 'negative evaluations'. Nova penalizes teachers financially for even a single sick day. Other schools have been known to write in penalties for tardiness or breaking rules in the classroom. While Article 91 does allow that companies may 'Decrease wages as a sanction or in order to maintain discipline,' having loose shoelaces or neckties, taking a sip of water or pushing up one's glasses during class time stretches the definition of a breach of discipline. Those who challenge such practices without union help are risk being dismissed or non-renewed.

The guide warns that companies must offer a guarantee of wages and minimum wages. According to Article 26, employers must pay an allowance *at least* equal to 60% of the employee's average wage in the event of a suspension of business attributable to the employer. In the case of ALT dispatcher Interac, this depends on the value of Interac's contract with the board of education. Some teachers do get reduced wages over the summer and winter holidays. Others however are reduced to two *itaku* contracts per year that neatly avoid the holidays leaving them effectively unemployed in those periods. Bruce noted that Nova pushed several contracts on him in the space of a year, all before his previous one had expired. Each new 'offer' reduced pay and benefits further than the last. In the latest iteration, teachers *must now pay the school* for the privilege of using the classroom (chapter two).

Though Article 27 makes allowance for companies to offer piece work or subcontracting work at fixed hourly rates, many eikaiwa schools and dispatchers promise hours and schedules that never materialize or insist on teachers putting in many hours of unpaid work. Aeon has been taken to task over unpaid overtime. Berlitz is still in a struggle with the union over the so-called breaks between lessons. Teachers from one end of Japan to the other have complained of having to write reports and lesson plans for many unpaid hours each semester. Article 25 states that 'In the event an employee requests the payment of wages to cover emergency expenses for illness or accident...an employer should pay accrued wages prior to the normal pay day.' More often, schools threaten and intimidate teachers against taking time off to deal with medical emergencies.

Overtime is sometimes paid, but as in the case of Aeon, it usually takes a spat with the union to wring it out of an employer. Even those teachers lucky enough to be salaried employees are usually listed as working below thirty hours a week to avoid the national health and pension obligations a company would face above that threshold. Yet in reality this means the downtime between lessons that is used for filing class reports and notes, or the overtime after closing, is not counted as 'work'. By narrowly defining the teacher's work as classroom time only and disregarding the many hours a week of preparation time and report-writing required, eikaiwa schools avoid paying overtime. Article 36 of the law stipulates that employers must pay workers a premium of 35% overtime for working public holidays and conclude a written agreement to work on a holiday beforehand. Few English schools have ever done this, though almost all the big brands are open on public holidays. Gaba avoids this because the teachers are 'small businesses' rather than 'employees'. They are strong-armed into working on these holidays as independent contractors at the same flat rate for every lesson, regardless of the day.

Under Article 39, 'An employer shall grant annual paid leave of 10 working days to an employee who has been employed continuously for six months', but again the definition of employee appears to be subjective. By insisting its teachers are subcontractors, Gaba avoids the commitment to offer annual leave, even though its teachers are some of the hardest-working in the business. Dispatchers such as Interac make sure their teachers have unpaid breaks by writing the school holidays out of the contract altogether. Other schools, especially smaller regional ones, simply tell their native teachers the rules are 'different' for foreigners.

Leave must be given for child care, maternity, or to care for a sick relative (Articles 2, 9, 11, 15), but it doesn't have to be paid. Yet paid or not, all workers are entitled to it. ECC's Japanese employees are generously allowed to take paid time off for a death in the family; foreign staff are still unpaid. Interac has non-renewed teachers for even *expected* absences during pregnancy or even the death of a newborn.* At Gaba teachers are pressured and punished by their supervisors for taking time off for their own illnesses, even though as 'subcontractors' they are not entitled to paid sick days and should in theory be in charge of their own schedules.

Employers must follow certain procedures in the event of a dismissal or resignation (Article 628 of the Civil Law Code), but it is often the case that English teachers are dismissed arbitrarily and without proper notice. Some employers impose a fine in the contract for resigning before expiry (invalid under Article 16), but reserve the 'right' to dismiss employees immediately if they see fit. English schools and dispatchers have

---
* See Chapter 10; Michael Collison case.

removed teachers for pregnancy or illness, whether they had to take time off or not. Teachers are also routinely dismissed without notice or a payout, when their contracts are not renewed. Many teachers working for smaller schools do not even have formal written labor contracts to begin with, or their contracts are in Japanese and the conditions are vague.[2]

The guidebook notes the labor ministry's requirement that employers must give 30 days' notice when dismissing an employee. Furthermore employees have the right to demand a letter or certification that clearly states the reasons for dismissal. Gaba and others keep teachers on short contracts of four to six months that can be arbitrarily non-renewed. Dispatchers such as Interac often do not know themselves until only two weeks before the start of a school year whether they will need to keep their teachers on or non-renew them. Interac has been accused by the union of forcing teachers to 'resign' when it has lost out on a contract, avoiding the responsibility to pay them out in lieu of thirty days' notice.

As far as Article 7 of the Labor Union Law is concerned, 'An employer shall not refuse to bargain collectively'. Yet, when the time came to negotiate, at Gaba, at Berlitz and a raft of smaller schools, the company's first response was to ignore the union's grievances altogether. Nor under the same law, can an employer attempt to 'control or interfere with the formation or management of a labor union by employees.' During the Berlitz and Peppy Kids Club strikes, company staff called teachers intimidating them for information or threatening them with discipline.

The law is also very clear on a company's responsibility regarding union-busting, as well as restrictions on punishing workers who speak out. Article 104 of the Labor Standards Law insists a worker cannot be dismissed for reporting an employer to any relevant supervisory agency.

Article 7 of the Labor Union Act protects workers against dismissal due to union membership or activities. Article 3 of the Whistle-Blower Protection Act does just what it says - protects whistle blowers. Yet most of the major chains such as Gaba, Berlitz, even Peppy Kids Club, have been taken to court for firing or non-renewing union representatives. Article 16 of the Labor Contract Act states a dismissal will be treated as an abuse of power and invalid, 'if it lacks objectively reasonable grounds and is not considered appropriate in general societal terms.' Big Eikaiwa has its own interpretation of 'appropriate'.

The guide has also identified the national health insurance and employee pension schemes as an area where foreign workers are woefully unprotected. Page 72 points out that the responsibility to enroll staff applies to all companies with more than five employees and that those employees must work at least three quarters of a full time schedule. This definition almost certainly applies to the vast majority of eikaiwa teachers at major schools and dispatchers. Yet pointedly most teachers do *not* have company support in the national health and pension arrangements. Some employers such as Nova and Interac attempt to get around this by enrolling staff in private health insurance. The rest simply write their teachers off as 'part timers'.

The first chapter of the handbook states that a contract violating Labor Standards Law is invalid. If any of the conditions, demands or omissions in the contract contravene the law, the contract is illegal and cannot be enforced. Most teachers in eikaiwa and dispatch are laboring under such contracts, but are either unaware or feel powerless to challenge their second-class status. Moreover companies that know full well their contracts are illegal also know that the teachers have little recourse to challenge them: if the entire contract is invalid then either party is free to break it. This can often work in favor of unscrupulous employers, reducing it to a mere talking point for the disadvantaged English teacher. Michael contends that, 'eikaiwa schools are like neighborhood bullies. When the boss cuts your wages, or reduces your paid leave and you complain, he can just say, "what are you gonna do about it?" In most cases, the teacher backs down.'

Every year thousands of young English speakers fly to Asia in search of an adventure, financed by work as English teachers. They come from Australia, New Zealand, the US, Canada and more. But it can be risky leaping into another country on the promise of an 'easy' job. In Japan's competitive English teaching market, foreign language instructors are on shaky ground. Subcontracting teachers at corporate giant Gaba fight in the courts for recognition as employees. Berlitz and ECC instructors have become embroiled in near-decade long industrial disputes, complete with strikes and legal action. ALTs contracted by dispatch agencies arrive to find the salary they'll receive was less than promised and that they may not be paid at all during school holidays. Schools across the country have slashed benefits and reduced wages, forcing teachers to work longer hours, split shifts and multiple jobs just to make ends meet.

With a monthly take-home income now nudging as low as 200,000 yen ($1,800) a month, many part time English teachers make about half the education sector average ($4,000) and a little over half of the average for a regular schoolteacher ($3,500). Even a salaried position in Big Eikaiwa pays far less than being a janitor (average $3,000), an office clerk ($2,700) and is barely on par with a starting car mechanic ($2,100).

With unpaid furlough and other deductions factored in, a part time teacher or dispatch ALT can earn roughly the same as a taxi driver (192,000 yen) or even a supermarket cashier (168,000 yen).[3] Service wages for the service sector. Just don't forget to smile.

Big chains such as Aeon, Gaba and ECC send recruiters to Australasia, North America and the UK and lure fresh graduates with slick websites and flashy recruiting videos. New hires come expecting to have weekends and vacations full of temples, shrines and exotic locales. Newcomers may also be tempted by the prospect of utilizing that TESOL certificate they've worked hard for. Yet from the start, they'll be effectively front counter staff, delivering a standardized product. In some schools, such as Aeon, teachers are even expected to act as salespeople, promoting self-study materials and CDs. Recruiting campaigns take good advantage of the prospective teacher's altruistic angels. They look for suckers.

Once the work starts, eikaiwa keeps teachers busy and broke. At considerably less than the average Japanese salary, most English schools pay teachers just enough to get by in Japan and not much more. The recruiting videos do not mention that they'll have barely ten paid holidays off per year, if they're lucky, and find themselves trudging into the language center on public holidays and at Christmas. Nor do eikaiwa schools warn the cost of living and the expense of domestic travel in Japan will stretch a teacher's salary. Many can barely afford a trip home once a year, time permitting. If a teacher stays for a couple of years as most do, they can afford a ticket home and again, not much more. Gone are the good old days of the bubble years when foreigners would teach for two or three years and return home with a deposit for a house or funds to buy a new car in cash. When industry leader Nova collapsed in

2007, thousands of foreign teachers were stranded penniless in Japan. Australian nationals were reduced to accepting the charity of heavily discounted flights home from their national airline.

Teachers can also be locked into apartment contracts that make leaving the company difficult or expensive. Nova teachers living in company sponsored apartments found themselves facing eviction when the troubled chain stopped paying its bills, even though teachers had their pay docked for rent; Aeon teachers have been warned by the company that if they move out of their company flat, they still have to pay the rent for the duration of the contract. The work schedule keeps teachers too busy to get many private students and many contracts insist on exclusivity, making it problematic to get outside work through private teacher matchmaking agencies. While Japanese law allows teachers to work elsewhere, it is also perfectly legal for schools to draft contracts that forbid it, making it easy for them to fire teachers for breaking the rules, or at least pressure them into toeing the line.

Big Eikaiwa limits the teacher's professional scope as well. In a traditional Japanese company skills are rarely transferable because the Japanese view company loyalty in an almost feudal sense, hence the term 'corporate samurai'. A former Toyota manager is rarely welcome at Mitsubishi because whatever corporate conditioning he's had, regardless of the similarities, is tainted by the competition's way of doing things. The same applies to an ECC teacher looking to move to Berlitz or Aeon. It is sometimes possible but frowned upon. A teacher might as well be a divorcée, trying to land a date while they're considered damaged goods: Stan ran into trouble at Aeon, where he felt his prior experience was a hindrance. Even when possible, moving from one big chain to another is usually just a step sideways; moving to a smaller school usually means even lower pay.

Gaining experience in Big Eikaiwa also limits development when teachers do move out of the rigid corporate environment. Often a teacher indoctrinated in corporate methodology finds it hard to adjust to a more parochial setting. Yet the drop in income may be offset by a reduction in stress: James recalls a former Aeon teacher who came to work at his school. 'He asked if it was alright to sit during a lesson. At Aeon he had to wear a jacket and tie and stand the whole time. It's no wonder they'll take a pay cut just to be treated as human beings again.'

The foreign owned Tokyo chain Dean Morgan Associates once had 850 applicants for only six positions when it advertised for new teachers. There are unlikely to be 850 unemployed English instructors at one any time even in a big city like Tokyo, and the money is about average, yet still hundreds of people applied. For teachers lining up to escape bonded servitude under Japanese management, a foreign-run language school looks like the last helicopter off the embassy roof. However even a foreign-run school can be as bad as the rest, as in the case of a teacher of over twenty years at Tokyo school ICC, who was non-renewed in early 2014 when he asked for his paid holidays.[4]

Owning your own school is an expensive and risky ticket out of eikaiwa drudgery, but may be the only way to make any meaningful decisions at the top. The glass ceiling is alive and well in Japanese companies. Few foreigners climb to anything above middle management and the most a foreign teacher can normally aspire to is head instructor at a branch or a cluster of branches, where they are usually limited to overseeing other foreigners. Most branch managers are Japanese and have ultimate authority over head teachers. At Gaba, even when teachers complained of sexual harassment by students, foreign supervisors were powerless to remove those clients from the roster without consent from Japanese management, at a far flung head office, who can take a week or more to decide.

Foreign supervisors can barely even recommend a promotion and are often bound by the rules of the game. Subjective student evaluations, based on wooly customer service goals rather than learning results, determine a teacher's raises, bonuses and promotion prospects, if there are any at all: the Berlitz union action started after the parent company posted record profits, while the teachers' pay had been frozen for sixteen years. At Gaba, targets for advancement such as total lessons taught or the number of positive evaluations have been revised upward, making them harder to attain.

Why are the star players in the game on the lowest rung? In an English school the organization's greatest asset should be its teachers, yet these are more often than not insecure, temporary positions. Now, two thirds of all English teachers are officially 'part time' or 'subcontractors'. The product is more important than the person who delivers it; a school's methodology is of greater value to the brand than the professionalism of its instructors. The industry has put this commitment to uniform service at the forefront. ECC for example likes to, 'think of our students as customers, as this term reflects our commitment to their complete satisfaction.'[5]

There is nothing wrong with reinforcing the notion of service - in Japanese the word *kyaku-san* stands in for a variety of English terms: customer, guest, passenger, client and yes, student. But in the wrong hands it can also be used as leverage to hold the teacher down, to remind him of his lower status, to devalue his credentials and expertise, to remind him he is just providing a service and to validate any complaints made against him, no matter how trivial. A teacher can be marked down for taking a sip of water, for wearing a loose tie, for 'looking tired' or for ducking out to the bathroom because he has a stomach bug. These complaints may seem like small change but one might argue such conditions undermine basic human dignity. At the harsher end of the scale, a teacher can feel pressured into seeing out a lesson to the end even while she is being sexually harassed by the student, because to terminate the lesson on any grounds and report the client could spell career suicide. The term 'career' here is relative.

Such lack of respect for teachers is often blamed on simple racism. Certainly the idea that it is easy to pull one over on the foreigners must play some part, but so-called 'black companies' are on the rise in many sectors of the Japanese economy and maltreatment is not restricted to foreign workers anymore. As Berlitz veteran Kieran suggested, globalization has brought *laissez-faire* western attitudes to the Japanese labor market. For foreigners in Japan, ironically foreign rules may have come back to bite them in the ass. Grant wonders if the rise in so-called NEETs (the long-term unemployed youth who are not in education, employment or training) and *'freeters'* (the Japanese slang for casual and temporary part timers who flit from job to job without settling) can be blamed on this drop in labor standards. 'Without the traditional protection employers used to offer, many young people are thinking, "Why bother? I'm not going to play their game; I'll go my own way".'

Yet the exploitation of foreign workers predates the recent media hype over poorly-treated workers in Japan so there must be other factors.

Perhaps more directly to blame would be the way Big Eikaiwa views its service as a product and the teachers not as professionals but as customer service staff trained to deliver. In a large eikaiwa school there is no need to hire professional teachers, because as Troy once observed, 'Anyone can learn to teach out of a book.' All an English instructor need do is follow the steps marked out in the lesson plan, deliver the right point or conduct the right role play at the right time and the job is done. Wrap the burger and place it on a tray. And again, don't forget to smile.

When a school takes it a step further and develops its own material, the need for outside, professionally developed texts evaporates and the brand identity is reinforced. The steps in the text become the *only* way to teach a lesson. The product becomes more important than the teacher, therefore it doesn't much matter who the teacher is, except as the face or image of the brand. Andre reminds us, 'what you can do is unimportant compared to how you look. If the customer doesn't like the way you sit, or knot your tie, or that you needed a sip of water, then you haven't only acted unprofessionally as a teacher, but you've diminished the brand's reputation.'

This reverence for the customer also partly explains the ambivalence or inertia eikaiwa management experiences when confronted with teachers' claims of harassment by students. If a customer is God, how do you tell the deity he is out of line? There is no ritual for rebuke. It is a small matter to warn an employee over the smallest of infractions, but quite another to tell a customer he is wrong. The consequences of disciplining a foreign teacher are minimal - she'll be gone in a year, and there's no need to keep her particularly happy till then. Yet with customers, schools are faced with a stark choice. They risk accusing a customer of inappropriate behavior and being wrong, or of being right and gaining a reputation as the school where students harass the instructors. With two equally damaging prospects and the usual Japanese penchant for seeking 'harmony', it is not surprising that rather than stand up for teachers' rights, the first impulse is to placate the customer and bury the issue.

Because Japanese society views foreigners as temporary, transient workers, the perception becomes a self-fulfilling prophecy. Schools don't expect teachers to stay, so they do not nurture them. Teachers are not encouraged, so they do not stay, and the circle is complete. The big chains have had an advantage because there has always been a steady stream of applicants looking to fund their Japanese adventure. Some schools may even believe a high turnover is good for business, and that they can keep a fresh image with a regular intake of new faces. They also know the teachers lack the resources to challenge them when it comes to dismissal. They certainly don't pay enough to afford a lawyer. They'd be crazy to.

There is little advocacy for foreign workers in Japan. With foreigners making up less than 2% of the population, and with an aging society, declining birthrate and associated economic difficulties on the horizon, the plight of a relative handful of foreign teachers is hardly a societal priority. Moreover the fees students often pay, along with memories of the bubble years, lead them to the erroneous conclusion that English teachers make good enough money as it is. They're often shocked to learn eikaiwa instructors get such a small cut for their efforts: at Berlitz or Gaba about a quarter of the lesson fee and in slow months barely enough to pay the bills. There is no broad awareness of the discrepancy between lesson fees and instructors' salaries.

The law does help somewhat. Although labor disputes in Japan often result in findings that favor the company, the courts are not wholly unsympathetic toward workers. However litigation is costly and time-consuming and again, foreign teachers are disadvantaged in both respects. In Japan there is the saying that, 'the stake that sticks up gets hammered in', adding an element of shame to standing up for oneself. This hampers the notion of industrial action in general. For a society where uniformity and complacence are considered virtues, the idea that foreign workers should be entitled to 'special' privileges is perhaps asking too much, except they're not asking for any more than basic labor requirements.

It is said that if you can't change company, change the company. Union activity at major *eikaiwas* has spiked in recent years. Companies have been searching for the bottom for a decade now, the bare minimum a foreign teacher will work for. They may have found it. Fewer teachers are coming to eikaiwa and the unions are starting to push back. At Gaba and Berlitz, where the management has dug in its heels and dismissed union members, this has led to more tension and ongoing court battles. In the small schools where teachers have been unable to fight back by weight of numbers, their benefits and rights have been largely at the whim of the employer. Some are benevolent, others shady. Most fall somewhere in between, as struggling schools do the best they can and are always looking to cut costs. This leaves collective bargaining the only viable option: in the big schools where large unions have been possible, industrial action and lawsuits have helped keep the most egregious exploiters in line. It pays to unionize.

Just being in a union doesn't confer automatic protection. As Ian Raines pointed out, all most unions ask for is that Japanese companies follow existing laws. Eikaiwa and dispatch have had a history of union busting. One year contracts make it easier to dismiss a worker and non-renewal has been used to attempt decapitation strikes against union heads, despite laws that insist companies cannot fire a worker because he or she is a union member. Gaba tried to fire its union chair and was forced to rehire him; Berlitz non-renewed several union members during the strikes. As recently as 2012, nationwide chain Peppy Kids club non-renewed the head of its newly-formed union. The company claimed 'performance issues' despite his evaluation record of 97%. Peppy was forced to rehire him, but tried to dismiss him again a few months later.[6]

Unions thus have to fight hard for every scrap of dignity. The Peppy Kids union's first action was over unpaid hotel bills for emergency dispatch teachers. Apparently it was too hard for the company to give them cash up front and teachers were being forced to dig deep then claim back expenses. Yet that small victory caused the company to dismiss the union chair several months later. ECC teachers are still battling for a meager contract completion bonus of about $1,000, while Japanese staff at the company get two bonuses of at least several times that amount each year.[7]

Big Eikaiwa fears that if given an inch, teachers might take a mile. This is something employers cannot abide, even if the law says teachers are entitled to that mile and then some. If the Berlitz union can get five minute 'break' slots between lessons recognized as paid working time, it would add up to several hours a week for most Berlitz teachers, who would then fit the definition of full time workers. They would become eligible for the national health and pension scheme, better paid holidays and more worker protection. A court ruling might oblige other schools to fall in line. Forcing the industry's largest employers to admit their teachers are indeed full time workers will leave hundreds of smaller schools out there following their lead a shakier legal leg to stand on. Of course, if all precedents are to be trusted, the large chains will fight tooth and nail to avoid such an outcome.

Teachers who don't have the union behind them still have some options to fight back. In 2012, Tokyo teacher Neil Grainger was working at Waseda University International Corporation, an English school affiliated to the prestigious Waseda University. He was diagnosed in the same month with HIV *and* terminal cancer, beginning a long battle for his health that required lengthy periods of hospitalization. Despite having been promoted to Senior Tutor only the previous year, suddenly the school was 'worried about his performance'. He was due for promotion and a contract renewal of three years owing to seniority, but instead the company sought non-renewal. After a fundraiser and media campaign, Grainger's supporters forced the school to back down on dismissal but he was still only offered a six month renewal, no doubt as a path to compulsory retirement. Grainger passed away in March of 2013 at age 44.[8]

A colleague once complained, 'teaching English is about squeezing. The employers and students, the tax man, squeezing as much as they can out of foreigners while we try to squeeze as much as we can out of Japan before we leave. It is not an amicable business relationship.' Such apathy leads to shoddy workmanship in the classroom and lax standards. The students aren't fooled and will quickly trade up on a school that under-performs. But in many ways the industry has brought this on itself.

Amid profits and expansion, what makes Big Eikaiwa keep slamming teachers – and teaching standards - down year after year? Because the teachers put up with it, and because the schools have figured this out. In all but the largest schools, scraping together a union is a tall order. It is very easy to intimidate temporary or part time staff living from paycheck to paycheck. It is time consuming and expensive for a small faculty to challenge the management in court or otherwise. Strikes and walkouts mean lost hours of pay, which few part timers are willing to risk even for a day. Add to that the threat of dismissal and the general mood is one of resignation and fatalism. It can be too much trouble to rock the boat.

When discussing this project, a friend in New Zealand asked whether the decline in working conditions was simply the market reacting to a glut in the supply of teachers. Yes and no. Of course a weakening economy, fewer customers and a labor supply exceeding demand are all conditions that contribute to a drop in prices, therefore wages. However, the lawbreaking, the unfair treatment, shady contracts, excessive discipline and effective wage discrimination cannot be so easily dismissed as 'the free market' at work. Respect is a uniquely human concept. It takes a human being to decide whether or not another is worthy of it. The daily disrespect endured by English teachers in Japan falls on squarely the shoulders of their employers, and sometimes the customers.

A similar refrain echoed even by some English teachers is that eikaiwa is just an entry level position, and that it's the nature of the beast. This is a fatalistic cop out at best, at worst the excuse of free market apologists. Many eikaiwa schools do ask for experience and even the large chains demand university-educated teachers. Yet that experience rarely equates to a paycheck on par with Japanese workers of a similar age and level of qualifications. There is also a difference between entry level and *exploitation*: an entry level Japanese graduate working in the office at a large company – even an eikaiwa chain - gets a steady salary, national pension and health coverage, bonuses and career progression. These are all benefits denied the foreign worker. Once again, the problem is not the market, but *people* deciding other people are worth less.

There was a time that as long as there were people willing to take a leap, and see what Japan holds for them, there were employers willing to exploit that desire. Even that may now be changing. Head teachers I have spoken to cited a drop in good candidates over the years: 'Where we used to get half a dozen applicants for a position, now we're lucky to get one. More and more the schedulers rely on shuffling people around to fill the gaps.' Shuffling doesn't always work either. In James' opinion, 'the school has pushed teachers so far out at arm's length that they've filled their empty slots with more lucrative work elsewhere. When a temporary corporate class comes on board or a new regular private lesson, nobody is available for it, and I can't hire new teachers for just one new class. Fact is people don't want to work in the business anymore. They can do better on their own with private clients.'

Resignations are on the rise too. Turnover is notoriously high at Gaba and Interac and even Nova is advertising year-round on local job-search sites like Gaijinpot, suggesting the need for quick hires who are already in the country. Bruce recalled one Nova teacher in Sapporo walked out after only a month, citing different contract conditions to those promised;

another called the company from the airport after going AWOL announcing he quit. A dearth of teachers may force the industry to either start paying better to attract talent, or to accept an even deeper drop in standards. It may be eikaiwa's ultimate own goal: Bruce learned his classroom skills at Nova, but earns more than double the hourly rate in eikaiwa, teaching ESL part time at a college in the US. Increasingly, there is a future and a career for experienced eikaiwa teachers back in their home countries, far better than what scraps are left in Japan.

Yet Japan will always attract its share of adventurers, romantics, romanticists, fantasists and those just making a living. The industry will shrink in step with the population. The worst projections show the declining birthrate will leave a country that stands at over 127 million today with just 90 million by mid-century. Given Japan's limited space and resources that may be a good thing in the long run, but in the near term, with a graying population and a shrinking tax base to pay for pensions, it will mean consumers have less money to spare on a lot of things, including commercial English lessons. Wages may continue to shrink, and the few benefits left pared back even further. There will be more scam-artist employers and fly-by-night teachers. Some may leave but others will start businesses, take on private students, get qualified and move into colleges. They'll join unions and try to better their working conditions. They will pound the pavement, fill the gaps, pull the hours, and make it work. Survivors.

Glossary

AEON (Aeon) – large national chain of language centers

ALT – assistant language teacher in public schools; or **AET** for assistant English teacher.

Berlitz - International chain of language schools with a large presence in Japan

Begunto – The Berlitz branch of the General Union in Tokyo

BOE(s) – local Board(s) Of Education

CELTA – Certificate of English Language teaching to adults, issued by Cambridge

Coco Juku – a recent entry into the language center arena, several dozen branches nationwide

DELTA – Cambridge Diploma of English teaching: a more advanced certificate than CELTA

ECC – a large chain of language schools, by some estimates the current industry leader

Eikaiwa – Japanese term for English Conversation; generic term for language centers

Eiken – Japanese standard English test for business world or college entrance

ELS – a large global chain of schools with several branches in Japan; collapsed 2009

ESL – English as a Second Language; generic

GABA (Gaba) – Large eikaiwa chain specializing in one-to-one lessons. Based in Osaka.

GEOS (Geos) – Large English school chain; collapsed 2010, temporarily revived until 2013.

IELTS - International English Language Testing System; UK standard for university entrants

Interac – A dispatch company that hires teachers and sends them as ALTs to public schools

IS – Instructional Supervisor: head teacher at a Berlitz Branch

ISL – Instructor Support Leader: head teacher at a Gaba Learning Studio.

Itaku – independent subcontractor

izakaya – a typical Japanese tavern with food and drink in equally abundant quantities

JET – Japan Exchange and Teaching Program; a govt initiative to hire ALTs from abroad

J-Staff - Japanese staff at language schools (slang term among teachers)

JTE – Japanese teacher of English in the public school system

Juku – private cram school: children visit them after school hours to prepare for exams

Kokumin Kenko Hokken – public health insurance, paid entirely by insured member

LC – Berlitz Language Center, or branch

LS – Gaba Learning Studio'; other name for branch school

Maxceed – dispatcher of ALTs; a subsidiary of Interac

MEXT – Ministry of Education, Culture, Scient, Sports and Technology

NAMBU – Tokyo branch of the NUGW, covering some districts in Southern Tokyo and East Japan

NOVA (Nova) – Industry leader until 2008 collapse; since revived and slowly re-expanding

NUGW – National Union of General workers – a trade union umbrella organization

Salaryman – (*sarariman*); stereotypical male Japanese corporate employee

Seishain – full time, permanent company employee

Shakai Hokken – National social insurance, including medical; payments matched by employers

TEFL – teaching English as a foreign language; generic

TESOL – teaching English to speakers of other languages; generic

TOEFL - Test of English as a Foreign Language: US standard for university entrants

TOEIC - Test of English for International Communication: US standard for business English

English to Go

Appendix I - Money

For convenience, the Japanese yen is often converted into its rough equivalent in US dollars at the time. Therefore when a figure for 2009 is given it is based on the average rate for that year, around ¥77 to the dollar, and for 2013, close to ¥100. Some calculations are done from memory and some mined from economic data, but is accurate enough to within a few yen.

The Japanese only count in 'cents', ¥100 being the equivalent of a 'Japanese dollar'. To make a quick calculation assume roughly ¥100 yen to the US dollar, or when converting back, subtract two zeroes. This is not entirely accurate, as the yen has fluctuated from over ¥120 to the dollar in the mid nineties to ¥75 in 2009 and back to ¥120 in 2015. Roughly ¥100 buys a soft drink from a vending machine or a candy bar at the convenience store, so prices for many goods as a share of personal income are more on par with Europe or Australia for the average consumer.

Tax rates are similar to other developed countries. The basic rate is around 10%. Full time workers must pay into national pension and social insurance plans, in which employers match contributions. Tax included, all this can add up to over 20% of a worker's income, but for that they have unemployment protection, government-subsidized healthcare to the tune of 70%, and a pension when they retire (economic forces notwithstanding).

The typical fixed salary for a starting English teacher at a large eikaiwa chain is around ¥240,000 a month, or $2,500. Of course fixed salaries are increasingly being reduced. Hourly pay for a part time teacher ranges from ¥1800-2600 (up to $26) at most schools, whereas private lessons and corporate training can pay as much ¥3,000-4,000 ($30-40). Some part timers earn as little as ¥150,000 in lean months. Assuming one pays into the national plans, take home pay from a ¥240,000 salary would be around ¥200,000.

How far does this monthly income get a foreigner in Japan? Rent in Tokyo for a dingy one-room apartment ranges from ¥70,000-100,000 a month, up to half of a teacher's salary in a reasonable month. For a separate bedroom and living area, the costs ramp up. Likewise for a newer or more modern building. Some teachers mitigate this by sharing with roommates or moving in with a partner. A 'family-sized' apartment with two bedrooms could be double. Rents are about a half to two-thirds of Tokyo prices in large regional cities such as Sapporo, Sendai or Fukuoka. Utilities average about ¥15,000 a month for gas, power, water and phone or internet lines.

Public transport is convenient and extremely efficient, but teachers who must commute to several workplaces could run up a bill of ¥20,000 or so per month. Owning a car is quite expensive, with high road taxes and fuel prices. Groceries are of a similar price to Europe - that is, more expensive than the US or Australasia. Eating and drinking out can be very cheap or very expensive. One of Japan's attractions is the food culture and there is no shortage of places to dine. Some teachers have even found that eating regularly at cheap beef-bowl or noodle shops is more cost-effective than cooking at home. Most teachers I've met could save about $500 a month if they were on a steady salary, or a fifth to a quarter of their take home pay. Those with more austere tastes can save as much as a third.

Appendix II - Unions

Though the words 'the union' frequently appear, there are actually several unions and overlapping union jurisdictions involved in this story. Most unions involving foreign teachers fall under the banner of the National Trade Union Councils, the smallest of Japan's three national trade federations. The National Union of General Workers is an umbrella group within the larger organization which itself covers 40 or so smaller unions including the General Union, based in Osaka, which has managed to enroll chapters from most of the large eikaiwa chains.*

General Union branches in Fukuoka, and Tokyo (*Tozen*) also handle their cases regionally. In Tokyo there is another branch called *Nambu* which splits the area with Tozen. At Berlitz, their chapter of the Tokyo General Union is called *Begunto*. In each case, schools with union representation have their own chapter of the local General Union, which also includes workers Japanese and foreign, from other businesses and industries. Union action in Tokyo is not necessarily in coordination with activity in Osaka or Fukuoka, although they are often all aware of what is taking place. Though one union's activities may encourage or influence another's, they are not necessarily working under the same direction.

Because of the somewhat bewildering array of branches and apparent overlap of responsibilities, union sources are generally introduced by their company names. For example, Adrian from the Gaba Union is a Gaba employee and Gaba union representative, whereas, Ian from the

General Union is a union official covering many schools in his region. As the branch unions work closely with their regional overseers, the book often seems to refer to 'the union' as a kind of monolith. This does not mean national-level operations in most cases. Unless otherwise stated, 'the union' or 'union rep' should be taken as representing the local or regional union chapter of the school in question.

Likewise government ministries have been abbreviated to the area most relevant. When discussing activities or rulings from the Ministry of Health, Labor and Welfare, it is usually the labor section that is most relevant so it is referred to as the Ministry of Labor. Likewise the colorfully named and no doubt task-saturated Ministry of Education, Culture, Sports, Science and Technology appears most often as simply the Ministry of Education, or the official abbreviation MEXT.

* See Wikipedia for a more in-depth description:
http://en.wikipedia.org/wiki/General_Union

Notes and References:

Wikipedia is used as a reference where reliable sources are provided on the wiki page, and only for convenience when the subject is a large one containing multiple references.

1 A New Breed:

1. Brian J McVeigh, J*apanese Higher Education as Myth*; M.E. Sharpe, 2002; p167

2. The center is still in operation at the time of writing: http://plaza-sapporo.or.jp/citizen_j/en/

3. American club history:
http://en.wikipedia.org/wiki/American_Club_(eikaiwa)

4. Asahi Shimbun, Jan 25 1996; *School closes while director absent, teachers to take legal action over pay*; (original Japanese)
http://isaokonno.webstarts.com/index.html?r=20110516115155

5. Don MacLaren, Business Week, Dec 7 1998; *Corruption is De Rigeur in Corporate Japan*

6. American Club advert:
http://en.wikipedia.org/wiki/American_Club_(eikaiwa)#Current_status

7. Phillip Seargeant; *The Idea of English in Japan*, Multilingual Matters 2009, p99

8. Brian J McVeigh, J*apanese Higher Education as Myth*; M.E. Sharpe, 2002; p175

9. Phillip Seargeant; *The Idea of English in Japan*, Multilingual Matters

2009, p112

10. Bloomberg, Sept 7, 2007; *Japan's Elderly Population Rises to Record, Government Says*

2 Champagne Supernova:

1. Nova method: http://en.wikipedia.org/wiki/Nozomu_Sahashi
2. Percentage of market: http://en.wikipedia.org/wiki/Nova_(eikaiwa)#History
3. Osaka Bar ruling: http://en.wikipedia.org/wiki/Nova_(eikaiwa)#Anti-fraternization_policy
4. Dating award: http://en.wikipedia.org/wiki/Nova_(eikaiwa)#Anti-fraternization_policy
5. Kara harris: http://en.wikipedia.org/wiki/Nova_(eikaiwa)#Contested_dismissals
6. Drug testing: wikipedia.org/wiki/Nova_(eikaiwa)#Drug_testing
7. Mainichi Daily News, September 1 2007; *Parents seek recognition for their son's suicide*
8. The Asahi Shimbun 17 February 2007; *Nova searched in contract row*
9. The Japan Times. 12 April 2005; *English schools face huge insurance probe*
10. Sydney Morning Herald, 19 September 2007; *Teachers unpaid as company falters*
11. The Japan Times Nov 2, 2007; *Nova share trading shady near the end*
12. *Yano Research Institute Report* - Yano Research Institute. September 2, 2008
13. The Japan Times Nov 6 2007; *Nova fall simple: it just bled red*
14. generalunion.org, Mar 2016; *Truths About Nova's Independent*

Contracts - #2 Paying To Use The Classroom.

3 The Battery Hens of Berlitz:
1. Berlitz homepage: http://teach.berlitz.co.jp/aboutus/location.html
2. Berlitz union history: http://generalunion.org/Joomla/index.php/en/berlitz
3. The Japan Times, May 6 2008; As parent firm posts record profits, Berlitz teachers strike back
4. The Japan Times, Feb 17 2009; Berlitz launches legal blitz against striking instructors
5. Union member dismissals: http://en.wikipedia.org/wiki/2007%E2%80%9308_Berlitz_Japan_strike#Berlitz_fires_teachers
6. Union achieved benefits: http://berlitz.generalunion.org/news/1007
7. Begunto home page, Jan 30 2014; You can bill Berlitz for extra work outside the class, http://berlitzuniontokyo.org/
8. http://www.berlitzunion.generalunion.org: Don't give Berlitz a free ride: organize
9. The Japan Times Dec 7, 2014; Quarter of workers suspect they are trapped at 'black firms'
10. Clawbacks on union homepage: http://generalunion.org/Joomla/index.php/en/berlitz/1144-sound-berlitz-a-resounding-no-to-clawbacks-sign-the-union-petition
11. Berlitz-ELS Sapporo Language Center; Overview for New Instructors, p4.

4 Aeon's Cult of Impersonality
1. The Washington Post, July 13 2008; *Japan's Killer Work Ethic*

2. Geos background: http://en.wikipedia.org/wiki/Geos_(eikaiwa)

3. The author once worked at Geos in New Zealand before it became NZLC; the overseas branches were not typical eikaiwa schools, but genuine language centers.

4. The Japan Times, March 2 2001; *Geos Affiliates fined for hiding 280 million yen*

5. The Japan Times, Apr 22, 2010; *Geos school chain files for bankruptcy*

6. Pension contributions; http://generalunion.org/Joomla/index.php/en/aeon/634-aeon-raises-pay-with-shakai-hoken-health-and-pension

7. The Japan Times. April 12, 2005; *English schools face huge insurance probe*

8. Asahi Shimbun Nov 6 2014; *Labor office emulates teacher's work at home, recognizes suicide as job-related*

10. *Aeon – 150,000 reasons to be happy:* http://generalunion.org/Joomla/index.php/en/aeon/

5 Life on Mars

1. The Japan Times March 22, 2015; *University teachers work under shadow of falling ax*

2. Brian J McVeigh, *Japanese Higher Education as Myth*; M.E. Sharpe, 2002; p162

3. Brian J McVeigh, *Japanese Higher Education as Myth*; M.E. Sharpe, 2002; p197

4. Japan Today Dec 4 2012; *More Japanese youth wearing surgical masks to hide their faces*

5. Sally Jones: *Speech is silver; silence is golden, the cultural*

importance of silence in Japan; Australian National University, ANUUJ Vol 13 No. 11

6. Ishin-denshin is the Japanese concept of non-verbal communication. Like other aspects of Nihonjinron, it is considered an innate ability unique to the Japanese. For more read Peter N. Dale, Alex Kerr and Ian Buruma.

7. Nonverbal communication: http://en.wikipedia.org/wiki/Nihonjinron

8. http://en.wikipedia.org/wiki/Asahi_Shimbun#Controversies; The Japan Times, Jan 29 2015; *Abe pledges to 'correct' the record on wartime sex slaves*

9. The Japan Times, Mar 4 2015; *U.S. author recounts 'lecture' he got about 'comfort women' from uninvited Japanese guests*

10. Phillip Seargeant; *The Idea of English in Japan*, Multilingual Matters 2009, p.49

11. Phillip Seargeant; *The Idea of English in Japan*, Multilingual Matters 2009, p.72

12. http://nihongonews.wordpress.com/2012/12/13/coco-juku-dogs-and-demons/

13. The New York Times, Jul 10 2010; *Japan training program is said to exploit foreign workers*

6 Gaba Moves the Goalpost:

1. Gaba website: http://www.Gaba.co.jp/companyinfo/gaiyo.html

2. 2010 Stock Exchange Report: http://pdf.irpocket.com/C2133/kzOO/UUri/iMyZ.pdf

3. Japan times Dec 20, 2011; *Gaba 'contractor' status under fire from staff, courts.*

4. Average wages:

http://en.wikipedia.org/wiki/List_of_countries_by_average_wage

5. Rough calculations based on figures from the Gaba Wikipedia page. The swings in pay are corroborated both by Adrian Ringin and in Japan times Dec 20, 2011; *Gaba 'contractor' status under fire from staff, courts.*

6. Minimum wages: http://www.minimum-wage.org/international/en/Japan

7. For more satire on Gaba and the eikaiwa business visit the *Gaba Teacher's Association* site; http://www.angelfire.com/apes2/gaba/

8. The Japan Times Apr 14, 2014; *Suit over dismissal to tackle thorny issue of language teachers' employment status.*

7. ELT news, July 22 2004; *NIF buys Gaba*: http://www.eltnews.com/news/archives/2004/07

10. The Japan Times July 3, 2012; *The curious case of the eroding eikaiwa salary*

11. GU News Jan 27 2010: *Gaba – round one to the union*; http://Gaba.generalunion.org/news/650

12. GU News Feb 28, 2012: *Gaba does about face, rehires branch chair, drops lawsuits*; http://gaba.generalunion.org/news/901

13. Belting system: wikipedia.org/wiki/Gaba_Corporation: Belting and debelting statistics

14. Lessons taught incentive: wikipedia.org/wiki/Gaba_Corporation: Incentives

15. Gaba recruiting page: http://teaching-in-japan.Gaba.co.jp/teaching-with-Gaba/earning-potential/

16. The Japan times Oct 19, 2010; *Gaba teachers challenge contractor status*

17. General Union Website: *New Nova contract is fishy*;

http://generalunion.org/Joomla/index.php/en/nova/1156-new-nova-contract-is-fishy

18. Laws regarding corporate interference in unions: Foreign Worker Guidebook p50; http://www.hataraku.metro.tokyo.jp/soudan-c/center/all-e2008.pdf

7 Love, Marriage and Charisma Men:

1. Charisma Man: http://charismaman.com/; The Alien may be a play on the tactfully named 'Alien Registration Card' that foreign residents were issued until 2012, making them feel just that much more 'welcome'.

2. Debito Arudou, The Japan Times, March 1, 2011; *Charisma Men, unite against the identity enforcers*

3, 4. Roslyn Appleby, TESOL Quarterly Vol 47 No 1, March 2013; *Desire in translation – White Masculinity and TESOL* (p141-144)

5. The handcuff poster can be seen at: http://www.letsjapan.org/forum/viewtopic.php?f=1&t=255552

6. The Japan Times, Nov 10 2014; *36,000 don't want 'pick-up artist' to drop in on Japan*

7. Roslyn Appleby, TESOL Quarterly Vol 47 No 1, March 2013; *Desire in translation – White Masculinity and TESOL* (p128)

8. Associate Press, April 2, 2014; *Ashley Madison is big in Japan where marital form counts, guilt is low for cheating on spouse*

9. Website banned in Korea: thestar.com, Aug 8, 2014; *Ashley Madison sues South Korea.*

10. Teenage prostitution: Osaka Prefectural Center for Youth and Gender Equality, 12 October 2007; *The meaning of enjo kousai*

8 Stalkers, Gropers and Serial Masturbators:

1. So-called 'hentai' ('deviant') comics are perfectly legal and available on convenience store shelves in Japan, part of an ongoing dispute with the UN over child pornography laws;
http://asiancorrespondent.com/91978/japan-the-un-human-rights-council-and-child-porn/

2. Chikan culture: The Japan Times, Oct 11 2009; *Campaign against groping*

3. Waseda university rape comments: BBC News June 27 2003; *Fury over Japan rape gaffe;* http://news.bbc.co.uk/2/hi/asia-pacific/3025240.stm

4, 5. Harassment survey: GU News March 23, 2014;
http://www.generalunion.org/News/1130

6, 7. The Japan Times, June 16, 2014; *Harassers exploit Gaba's 'man-to-man' lesson format*

9 ECC - Appetite for Compromise:

1. ECC recruiting pages: http://recruiting.ecc.co.jp/about/index.html

2. For a scathing critique of Coco Juku on Halloween costumes and other issues, see: nihongonews/wordpress.com, Dec 13 2012; *Coco Juku – Dogs and Demons*

3. Halloween costumes survey:
http://generalunion.org/Joomla/index.php/en/ecc/146-halloween-costumes-take-the-online-survey

4. ECC union achievements:
http://generalunion.org/Joomla/index.php/en/ecc/863-ecc-branch-some-of-our-many-achievements

5. The Japan Times, Dec 17 2013; *4,200 firms hit over labor violations*

6. Guarantee of wages and minimum wages: Foreign Workers' guidebook, Tokyo Metropolitan Govt, 2009 p12; (http://www.hataraku.metro.tokyo.jp/soudan-c/center/e/)

7. The Japan Times, Aug 4 2012; *Diet Revises Labor Contract Law*

8. National Pension system: http://en.wikipedia.org/wiki/National_Pension_(Japan)#Lump_sum_withdrawal_payments

9. GU News Apr 11 2013: Job security at ECC...coming soon? http://www.generalunion.org/ecc/news/1023

10. Epion Mabuchi dismissal: http://generalunion.org/Joomla/index.php/en/independents/820-epion-back-in-the-classroom

11. ECC salary graphic available at: www.generalunion.org/ecc/news/1024

12. Summer bonus for Japanese staff: http://www.generalunion.org/ecc/news/1095

13. The Japan Times, Oct 29 2014; *Maternity harassment verdict benefits women, men, humanity*

14. ECC recruiting page: http://recruiting.ecc.co.jp/

10 Interac's Phantom Jobs:

1. Collison: www.debito.org: *Michael Collison Case: Fired from Interac after death of infant daughter*

2. The Japan Times, Jan 5 2008; *Assistant language Teachers in Trying Times*

3. Interac history: http://en.wikipedia.org/wiki/Interac_(Japan)#cite_note-5 Retrieved from Ministry of Education, Culture, Sports, Science and Technology Japan.

Retrieved 10 December 2012.

4. Interac recruiting page: https://www.interacnetwork.com/recruit/jaltjobs/jsalarytaxesandinsurance.html

5. Olympus story: Nikkei Business, Oct 31, 2011; *Dismissed CEO Turns Focus on Troubles at Olympus.*

6. Dispatchers' misinformation - http://fukuoka.generalunion.org/alt/doanddont.htm

7. The full *Nihon Terebi* documentary can be watched at http://interacunion.org/2009/08/31/stop-illegal-dispatching-in-tokyokanto/

8. Unpaid transportation: https://www.youtube.com/watch?v=z4E1qzn1PL8 ?v=z4E1qzn1PL8

9. Forced resignations: http://interacunion.org/2012/03/13/dont-let-interac-force-you-to-resign/

10. Drug testing: Tozen Interac website http://interacunion.org/2012/06/04/collective-bargaining-demands-over-interac-drug-testing/

11. Nonrenewal over pregnancy: interacunion.org, Sept 21 2009; Interac and Pregnancy: Getting Fired for Being Pregnant

12. Illegal contracts: http://alt.150m.com/ Gyomu Itaku Contracts Are Illegal

13. Insurance: http://interacunion.org/wp-content/uploads/2009/11/FAQ-Insurance-System-in-Japan.pdf

14. Health insurance disclaimer: http://interacunion.org/wp-content/uploads/2009/11/HealthInsDis.pdf

15. Non-enrollment in health insurance: http://interacunion.org/wp-content/uploads/2009/11/Social-Insurance-Letter.pdf

16. Open letter to management: http://interacunion.org/2010/10/01/open-letter-to-kevin-salthouse/#more-399

17. Dismissal period: http://www.hataraku.metro.tokyo.jp/sodan/siryo/H23_handbook_all.pdf *Foreign Workers Guidebook*; p40

18. Forced resignations: http://interacunion.org/2012/03/13/dont-let-interac-force-you-to-resign/

19. Japan Times, Jan 5 2008; *Assistant language teachers in trying times*

20. General Union: *Shakai Hokken laws are changing in 2016- how will you be affected?* http://generalunion.org/Joomla/index.php/legal-issues/1346-shakai-hoken-laws-are-changing-in-2016-how-will-you-be-affected

11 How Does Eikaiwa Get Away With It?

1. *Foreign Worker Guidebook*: http://www.hataraku.metro.tokyo.jp/soudan-c/center/e/

1, 4. The Japan Times, Apr 14, 2014; *Suit over dismissal to tackle thorny issue of language teachers' employment status*

3. Average salaries: http://www.worldsalaries.org/japan.shtml

5. ECC website: http://recruiting.ecc.co.jp/about/index.html

6. Peppy Kids Club union: http://www.generalunion.org/peppykids/news/998

7. ECC bonus: http://www.generalunion.org/ecc/news/1095

8. *The Japan Times, Oct 21 2013; Medical bills mount for 'fired' Tokyo English teacher fighting cancer, HIV*

ABOUT THE AUTHOR

Craig Currie-Robson studied history and literature at the University of Auckland. He has taught ESL in Japan, Hong Kong and New Zealand, and has worked in the airline industry in the UAE. He has published articles in The Japan Times and is currently working on his next book.

craigkneedeep.blogspot.com

www.ingramcontent.com/pod-product-compliance
Lightning Source LLC
Chambersburg PA
CBHW020854180526
45163CB00007B/2497